ALSO BY JAMES BROUGH

Ed Wynn's Son
A Victorian in Orbit
Auction!
The Dog Who Lives at the Waldorf
Princess Vic
We Were Five
The Whole Truth and Nothing But
Every Other Inch a Lady
The Fabulous Fondas
Princess Alice
The Prince and the Lily
An Untold Story
A Rendezvous with Destiny
The Ford Dynasty
Mother R.
Margaret
Miss Lillian Russell
Consuelo

The Vixens

A *Biography of*
Victoria and Tennessee Claflin

James Brough

SIMON AND SCHUSTER

NEW YORK

SIMON AND SCHUSTER and colophon are trademarks of Simon & Schuster
Designed by Eve Kirch
Manufactured in the United States of America

1   2   3   4   5   6   7   8   9   10

Library of Congress Cataloging in Publication Data

Brough, James, 1918–
The vixens.

1. Women—United States—Biography. 2. Martin, Victoria Claflin Woodhull, 1838–1927.
3. Cook, Tennessee Celeste Claflin, Lady, 1845–
1923. I. Title.
HQ1412.B76   305.4'2'0922 [B]   80-21780
ISBN 0-671-22688-6

To Roland Morin

I am a prophetess, I am an evangel, I am a Savior, if you could but see it; but I, too, come not to bring peace but a sword.

> —Victoria C. Woodhull
> 1838–1927

Women must *come up,* or men must *come down.* Our mission is but commenced; the battle is opened. We ask no quarter and take no prisoners. Having set our hands to the plow, we will not look back nor turn aside until our work is done.

> —Tennessee Celeste Claflin
> 1845–1923

Equality of rights under the law shall not be denied or abridged by the United States or by any state on account of sex.

> —proposed Amendment XXVII to the
> Constitution of the United States

None of the principal characters referred to in these pages is a creation of the author's. Neither has any license been taken with the sequence of events in which they were embroiled. They lived, behaved, believed, and in print or recorded word expressed themselves in the manner reported here.

One

---◦◦◦---

Homer, Ohio, where the worth of a woman was judged by the washing she hung out on a line and the crust of the pies she baked. Not a whole lot more than a clapboard church without a steeple; a subscription school of split logs and greased-paper windowpanes that the Claflin children rarely entered; the post office; the Pioneer Farmers Bank; and Harrison's general store, where mice scuttered behind barrels of flour and molasses.

A one-horse hamlet about four hundred feet long end to end, set in the center of the state at the northern edge of Licking County. On a rutted road that led no place in particular, only on between high-standing corn and up into hardwood forests where axes thudded and wood smoke rose to the sky. The two sisters might have wasted their lives there if Buck Claflin hadn't gotten it into his head to burn down the mill.

The family lived on the fringe of town beside the creek that turned the mill wheel except when the rain held off and the boys would jump down to catch crawfish in the water that puddled around the rocks. Buck didn't object to droughts; anything sat well with him that provided an excuse to cut back on work. If he had been like most men around he might have spent time smartening up the house, which had no more paint left inside or out than could be found on the cheeks of a nun. Or he'd have nailed the boards of the porch, which a red-berried vine of bittersweet had pried so loose they sounded like the tail end of a rattlesnake when they were stepped on. But Buck didn't believe in frittering energy away.

The neighbors rated the place a downright disgrace. They told each other the Claflins were "dregs of the earth," but the family knew better. By the father's account the Claflins were originally Maclachlans, who had won respect east of the Mississippi River for more than two hundred years, ever since the first of them was shipped over to Boston as a bondman when Oliver Cromwell captured him in the Battle of Dunbar, which followed King Charles's execution.

Children who came to visit and wrestle or skip rope with the Claflin young were likely to be whipped as soon as they got home to teach them to stay clear in future. They still stopped by to pick green apples off the trees that never saw a pruning in the orchard behind the house, where hogs rooted through the brush for windfalls. To keep the score even, Buck would go after visitors with the switch of braided walnut twigs he stored in a rain barrel for service in maintaining order and discipline among the seven survivors of his own brood, whenever he stirred himself to try.

The sassiest of them, the one whose bare legs got switched most, was Victoria, named for the new queen in London, England. Victoria could rile him just by looking at him with her smoky blue eyes that sometimes seemed to stare right into his skull. He would beat her until blood began to trickle, but she wouldn't allow herself to let him hear so much as a whimper.

The only one spared even an occasional slash or two was Tennessee, the youngest living. If he raised a finger at her, her mother would interrupt the proceedings by waving a length of cordwood under his nose. Before she met Buck Claflin, she was Anna Hummel, daughter of Jacob, who kept a tavern at Hummel's Wharf, Pennsylvania. The German still bobbed up, especially when she was sore. "*Schweinhund!* Monster! You hit Tennie and with this stick I crack your skull!"

She was past forty when Tennessee was hauled out into the world, feet first. "A sweet little footling," she called her. "I rub your feet with laurel leaves, *liebchen,* so you not walk lame." A footling, she vowed, was blessed with the gift to heal rheumatism and lumbago by tramping up and down a sufferer's spine. She was sure Tennie was destined to be something special. Two more babies arrived afterward, but Anna's milk dried up and both of them died within a year, as another had done soon after she was married in 1825. Her father, who rated Buck as riffraff, never spoke to her again.

Tennie was the seventh of her children by her reckoning, and she was a seventh child, too, which meant Tennie could tell the future and know about events without actually seeing them happen. There was something else going in her favor: by the pocket watch Buck took off a Bible salesman in a dice game, she was born in front of the kitchen fireplace at three o'clock of an October morning, "a chime hour" according to her mother. Tennie would always be able to see ghosts, and always be safe from witches' spells.

She was named Tennessee not because that was what the label said on the bottles of bright yellow liquor Buck liked to pull on now and then, nor because it was what some people called the wagons they drove west in when they got smitten with Ohio fever. She was Tennessee for no better reason than it sounded pretty with the middle name chosen for her, which was Celeste.

Anna couldn't figure where two more young Claflins could have been fitted into the house if they had lived to grow. There was only a smidgen of space left after Uncle Samuel, Buck's twin, moved in along with his wife and a Cousin Corintha. Samuel was the image of Buck but for one important detail. These additions to the family came about after Sam got his right arm broken as the keelboat he was poling upstream struck a snag near Louisville. After the arm was fixed, he couldn't handle bigger jobs than sawing wood or helping with milking, but Buck refused to put him out and insisted on his relatives' having the only decent bed in the house.

That stood in what Anna referred to as "our best bedroom"— there was no other—which opened off the kitchen and with it made up the entire ground floor. She and her husband bedded down in the kitchen on a lumpy straw tick she spread out when everybody else was out of the way. The whole flock of children slept on ticks of corn husks under the leaky shingles in the attic, freezing in winter, frying in summer, skipping down into the root cellar when thunderheads piled up in the sky and lightning flared and shimmered. A tornado would have taken off the roof and sucked them out like so many wisps of straw.

The squeeze was relieved some when Margaret Ann, the eldest, went off to Mount Gilead to be married to Enos Miles one Fourth of July. A girl was counted well provided for in Homer when her mother furnished her with a good bed and bedding, a sidesaddle, cutlery, plates, a teakettle, a Dutch oven, and a washtub as her dowry. The fanciest present Margaret Ann collected was a washtub that her mother hadn't much use for, anyway.

Life took another turn for the better when Buck landed an extra job that gave him steady pay without much work to do. How he wangled it nobody knew because he told nobody. He simply walked back from one of the excursions he had a habit of making and announced that henceforth, besides running the mill, he was Postmaster Reuben Buckman Claflin.

He may have felt the call to set the fire as a result of what happened after another trip he took one November weekend. He came back in through the kitchen door while the family were sitting together around the table where hog and hominy served as the regular staff of life.

He undid his fusty coat that had been buttoned to the neck against the chill and pulled out a roll of ten-dollar bills, fresh and crisp, to slap them down with triumph gleaming in his eye. "Eye" in the singular; that was what marked the only visible difference between him and Sam. Buck used to explain away the absence of a second eye by claiming he lost it to a bow and arrow playing Indians as a boy. The truth was it was extracted by way of recompense on the thumb of a Susquehanna boatman who caught him out with one jack too many in a game of sledge back when Buck was in his twenties and scratching up a living as a horse trader in the Pennsylvania river towns.

"What d'you say to this, Sam? Two hundred dollars' worth. Go

ahead. Pick 'em up. Smell 'em. Ain't they just exactly like real? I
bought the lot for a sawbuck from a feller that prints 'em."

Anna reached out first and covered them with a corrugated hand.
"What you up to, Reuben? You playing hanky-panky again?"

He pushed her away and grabbed the bits of printed paper. "Keep
your snout out of my affairs, you scrawny old sow. Starting A.M.
tomorrow, I can spend this stuff like it was the genuine article, and
there's more where these come from."

Anna and Sam exclaimed together: *"Dummkopf!* Idiot!" and
"What you aiming to do with it, Buck?"

"First off, I'm going to buy myself a new outfit, and then a horse,
since I ain't partial to perambulating around in rags. I don't relish
passing the rest of my days milling corn neither, so next thing is I
apply to the county court for a license to open a hotel. Town could
use one. A nice little tavern with my post office set up right
there in the lobby. A back room for some quiet games of cards.
Maybe some female entertainment on tap up the top of the
stairs."

Anna would have taken herself to bed if she could. "You want
license for a tavern? I remember about this from my own papa. To
apply, you must prove to the judge you have good morality and
clean character. How you propose to do that, postmaster?"

"Don't ruffle your feathers. I'll find men to vouch for me when I
make it worth their while."

His frolic lasted one more day. In the morning, he did his shopping at Harrison's and brought back a new beaver hat, leather boots,
and a three-piece suit of black worsted, but the shirt he wore had
not been washed for close to a month. In the afternoon, he settled
himself by the fire, one hand rubbing his bare feet where the boots
had raised blisters, fingering the balance of his imitation cash with
the other. Nobody else was in the house. Sam's wife, Abigail, had
steeled herself to go up to the trough by the spring to launder the
shirt. Anna was down at the church, raising a hubbub because her
children had been seated too far back from the stove in Sunday
school. The rest of the tribe was out somewhere, Malden and
Hebern hunting for coon, Polly helping Utica make corn dollies.
Victoria sat on the porch with Tennie, spinning a yarn about the

trouble she would run into if she ever risked digging into the old earth mound that rose from the ground behind the house.

"As soon as you stick a spade in, Tennie, evil spirits would come flying out to torment you. There's spirits of dead people inside who've been buried there for millions of years, before even Indians was living here. Ma says there was a young feller who tried it once, and the spirits crazed him so with the horrible things they did that now he's kept locked in chains in somebody's cellar, gibbering and moaning all day and all night."

Tennie was not easy to scare; she took her mother's word that she was immune from witchcraft and hauntings. Something more alarming was coming up that hill toward them. "There's two men wearing badges and, lookit, *guns!*"

One glance told Victoria who they were. "That's Sheriff Dodds and a deputy! I bet they're after *Pa.*"

With Tennie at her heels, she raced into the kitchen to blurt out the news to him. "Christ forever loving mighty! It's the money. I got to hide it. But where, for God's sake, where?" He pranced around like a lassoed mule, the bills clutched in his grasp. The room was so frugally furnished it offered no place to cache anything away. He finally tugged open the front of his union suit but got only a single bill in before the rest fell from his trembling hands onto the floor.

The boards of the porch were rattling under two pairs of boots when Victoria stooped down to gather up the scattered paper and feed it into the fire. Buck groaned, went to salvage his smoking fortune, then checked himself and opened the door.

Mr. Dodds hitched his gunbelt up an inch or two. "Howdy do, Buck. I got a warrant. They've swore down at Harrison's that you been passing counterfeit to fit yourself out with new duds."

Buck cooled off fast. "I don't know nothing about what you're saying, sheriff, but you're welcome to step inside and ferret all you please." On the far side of the room the two girls watched the bright green flame that had flared up a moment ago subside into innocent flickering red.

Mr. Dodds's jowls wobbled appreciation of Buck's cooperativeness. "Me and Ben here's gonna have to conduct a search. If we don't uncover nothing, you can call yourself in the clear. If we do come across any more funny money, it'll be a case for a judge and jury."

Unrolling the straw tick that lay in a corner and pawing through the bed in the room next door were the only jobs that slowed them down. They had finished in the attic when the Claflins heard Dodds grunt as he creaked down the ladder, "That about does it, Buck. I just want to take a look at your own person."

Buck dipped inside his red flannels, fumbled around until he located the last of his fleeting fortune, crumpled the paper into a ball, and stuffed it into his mouth to swallow. The sheriff, descended, knew right from wrong. "I'll have to ask you two young ladies to step into the bedroom while your Pa shucks off his drawers."

As they complied, Victoria grinned, and Tennie followed suit. They were certain by then that everything would work out. The rubes had tried to down them and had failed once more.

That evening Buck crooked an arm around Victoria's skinny shoulders; he had returned his new clothes to Mr. Harrison and found him agreeable to forgetting he'd ever been taken for a jackass.

"We foxed 'em good, girl, didn't we? I allow as I couldn't have done without you. It's like I always says: Claflins was born to stick together when the going gets rackety."

But the townspeople took to muttering to each other, "Where there's smoke there's fire." Men would sooner spend half a day driving a wagon to the next nearest mill than do business with Buck Claflin. Most were outright surly when they went into the post office. All his children fancied his cold blue eye combined the powers of spyglass, watchmaker's loup, and gas microscope. He left customers with the same queasy notion that he could probe their minds with it as they stared at him across the splintery counter, sorting letters and slipping them into the slots as fast as he could deal a deck of cards.

They couldn't be expected to understand how he came to be acquainted with so many of their dealings, but behind the dusty green curtain strung on a wire toward the rear of the shack, he kept a kettle boiling on top of the wood stove, ready to steam open

envelopes that stirred his curiosity. It was a point of pride with him
to stay abreast of other people's affairs especially if he heard money
crackle inside the envelopes. In that case, he didn't lose a minute
extracting it and disposing of the correspondence under the stove
lid.

It was a letter addressed to little Widow Wycherley, who was
never far from starving to death sewing dresses, along with a paragraph in the penny newspaper which arrived each week for Mr.
Harrison, that sparked Buck's serious thinking about ridding himself of the mill.

He had given the idea some serious thought by the time he
hurried home for supper, flushed with excitement, bringing Mrs.
Wycherley's letter and Mr. Harrison's paper tucked into an inside
pocket. He considered it best to retain both of them on a confidential basis for the present to prevent the news they carried from
spreading too far and wide. He came straight through the doorway,
shoved aside the dishes on the table, sat himself down, and produced
his two exhibits.

"You know what it says here?" He jabbed a finger at a few lines
of small print. Of course nobody did and nobody would unless he
told them because he was the only one who could read more than a
word or two without a struggle. "Turn your minds to this then. 'By
magnetic telegraph, Washington, D.C.: President Polk announced
the discovery of gold by James W. Marshall, who was erecting a
sawmill in partnership with Captain John A. Sutter on the American River, branch of the Sacramento, near Coloma, California. Finds
of ore have previously been reported northwest of Los Angeles, but
only in quantities infinitely smaller than appear in these new
lodes.' "

His eye burned bright as flame. "There's more. This letter here
was wrote to his ma by Tom Wycherley, that moonfaced feller who
lit out for San Francisco. This is the important bit: 'Everybody's
rushing off prospecting for gold, sailors jumping ship in the harbor,
men leaving cattle and crops to the crows, store clerks quitting in
droves, and the owners hurrying in their footsteps. Word is all you
have to do is walk around to fill your pockets with nuggets big as
hen eggs. So I'm giving up waiting on tables—I've been sleeping

under one at night because there's not a room to rent anyplace—
and I'm off to the gold fields in the certain hope of making more
than enough to bring you out to join me and enjoy ease and comfort
with a big house and servants and everything I ever dreamed of for
your happiness.' Now what you say to that?"

Anna sniffed. "What we supposed to say? What's it to us except
you stole a widow's mail?"

"For one thing, you can say goodbye to me as soon as I can get a
start. I'm going out there and pick me up so many gold nuggets I'll
be richer than John Jacob Astor. Sam, you come along with me,
and we'll both make our fortunes." His imagination was soaring
higher than a kite, but his meaning hadn't sunk deep into anybody's
head yet.

Sam was no more enthused than Anna. "When you reckon on
leaving?"

"Have to wait for spring. Getting there would be too damn hard
in winter. There's things to tend to first, besides."

"What you going to use for stake, Buck—more funny money?"

Buck could not be drawn. "I worked that out, too. Insurance."

Anna snapped at daughter Polly, who was eighteen and the eldest
left at home, with Margaret Ann married. "Too much talk and no
eating. Go get the stew out the pot. What is with this insurance,
Reuben? We got no insurance."

"We will have. I'll hold a confab down at the bank with George
Bell, goddam son of a bitch, and fix it up with him."

Uncle Samuel carefully cleaned a nostril with a grimy fingernail.
"You didn't get far last time you went to borrow, trying to invest
in that quarter-section of land."

"No comparison. I'll be paying him money for protection in the
event something happens to the mill. Say it gets struck by lightning, or there's a flood, or maybe a fire. Then he coughs up the
price of the damage that's been done to my property."

"How's forking out cash to a bank going to stake you to California?"

Buck's eye grew sharp as an awl. "I said there just *might* be a
fire."

"*Gott behüte!*" Anna leaped up from the table and went out the door. The porch boards began trembling as she stomped to and fro. When Polly served supper—possum stew—the children split Ma's helping among themselves.

In the attic, squashed between Victoria and Utica under two frayed blankets that had never lost the smell of horse, Tennie heard her mother's voice from the top of the mound. She went there most evenings, but never this late, turned her face west to where the sun had set, and shouted out her prayers. What God received from her was mostly a rundown on the neighbors' shortcomings and the wrongs they were doing to the Claflins, though she made a point of saying she didn't bear grudges and asked for God's forgiveness.

This time Buck came first on her list. There promised to be frost before morning, and she hadn't bothered to collect her shawl before she left the house, so she was working herself up to fend off the chill. "Lord God of Heaven, there is such wickedness going on here below right close to where I'm standing here in the cold it could make your head swim. Tonight the sinner I am telling about is my husband. Lord of all spirits and all flesh, blessed be Thy name forever and ever!" She threw in a few bars of "We Shall Gather at the River" before starting in again. "Hallelujah! He's bent on going to California, God, and leaving us alone to starve. *The judgments of the Lord are true and righteous altogether. More to be desired are they than gold, yea, than much fine gold.* Lift up Thy hand and strike him dead, Lord, before You let him go!"

Utica was apt to be pettish, on account of feeling neglected from the time Tennie was born two years after her. She yanked at the blankets to pull them up over her head. "How much longer's she going to rattle on?"

Victoria gave the covers a compensating tug. "You'd best simmer down and get to sleep. It does Ma good to work off steam."

Sometime before morning, Tennie dreamed she was standing on the porch, watching her father and her brother Malden as they sidled into the mill. She could see them as clear as day, though in the dream it was a moonless night, with peepers chirruping in the buckeye chestnut trees along the creek. Between them they were carrying a pail of something that gave off a smell of evil.

Buck was true to his word in the matter of Mr. Bell. The bargain they struck, spelled out and signed by both of them, called for Buck to contribute a dollar a week to the Pioneer Farmers to insure the mill. For its part, the bank was pledged to hand over four hundred dollars if any accident put the mill out of business. From reading Mr. Harrison's newspaper, which he waylaid every week now, he educated himself on the subject of California. Notices appeared in most issues to drum up recruits for the goldfields, inviting them to throw in with parties preparing for the trip. The usual amount of stake money quoted was three hundred dollars, this applying to departures from places as far off as Boston, Massachusetts. In his thinking, Buck added an extra hundred for emergencies.

Boats would provide a smoother ride; stages would rattle his bones like dice in a cup, but they'd probably prove quicker in the end. He wavered like a mule tied between two bales of hay. "What's our vote to be, Sam? Broiling in the Mohave or frostbite in the Rockies, two thousand and more miles to go before we're there even if we was fitted out with wings to fly with?"

"You can't count on any vote from me, but what you can do is count me out. I won't be leaving. It ain't going to work, Buck, and that's no cause for regret. I don't relish busting my balls or losing my scalp to a bunch of painted Indians."

Buck looked about as pleased as if he'd stumbled into a hornet's nest.

"You implying that you're chickening out?"

"That's your error, Buck. I never was into this thing, and I'd sooner be a live chicken than a dead duck."

Buck snorted, "You wouldn't have been much use, anyways, with a game arm. But you best not anticipate living off the fat of the land after I make my strike in California. I'll take my boy Malden along for company. He ain't overendowed with brains, but he's got a strong back, and he's willing enough."

"Maybe I'd best not anticipate more help from you now."

"You could be right. I don't hold much respect for chickens."

Sam and his wife and daughter had gone by the end of the week, and Anna wasn't sorry to quit sleeping on a floor instead of in the bed she'd brought with her into marriage.

Buck calmed himself by giving that week's newspaper a thorough going-over, which he'd done half a dozen times already. Feeding his dreams by poring over the print was his favorite pastime when the snow fell early and thick, threatening to bring him down with an attack of cabin fever if he hadn't found something to occupy him. He claimed reading aloud raised his spirits.

During that time he didn't pay too much attention to accounts of what the Abolitionists were doing, since slaves were prohibited in Ohio. In any event, he stood in no need of them when he had his wife and children running at his beck and call. But his interest perked up if a mob lynched an Abolitionist, which occurred now and then in the South.

He was always intrigued by reports about what Mrs. Elizabeth Cady Stanton, Susan B. Anthony, Lucretia Mott, and their like were tackling after they held their first meeting in behalf of "women's rights" at Seneca Falls, New York. "Them biddies don't know their rights from their lefts. I plan on sending you back a pair of them bloomers so you can strut around in them, aping a man, Ma. They'd suit you down to the ground. You've always hankered after ruling the roost and wearing the pants."

What Victoria liked hearing about best was something they called "spiritualism" in the tales the paper published concerning the crowds that flocked to a farmhouse at Hydesville near Rochester, New York, to listen to whatever Farmer Fox's two daughters might come up with. Margaret Fox was going on fourteen and Kate was a year younger.

They got going in the first place by exchanging a few taps and raps with a peddler who had been passing through Hydesville when he succeeded in getting his pack stolen and his throat cut. The method they used was to go through the alphabet letter by letter, one tap for an *A,* two for a *B,* and so forth. But the girls had made a business of it, with their father charging admission money, and there was talk of their being put on display in exhibition halls in Rochester.

This was the part in the stories that appealed to Buck. "Think of the amount of cash that slob can rake in! No end of people could be hornswoggled into believing they was getting through to their poor dead ma or some kid as was bowled over by typhoid."

Anna took offense at such ribaldry. "You got no faith, you heathen, and one day you pay dear for it. I know there is angels up in heaven because sometimes they say words to me, soft and sweet and gentle."

He ignored her. "I bet if Vic and Tennie was older they could handle all that buncombe and more. I'd be tempted to give it a try with Vic if I wasn't overdue in California."

Victoria put him down with a look before she spoke. "No way I would do it. I got faith like Ma. I've heard voices, too, when nobody was talking."

"You'll do as I tell you or you'll get what's coming."

"How can you force me when you won't be here?"

He shot up like a Fourth of July rocket. "I'll give you something right now to show you—what you might term a little going-away present."

She made no move to get away before he grabbed her, adding one more rip to the red calico dress on her back. He pushed her in front of him out the back door to the rain barrel where the ice was almost melted. Those inside heard the whishing of the switch as it swung against skin, to and fro, but there was no other sound from anybody. He didn't let go of her until they reached the ladder to the attic, which she climbed alone in silence. Utica was up there already, as she had been for days, fed nothing but spoonfuls of gruel that she could hardly swallow, and bundled away in a corner so the rest of them wouldn't catch the fever she had been struck with as a result of parading around barefoot in the yard too long when the thaw set in.

His breathing slowed. "Already smells like spring out there to-night. Soon be time to get moving."

At bedtime Tennie shivered herself to sleep with only a thread-bare blanket to warm her. Victoria was sitting up with Utica, who was tossing and turning and sniffling through her nose. First light of morning was seeping in through the chinks in the roof when Victoria woke Tennie with a finger stroking her forehead. Victoria's eyes were tired but bright and fierce.

"I had a vision come to me, Tennie, and Utie's mending now. I was trying to rock her to cool off the fever when two angels lifted her clean out my arms. They smiled at her and took turns fanning her face with their pale white hands until she was all cool and calm again. It's as true as I'm sitting here talking to you."

"You sure you wasn't dreaming?" Tennie was supposed to be the only one able to see things nobody else could. "What did they look like?"

"Like angels. With haloes and white robes and golden hair."

"Did they have wings?"

"Of course. They always do have, silly."

"Did they say anything?"

"No. Just smiled."

"Will you tell Ma?"

"Yes, but Pa mustn't know. He wouldn't understand."

When the hawk-nosed preacher rode into town to open the hell-fire-and-damnation season, the creek was racing so fast with melted snow it threatened to spin the waterwheel off its bearings if Buck hadn't checked the flow at the sluice gate. He was busy tackling what he swore to be the last corn he'd ever mill. He was chirpy as a cricket, singing to himself as he left the house:

> *Oh, Susannah, don't you cry for me,*
> *'Cos I'm off to Sacramento*
> *Wid a washbowl on my knee!*

Reverend Tupper came by every spring and set up shop among the white oak and birch and hickory just off the road where a brook ran sweet and huts had been put up years ago in a grove with a platform at one end to serve as a pulpit, facing rows of split-log benches. People drove their wagons in from miles around, drawn by the fact that he could be depended on to rouse them up pretty lively. If all the huts had been taken, they'd raise tents for an overnight stay because things went best when the torches were lit and the audience felt driven to let its hair down.

Anna would have liked the whole family there for opening night, but Buck dug his heels in as usual. He wouldn't let Malden go, since he had him in training for California. Polly cried off because she was being courted. Utica hadn't gotten her strength back yet.

Only Victoria, Hebern and Tennie were left to join in with their mother.

Victoria lugged bucketfuls of water down from the well to heat on the fire and wash the clothes they would all be wearing. For once, they were clean, on the evening they set off walking to the campground. The clearing was close to being filled when they got there, with teams unhitched from the wagons and tethered to trees, and families chatting with each other while they waited. Lanterns and torchlight made light enough for the Claflins to spot some people they knew perched on the benches, but nobody had a word for them, and they'd nothing to say by way of exchange.

Somebody down by the platform thumped out a tune on a wheezy harmonium, and Reverend Tupper showed himself on the platform with his hands lifted toward heaven, settling himself on one natural leg and one carved out of buckeye as a replacement for a limb he'd lost fighting the Iroquois. "Dearly beloved, I bid you welcome with joy in my heart, for tonight we shall join battle together to reclaim the world for Christ." The loudest "Amen" to be heard came from Anna. "We shall gird our loins and grab ahold of Satan to wrestle him down into the sulfurous pits of the abyss where he belongs. But first we must humble ourselves on our knees before Him. Let us pray."

In his case, this took some maneuvering, but he was used to it. He'd barely lowered himself to ground level and got launched before raindrops began to fall, but he covered that without a falter. "While Thou waterest the earth with refreshing showers, pour out showers to refresh our thirsty souls." The audience rewarded this sample of nimble thinking with a round of Hallelujahs.

Nothing could help Tennie from drowsing once in a while as the proceedings got under way: hymns, prayers, and the minister shouting himself hoarse; torches smoking and hissing from the sprinkling they were getting; mutters and moans on every side as he worked the crowd over, stirring them up for the tussle that lay ahead.

Reverend Tupper got down to particulars, spelling out a list of sins so comprehensive it had something to appeal to everybody. Once he was through with that, he tackled the main event, which was to wheedle as many as he could into marching up to the platform to tell about all the wickedness they'd been involved in up to now.

He thumped his wooden leg on the planking for punctuation. *"Vengeance is mine; I will repay, saith the Lord,* but He'll give you one final chance because He's fair-minded. He saith unto you, nay, friends, He beggeth you, each and every one—'Pray for redemption here and now before it's too late and you're tossed into the fiery lakes of hell, where the boiling billows roll throughout eternity and the screams and hollers of the wicked echo under the wrath of God forever and ever.' He says, 'Step right up while there's still a moment of time left to you and put your souls on the counter. He don't bargain; He don't cheat. He'll pay top dollar in the trade and grant you peace of mind for eternity.' "

Anna wasn't first in line. That privilege went to a young man with red whiskers who covered the distance between log and altar on his hands and knees, howling like a hound. Nor was she next; another woman skipped up ahead of her, jabbering without anybody understanding a word. But Anna showed up third, and Victoria fell in step behind her.

Between two sets of shoulders Tennie caught a glimpse of the preacher reaching down to help Victoria up onto the stage. He raised his arms to quiet things down for a minute, though one old man was flapping in the aisle like a landed trout.

"Verily, verily, as the good book says, 'A little child shall lead them.' This little child shall speak to us on this night of glory. O, harken to her, all ye that sin. Let her words sink deep into your hearts."

Hebern, who had the fidgets, wanted to cover his ears for shame. He'd no notion where Victoria had plucked up courage to make herself heard. "I just lately saw angels in our attic with shining wings and everything," she cried. The crowd yelled "Hallelujah!" "They spoke to me while they was curing a young sister of mine of the fever." The yells were louder now. "They said I was to come here with a message to you." The harmonium pumped out a chord or two. *"Cast out the devil, and give yourselves to Jesus!"* Tennie thought her sister was doing as well as Reverend Tupper and with equal force of imagination.

On Saturday, Buck left the house early, taking down no more than a mug of rye coffee and limiting himself to saying he'd be away until nightfall and was delegating Malden for duty at the post office. From the way Malden scratched his pimples, Tennie guessed he had some clue to what their father was up to, but she couldn't coax it out of him.

Buck arrived back late, looking so tired he must have walked most of the day, but perky as a blue jay. He was carrying a pail of something whose stench escaped even with the lid on. When he set it down on the floor and pried it open, it smelled that much worse. Rainbow colors swirled on top of the oozy brown liquid inside.

"Never seen the like before, have you? If you're out of luck digging a well in some places up to the northwest of here, this is what you find instead of water. Try burning it in a lamp and it smokes you like a codfish. The name they give it's 'magoozalum.' I been telling Malden about it."

Pinching their noses, his children asked how he'd come across magoozalum and what was its use. "Just happened to read about it and where to buy some in a letter the other day. Sells as a remedy for rheumatism. What else it's for you'll see tomorrow. Come on, Malden, we got things to do."

A jab between the shoulder blades convinced Malden to pick up the pail. Tennie hung behind for a moment or two, then skipped out onto the porch to watch them making for the mill. The peepers were chorusing along the creek, and the sky was dark as pitch. Suddenly she remembered her dream on the night Anna had gone out to the mound to cry down Buck. The girl didn't like remembering the next part, but there was no avoiding it. She knew Buck and her brother would collect deadwood and brush to build a bonfire in the mill. Her father would show Malden how to soak the floor and timbers with magoozalum, which would make a hotter fire than whale oil, then Malden would be ordered to strike a yellow phosphor match.

Sunday morning, Buck had dumbfounded his wife by saying he'd stroll down to church with them when she took Victoria, Hebern, and Tennie to Sunday school. She was bent on letting the superintendent, purse-mouthed Mr. Wheeler, know about Victoria's angels showing up in the attic.

Buck was on his best behavior every step of the way, giving a nod to every man he saw and tipping his hat to the wives. Outside the church he made a point of repeating much the same words to everybody willing to listen to him. "I'd planned on attending service today, but sad to say, I got an item of business to attend to in Mount Vernon. What'd that be, ten or more miles from here? Guess I may have to spend the night."

He buttonholed so many people before he left that the children were late entering the school hall, where Superintendent Wheeler was conducting the first hymn. Ma led them in procession up to the old rosewood piano his wife was pounding so heartily Tennie wondered whether it wouldn't fall apart before the benediction.

Anna grabbed hold of one of his wrists, yelling above the din. "You will listen to me, please. My child Victoria has been talking with angels. They fly down from heaven to call on her." He gave her a soapy smile without missing a beat, but he would need to be persuaded she was speaking the truth.

"You pay attention, please. These other children in Sunday school push mine away and won't say nothing nice about them. You stop them doing that or she will tell the angels how she is treated, and then those whelps will learn a lesson."

Most of his scholars had quit singing to goggle at them, but Mrs. Wheeler applied more muscle to her playing and built up the volume: "Wash me in the blood of the lamb so I can be purer than the snow."

Mr. Wheeler's smile had faded fast. "You're disrupting our service, Mrs. Claflin. I must ask you to take a seat. We'll have plenty of time to talk later."

"*Nein, nein!* Not later. Now, instantly. You warn them, please, to be good to my children."

Though his wife didn't give up, he did, to shoo Anna toward the door.

"Madam, you're causing a disturbance in a house of worship. . . . I really can't allow it. . . . Have consideration as a Christian for the others. . . . What will the children think of you?"

The faces of Victoria and Hebern had turned as red as turkey wattles. Anna let go with a stream of German that nobody could mistake for a blessing. In the doorway she gave a clearer hint of her feelings. "God curse you, blackhearted spawn of Satan, and your *zänkisch* wife also!" She crossed two fingers of her right hand and jabbed at him with the sign of the evil eye.

The Claflin children passed a restless day after that round of sparring. Buck was missing when they reached the house, and Malden was not to be seen anywhere. The dream about them wouldn't leave Tennie's mind, but her mother continued in such a passion that the girl wasn't inclined to relate it to her lest it threw her into a worse spasm. They all went to bed early, without a glimpse of Malden.

It was the wind blowing smoke in through the slits in the roof that roused Tennie from sleep, coughing. She listened for a moment, and above the wind there was a crackle like twigs snapping. She opened her eyes and saw the attic lit up with a flickering red glow.

A nudge of the elbow woke Victoria. "It's started. Look!"

She always woke up ready to go. "What you say—the mill!" She was on her feet in a flash. "I'll get Pa—I mean Ma. Utie, Hebern, Polly, get up! The mill's afire."

Pretty soon everybody was outside, pausing to stare at flames brightening the night while smoke filled their lungs. Anna, wispy gray hair done up in twists of paper, went down on her knees to pray. They left her there to get as close as they could without being singed by the sparks the wind was swirling around like snowflakes. Down in the town, somebody was hammering on the iron wagon tire that hung on a hook outside the jail to do service as an alarm.

Within a minute or two at most, half the population of Homer came panting up the hill, women clutching blankets and shawls around their shoulders, men stuffing nightshirts into their pants. Hebern had skipped out of the house in no more than a flannel shirt which was displaying more of his anatomy than his mother considered decent, but Widow Wycherley remedied that by insisting on lending him her shawl.

Sheriff Dodds arrived, heading up a team of men hauling the pumper, just seconds before the mill's roof caved in. There was such a leaping of flame and wrenching of timber that the crowd ripped out a roar as loud as if they were at a fireworks show. Mixed in with the smoke there was a smell like popcorn on a griddle. Tennie heard a sound of sobbing close behind her and turned around to Malden, tears leaving tracks in the soot on his face, one hand nursing the other, which was wrapped in a rag.

Everything was tried to douse that fire, half a dozen men working the pumper to draw water from the creek, three times as many passing buckets hand to hand to Banker Bell, who was at the top of the line bellowing for more buckets and quicker, too.

Tennie had known ahead of time it wouldn't work. Even Mr. Bell had reached the same conclusion and was standing by, chomping on his black beard, when a jaded livery-stable horse carried Buck to the spot at a canter. He put on a show of being horror-stricken, wringing his hands and groaning as if a dentist were pulling his teeth.

He edged up to Banker Bell before he started talking rationally. "I had a fearsome premonition this was happening. I took a room in a tavern for the night but couldn't sleep a wink. I had this feeling of doom as I couldn't shake, so I borrowed a horse. If I'd only left sooner I might have been able to do something. Now I'm ruined, wiped out, done for. Dear God, have pity on me and my young 'uns!"

Mr. Bell wiped sweat off his forehead and ash off his beard. The look he gave Buck was kin to those Victoria specialized in. A handful of men stayed on to wet down the embers, but Buck appeared so wrought when he offered to help that they advised him to go straight to bed. Inside the house, he insisted his family do the same.

The smell of smoke hadn't entirely cleared next morning and the atmosphere was continuing murky when Buck went off to the bank to collect the insurance. An hour later he was back, his eye twitching and face dark as thunder.

"Son-of-a-bitching bastard won't pay. Says he wants the sheriff to finish some inquiring first. I'll sue that prying Shylock for my money if that's what I have to do."

They didn't waste time moving against him. Before night, a committee of citizens tramped up onto the porch, Banker Bell in the lead, flanked by Mr. Harrison, the storekeeper, and the sheriff, who brought along the pail, burned clean and twisted out of shape, that had held the magoozalum. Malden took off through the back window as soon as he spotted them.

Mr. Bell took charge when Buck went out to meet them. "Show him the pail, sheriff. Do you recognize it, *Mister* Claflin? He found it in the mill, or what's left of it, this afternoon. I think you know what it once contained. Crude petroleum. How do you account for that?"

Buck swore he'd never seen it before, but not one of them believed him. He laid stress on the fact that he'd been away the previous night and could prove it, but that only set them off asking questions about the part Anna or any of the children had played in last night's affair.

Mr. Bell's jaw worked like a snapping turtle's. "It was your mill, and it's your loss. Attempted fraud and arson. What might a judge say about that, sheriff?"

"Ten to twenty years, depending on his humor. Maybe more if he got riled."

"I don't intend to press for prosecution right this minute, but you're plain criminal trash, Claflin, and this town can do without you."

Mr. Harrison nodded agreement. "A taste of tar and feathers might teach him better."

Mr. Bell summed up. "I advise you to leave, quick and quiet. If you're still here in the morning, I might have second thoughts."

Buck spluttered on about his rights and responsibilities, but they turned away and started down the steps. "What about my wife and family then? Who's going to fend for them? Am I supposed to leave 'em to starve?"

Mr. Harrison spoke over his shoulder. "We'll do something about that. Best get moving, Buck. You wouldn't look too pretty in a suit of feathers, rode out on a rail."

Malden had been listening outside the window. He was sniveling again when he climbed back in. "I don't want to go to California, Pa. Please don't force me. Please, Pa."

"I ain't going there, you goddam fool, and I ain't got the time to give you what you deserve."

He crammed his few belongings into an old carpetbag and pulled himself away from everybody when they tried to kiss him goodbye. All he said was, "I'll send for you when I'm settled," before he mounted the borrowed horse and rode south for the Cumberland Road, to turn east there for Pennsylvania, not west for gold.

Two

The number of social calls the Claflins received fell off after that night. In point of fact, nobody in any shape or form showed up either at the door or in the attic. Anna kept to the house, too proud to show her face outside. Malden was too unstrung to seek a job, and in any event he wouldn't have been trusted with one. He passed most days hiding in the woods, with the excuse that he was trying to snare rabbits or a possum for the pot. He usually had Hebern for company.

Polly was moping because her beau's interest in her had faded. Utica couldn't be coaxed to lend a hand for any chore now that her father wasn't there with his switch to persuade her. So Victoria and Tennie took on the task of going down to Harrison's to bring back whatever provisions he was willing to let them have on credit to supplement what was left in the larder.

They stopped by the post office every day to check on whether there was a letter from him that Victoria might be able to make something of, but the welcome that awaited them there from the temporary postmaster was cooler than anywhere else in town. He'd found a stack of empty envelopes Buck had been careless about, and he was denouncing Buck to everybody.

The two girls ran across Mrs. Wheeler from the Sunday school one morning. She told them the ladies of the church were getting up some sort of bazaar as a benefit for the Claflins. None of the family was on the invitation list, she said, because the ladies calculated that the sight of them was certain to put a dent in selling the aprons and pies they'd be making as soon as they'd set up a committee to oversee the jobs.

Victoria asked a favor. "I can't read too good, since I've never had much schooling, but I'd like to cipher what's in any mail that might come in for us. Do you think there might be someplace to borrow a book to teach me better, ma'am?"

Mrs. Wheeler looked as pleased as if she'd stumbled on a ten-dollar gold piece. She promised that if they called at her house she'd have something ready for them. And so Victoria laid hold of a copy of the New Testament, Weem's *Life of Washington,* and a collection of little stitched chapbooks handed down from Mr. Wheeler's grandfather featuring Tom Thumb, Dick Whittington, and Jack the Giant Killer. She soon got the hang of most of them, and she pulled Tennie along in her footsteps. She copied out words, too, to include handwriting in the curriculum and promised she'd pass the knack on to her sister as soon as she'd begun to master it.

The spring weather turned warm by the end of April, and there was still no news of Buck. The sun was beating down from a crystal-bright sky the afternoon she took Tennie and a book up beyond the mound into a clearing among the trees where nobody but the Claflin children had been known to tread. She stared at Tennie for what seemed forever before she undid the one surviving button on her torn red calico dress that no one had ever bothered to mend. After she pulled it off over her head, she took off her petticoat, which was as tattered as the calico.

Since Ma wouldn't permit shoe leather to be squandered by any child, nothing remained to cover Victoria except her drawers. She had those off in next to no time.

Tennie had seen her naked often enough before, but not outdoors. "Why'd you do that? Ain't you scared you'll catch a cold?"

Victoria took a breath that stretched her skinny ribs, reached up
with her arms, and gave out a sound like a cat being stroked. "I
want to feel the sun all over me. It's warm and good and soothing.
Want to try it?"

Tennie shook her head. "Somebody might see us, and if Ma got
to know we'd never hear the end of it."

"I don't care. If anybody steps by, we can take off and hide. I'll
help with your buttons if you like."

They spread themselves on the thick, soft grass. Tennie found it
a rare, satisfying feeling. Victoria put the book aside after she'd
finished a page. "Know something? I'm going to do the same next
time it rains. Wouldn't that be special, having rain trickle down
you?"

"Maybe. I reckon you'd catch your death for sure then."

"You'll learn more about yourself when you've grown. How you
feel things is every bit as important to you as brains. There's no
difference really. You have to know things with your skin before
you can think straight about them." She plucked a buttercup to
tickle Tennie under the chin with. "You miss Pa never kissing us,
Tennie?"

"He never chose to; us nor Ma either. But you and me do sometimes."

"It's not the same. I bet kissing a man gives you goose bumps."

She had plunged in too deep for Tennie. "You ain't supposed to
say such shameful things."

"I mean it. Soon as I'm old enough, I'm getting married. I'll find
somebody rich so Ma won't want for nothing, nor you either."

"You'll have to look real hard around here when that day comes."

"I shan't be here. I'll be living in a city. Cincinnati or Columbus
or Cleveland—somewhere that starts with a *C*. I've glimpsed it in
my mind."

"Angels been visiting again?"

A smile spread on her face. "Whatever you think, Tennie."
Shying off the subject, she talked about the marvels the two of them
would encounter and the fortunes they'd have when they were grown
women. Tennie did most of the listening and 50 percent of the
believing until the sun weakened behind the treetops. They had so

much of themselves for the bugs to bite that they hurried into their clothes and went home.

The church ladies took their time organizing themselves. The Claflins would have gone through their last cent but for Anna. She had always been a believer in charms and homemade tonics. She was never without a nutmeg in a pocket of her apron to stave off rheumatism. The past summer, when Utica caught whooping cough, Anna searched out a snail and set it crawling over brown sugar. She dosed Utie with it, slimy as it was, and followed that by serving her the drainings of black currant leaves boiled in water. Anna treated warts by plastering them over with brown paper soaked in spit or, in the absence of brown paper, with cobwebs rolled into a ball and set afire. She was her only patient in that regard. Warts didn't sprout on the rest of her family, but cobwebs did the trick whenever a scrape or a nick started one of them bleeding.

The children would stand watching her cook her potions over the fire, though there were some details she held to herself until they were farther along in life. Then she confided that yellow cedar cured the clap, a douche of hemlock lulled the itch in private parts of the anatomy, and a solution of mayflowers eased monthly cramps.

She had finished up a batch of lobelia one night when she paused to pull at her lower lip, which was a practice of hers to stimulate her thoughts. "Maybe I could prepare medicine to sell for money."

Polly quibbled, "Who'd buy off us, Ma? They'd figure we was out to do 'em in if only for spite."

"Not for people, I don't mean. Only for horses. Your father, when he was a young man selling horses, and we're still getting along good together, he was also selling medicine for them that I make." The wrinkles in her cheeks creased up tight so she looked almost happy. "I can hear him now. 'For cure of wind, galls, spavins, sprains, and strains, scratches, stiffness and swelling of the joints and limbs.' "

Mr. Harrison was cautious at first about letting them add the price of empty bottles to the bill, but when Victoria outlined what her mother had in mind, he offered to stock a few samples for sale provided they proved in advance there were customers to be had. The entire family except Anna and Malden took turns peddling

liniment from an old wicker basket, house to house and stable to
stable, then hanging around the hitching rail outside the store on
Saturdays. They didn't make a mint of money, but the task satisfied
Mr. Harrison and kept them fed once a day by his charity.

Malden, eighteen months older than Hebern, wasn't in on the
undertaking because he had left for parts unknown with only the
clothes on his back, saying nothing to anybody. After what had
happened on the day of his leaving, Tennie fancied he could see no
other course to take, and she felt no grief to see him gone.

That morning had clouded up gray and misty, and soft, warm
rain was soon falling. When Victoria slipped out of the house alone,
Tennie guessed she was off to test the touch of water trickling down
bare skin. Malden was up in the woods already, staying out of sight.

Hebern set out with snares to carry to him. Tennie went along,
too, thinking to join Victoria in their private clearing, where she
was certain to be. Brother and sister had reached the first line of
trees when Victoria came darting toward them, fleet as a deer,
naked, legs raked by brambles she'd met with as she ran. They
stopped short, then heard somebody hurrying after her.

She scurried behind the two of them. Three faces were turned in
the same direction when Malden pushed through the last tangle of
branches. Sweat beaded his forehead and a flush reddened his cheeks.
She was breathing hard, but she had breath enough to jeer at him.
"You couldn't catch me for all you tried, could you?" The next
thing she said was for Hebern and Tennie. "He sneaked up, pawing
at his pants, and made a grab for me, but I was too quick for him.
We're duty bound to tell Ma."

He spoke as if his mouth was full of slaver, damning her for a
wanton bitch, then turned back into the woods along the path he'd
just trampled. That was the last they ever saw of him. When everything was quiet again, they walked in with Victoria to pick up her
clothes. She was carefree as a kitten. What mattered to her wasn't
the scare she'd had; only winning the race. She heard once from
Anna much later that Malden had found work laying track for one
of the railroads that were spreading everywhere.

Victoria was making headway with reading and arithmetic and
Tennie could manage most three-letter words when Buck wrote at

last. He had settled, he said, in Pennsylvania and he'd collect his family if they would get themselves to Pittsburgh and send him a telegram from there to an address he gave in Williamsport. Since he omitted to enclose or mention money, they were free to choose their own route. That called for careful study, since their finances were tight even after Mrs. Wheeler, shading herself with a parasol, conducted a delegation of church ladies to drop in on Anna and hand over a purse, the proceeds of the bazaar they had finally come around to organizing. Finding a customer to buy the house would take too long, but in anticipation, Banker Bell advanced a few dollars on a note Anna scrawled her name to, though he claimed he was overextending himself when the Claflin place was fit for nothing except being torn down and sold for kindling.

Though track ran east from as far off as Iowa City, she had no use for railways. She had ridden once between Harrisburg and Chambersburg on the Cumberland Valley line in her younger days when Buck was in the horse trade. She recalled being jolted, rattled, and smothered in cigar smoke and locomotive cinders before the cars jumped the tracks at a switch and they were stranded all night. Victoria figured out the price of stagecoach fares.

They could not be afforded, apart from the fact that the stage wouldn't carry the Claflins' sticks of furniture, in particular the brass bedstead that Anna declined to abandon.

She elected for them to take a steamboat, which would cost a dollar a head for each hundred miles. All that had to be done was hire a carter and a road wagon to load everything and everybody down as far as the closest public landing, which would involve two nights of sleeping as best they could under a spread tarpaulin. The day of their leaving, the population of Homer down to babes in arms turned out to see them off and make sure there was no delay. Widow Wycherley made to press a folded bill into Anna's hand, but she refused to accept.

Anna had never sighted the Ohio before, and she was in as great a flutter as any of them as they clustered together on the landing that jutted out into a river so wide they could scarcely make out the opposite bank in the haze. Wagon wheels clattered over the timbers, and teamsters cursed to clear a road through the throng of waiting passengers. The rippling brown water was aswirl with every imaginable kind of craft—arks, skiffs, rafts, flatboats, keelboats with sails up to catch the fitful breeze, which barely fanned the flushed faces of the crowd. They stood bordered at back and sides by piled-up boxes and bales, kegs and trunks, crates and hogsheads. Victoria spelled out the stenciled letters marking them as shipments of flour, salt, and iron due to be borne west; molasses, lead, and hides that would soon be loaded for sailing upstream. The black men laboring in the stevedore gangs—and sharing swigs of the bottle with the rest—were a novelty. Tennie hadn't anticipated their being so sharp-looking, not much darker than whites, she judged, after what the weather had done to all their faces. As they wrestled the cargoes closer toward the water's edge, they were chanting above the bedlam of bells and whistles and toots from the bullhorns the keelboaters carried:

> *Hi-O, away we go*
> *Floating down the river*
> *On the Ohi-O!*

A suntanned, soft-faced individual with a mourning band on the right sleeve of his white jacket sauntered up, set down a good leather valise, and raised his panama hat to Anna. "Remarkable yet reassurin' somehow to witness members of our race and the offspring of Cain workin' harmoniously side by side, don't you think? But you know what they say about Ohio boatmen—half horse, half alligator. Is this your family, ma'am?" His voice sounded slow and peculiar, altogether different from what they were accustomed to.

Anna gave him a bob of her jet-beaded bonnet.

"Four beautiful girls, and this one here's the prettiest, if I may make a distinction." He chucked Tennie under the chin with a gentle hand ornamented with a big diamond ring. Utica sneered behind his back.

"But she's the smartest." Tennie pointed a finger toward Victoria.

"Ah, she brings to mind my own little girl, lost to this life consequent to a bout of typhoid seven months back. Poor, darlin' Adele! How I miss her! Are you all travelin' far?"

"To Pittsburgh, sir." It was Victoria's turn to speak. "It'll be our first time there." Anna was uneasy about talking to strangers. She wasn't to be distracted from mounting watch over their bundled luggage and the brass bedstead, taken apart and roped for traveling.

"Then let us trust the captain's runnin' to schedule." He fished out a gold hunter watch on a chain that straddled his vest. As he flicked open the case, Tennie spotted the likeness of a child with long ringlets, likely of a fair color, though she couldn't be positive from the sepia about that. "The *Telegraph* should be steamin' along any minute now. Pittsburgh's my destination, too, but I've been interruptin' a long trip up from New Orleans for a night of rest ashore."

The gleaming white stern-wheeler that showed up around a bend in the river on their right had to be it. She stood four decks high, looming over everything else on the water, creamy foam curling off her bow and churning up from her stern, gray streamer of smoke trailing from the coronet of iron that circled the top of her stack, then puffs of white rising from her steam whistle, signaling her turn into dock. The landing bell rang out sweet and clear from the campanile of the building behind them, and the roustabouts on the landing perked up their pace. Idlers stirred themselves from lolling against the bollards, chewing tobacco, to catch ropes thick as a man's wrist that snaked out from fore and aft.

Anna would have chosen to linger until the bedstead and the heavier stuff were safe on board, but a roughneck in a peaked cap informed her that was contrary to regulations. Soon they were caught in the crush squeezing up the gangplank to the open deck. The stranger in the white suit went by a different way into the first-class quarters with a black servant in green livery toting his bags.

The bell chimed again for departure, and the steam whistle shrilled loud above them. The stern wheel started to tumble and thrash up suds, the last rope was tossed back aboard, and they settled themselves on their share of the bony iron benches to gape at the trees on either side of the river sliding by faster and faster as the *Telegraph* put on speed.

They had been under way no more than ten minutes before they had another visit from the stranger in white. He spoke about how much Victoria reminded him of his dead daughter. He would take it as a privilege to converse with them, Victoria in particular. Would Anna permit him to make up the difference in the price of the tickets so he might enjoy their company in the first-class cabins?

Victoria cut in before her mother could refuse. "We'd welcome that kindness, sir. Mother would be a lot more comfortable sitting snug out of the wind."

Tennie and the rest of them weren't as successful as Victoria in controlling their gawking as they stepped inside. Their feet sunk deep into carpets, woven with flower patterns, the like of which they had never seen, covering floors that shook with the thumping of the engines down below. Every wall was paneled and inlaid with more designs. The whale-oil lamps fixed to them and swinging overhead were of shiny brass with real silk shades. In a vestibule a string band was playing without gaining any particular attention. They climbed one broad stairway after another, goggling at the oil paintings in carved frames that hung everywhere, passing a red-plush saloon with a mountain of liquor bottles stacked against sparkling mirrors, a barbershop, and rows of varnished doors, until he led them into the dining room. Nothing would satisfy him there but their agreeing to sit down with him as his guests for dinner, though he had yet to announce his name.

Tennie had never imagined such luxury even in a dream. Fresh roses in a crystal vase on the snow-white linen tablecloth; painted roses repeated around the rims of the plates, each of them flanked with more knives and forks and spoons than she could tally; chairs upholstered far softer than the bedding they'd slept on at home; an array of glasses sparkling at every setting; a black waiter in a starched mess jacket dealing a folded-over bill of fare to every one of them.

Victoria opened hers up and batted her eyes at their host. "Would you mind reading out what it says, sir? None of us is too good at distinguishing long words."

Tennie was about to point out she was underselling herself when Victoria threw her a sideways wink. He was happy to oblige, and then he ordered the same for all, starting with turtle soup, proceeding to rainbow trout and sirloin steak, rounding off with sherbet, a platter of cheeses, and a bowl of fresh fruit. He signaled a steward to bring a bottle of French wine, but Anna butted in. They had to stick to water until they reached coffee time.

By then they were feeling compelled to push back from the table, but Victoria kept the ball rolling by inquiring what was taking him to Pittsburgh.

He tilted his chair, lit a thin cheroot, and let smoke wander through his nostrils. "Well, I've a degree of inquisitiveness about a young lady who's advertised to make a public appearance in a hall in that city. Maybe you or your mother is acquainted with the name of Cora L.V. Hatch?" Victoria shook her head. "The Fox sisters, then? She's a kind of follower of theirs."

Victoria knew something about them from her father's newspaper reading. "The farmer's daughters who claim they raise spirits?"

"That's it. But this Hatch girl is some years younger—her manager's her father. I'm informed she's recently established communication with the shade of our late President, old Zach Taylor, regardin' the present incumbent of that office, Fillmore, one-time wool-carder's apprentice, who's riled the Abolitionists no end by signing the Fugitive Slave Law, requirin' the return of runaways."

"Is that what you want to see her about—freeing slaves and such like?"

"Not at all. Something far more personal to me. The current uproar over slave or free will simmer down eventually, and we'll get on with the important business of unitin' this great land. No, I intend to put her to the test and ask her, for a fee, to locate my little girl wherever she is in heaven."

Victoria's eyes fixed on his. "The one who looked like me?"

His voice blurred. "She was close to being your twin. I'd have done anything in the world for her, but that wasn't to be."

"Could my sister, Tennie here, and me help you out? We've done things similar to that. She's got a gift, you know, and me—well, I hear voices talking to me sometimes when nobody's there."

He wasn't out-and-out disbelieving, as Tennie figured he ought to be. Instead he warmed to the suggestion, and after she'd begged him two or three times to give it a try, it was arranged that they would rest up for a while in the ladies' retiring room, then Anna would take them along to his private cabin.

First, in a row of closets, they experimented with flushing the toilets, which had to be considered superior to the outhouse they were used to back home. Then as soon as the two girls had a moment alone, Tennie had a question to ask her sister. "What are you expecting of us when we don't even know his name?"

"It's Henry Caldwell—I seen it on his valise—and I bet he's rich, with a big mansion and a plantation and slaves and everything. I reckon she was his only child."

"I know how she looked, from a picture in his watch."

"You do? That's perfect. He only wants a true word of comfort."

"Do you think he'll pay?"

"I think so. He'll feel obligated."

"I shan't know what to say without you teach me, Sis."

"Do as I do. I'll start off, then you copy me. I'll help you out if you falter."

Mr. Caldwell was well informed about what was fitting for a session with the spirits. In the cabin a small round table had been covered with a green baize cloth and pulled up to the sofa where he was to sit. A folding chair had been added to two others for Anna and her two daughters to link hands with his. The wick of the lamp was turned down to the slimmest strip of yellow, with a red bandanna knotted around its glass for further dimming. Just before they closed the circle—Caldwell, Tennie, Victoria, and Anna in that order—Anna crossed herself, and he leaned forward to give Victoria a gentle kiss on the cheek.

She delayed doing anything until some minutes had ticked away on the marble clock standing on a piece of furniture that was part clothespress, part washstand. Her heart was beating in time with the throb of the engines. Then she set to swaying from side to side and mumbling, but not in words. Caldwell's fingers crunched Tennie's left hand.

The voice Victoria spoke with next was as gruff as a man's. "I come to guide you where you want to go. The gates of heaven lie open before me. I will lead you among the angels. Tell me your wish."

Her face was contorted in the glimmer from the lamp. Tennie doubted she'd be able to match her in a month of Sundays. Anna was shedding tears down either side of her bony nose. Caldwell was whispering, "Who are you? Where do you come from? What do you look like?"

The girl's voice grew deeper. "I am pathfinder, name of Flying Eagle, Indian chief, scarred from many battles. What you want of me?"

"I'd be much obliged if you could look for my Adele. She's been gone since last fall, a beautiful, lovin' child, and very dear to—" The steam whistle somewhere high above their heads let go with a blast that momentarily had all four of them in twitches, surmising it was an augury.

"I go seek her." Victoria let her head fall back while she muttered mumbo jumbo with no meaning to it. Then she laughed aloud and when she spoke her tone was pitched gentle and drawly like his. "Here I am, Adele Caldwell. Who's that callin' for me? I can't see a thing yet, it's so misty up here."

His body trembled, making Tennie fearful he was entering into convulsions. "It's your daddy, precious. Are you really there?"

"Why, certainly I am, daddy darlin'. I've been waiting the longest time to hear from you."

He could barely manage a word out for the sobbing that shook him. "Has the pain gone away, sweetheart? Are you happy the way you always used to be?"

"Everybody's happy all the time here, Daddy, in our flowin' white robes and all. Nobody suffers pain nor sorrow. My hair's still just as long and curly like you remember, and I love you more than I ever did."

"Have you seen anyone we used to know, Adele honey—your mother or Grandpa or Uncle John?"

Here it comes, Tennie told herself; she's going to be sunk unless she can maneuver out of it. But she should have had more trust. "Yes, they're all here," said Victoria, "and they're just fine as can be, but would you excuse me, Daddy? I have to go now. The choir's on the point of giving another concert. Will you talk to me again real soon? I miss you somethin' cruel."

He was too wrought to ask for more. Victoria kept them holding hands to provide him a chance to pull himself together. Tennie was glad she hadn't been given a turn at a trance, but she had gained some clues about performing in the future. When he was feeling more like himself, he ordered supper all around, though he himself ate nothing. He was convinced he'd witnessed something superior to anything in the Book of the Revelation. Anna shared that opinion, from all she said later.

Victoria hadn't before seen a man in such a glow of pleasure. He made her promise they'd return the following evening, and he handed Anna a five-dollar piece. The family slept well that night in the two cabins he paid for, lulled by the nonstop swishing of water against the hull and the comfort of featherbeds.

Tennie had a dream about a white-painted mansion shaded by trees from the sweltering sun, pillars framing the front door, surrounded by fields of cotton ten times bigger than anything around Homer. She knew in her mind the place belonged to Henry Caldwell, but now he was lying dead somewhere, shot by a soldier, and the house was empty and charred by burning.

Every evening for the rest of the trip, the party of four gathered for more seances while the remainder of the Claflin young kicked up their heels on deck. Tennie was called on to contribute no more than joining hands because Victoria was nimble at cutting off Adele if his questions stumped her. He asked for nothing of consequence apart from reassurance that Adele was staying happy. By the time the boat docked at Pittsburgh, Anna had thirty-five more dollars sewn into her corsets, and he doubted he'd go to the trouble of seeking out Cora Hatch.

Anna shied away from taking a railroad train for the next lap, but Victoria talked her into it. They still had something approaching two hundred miles to cover. They didn't qualify as emigrants, which would have entitled them to a special rate, as they discovered when she bought the tickets. Anna commissioned Victoria to telegraph to Buck that they were bound for Williamsport, but Victoria took it on herself to omit doing that in order to surprise him.

Anna had settled for what were known as the "accommodation cars," though they soon learned from the smoke and cinders that the accommodations hadn't been refined much since she had suffered her only previous ride aboard a train.

It was Victoria's idea to hire a buggy at the station to convey them to what proved to be a lodging house. There, Buck was accommodated in a third-floor bedroom which he calculated to be big enough for all. He and Anna would share the only bed, the five children the floor. With the landlady's steering, they found him outside the door of a stable in an alley in the rear, stirring something in a stew pot over a brazier, surprised but not overcome with joy at the sight of them.

First, Anna complied with his directions to hand over whatever cash she had, and then she explained how Malden came to be missing. Without a twitch of an eyebrow at the news, Buck reported on how he'd been occupying his time lately. This involved conducting them into the barn to show them the livery horse he'd neglected to return, together with a four-wheeled cart, roofed with tarred canvas and bought cheap, he said, after he had sold the livery stable's saddle. He marveled to find he was in the same line of work as Anna, peddling horse liniment made according to the same recipe as hers. He was currently engaged in boiling a batch of it over the charcoal.

He surveyed them with misgivings in his sharp-honed eye. "I been getting by fair enough on what I make, but I ain't so sure it'll cover feeding all. Maybe I been too hasty summoning you. How'd you come by the money, Anna?"

She set about relating Victoria's venture into trances for Caldwell's benefit and the part Tennie had played as helper. Buck prodded her with questions to catch the details. His brain was whirring, and from his tossing and turning on the creaking bed that night, it was clear the whirring was continuing.

By morning, he had everything sorted out: "Claflins got to stick together, and by God, you two are going to stick with me." He was enrolling Victoria and Tennie in a new family business, combining their talents and Anna's with his, he said.

"It's frittering time away selling liniment when there's a lot more people than horses in this neck of the woods. What you'll do, Anna, is stew up some of the people-medicine of yours. We'll stick a label on the bottles, and I'll take it on the road with me and the two girls; maybe Hebern, too, if he turns out useful."

Victoria spoke up for both. "What've you a mind for Tennie and me to do, trailing around in that little cart?"

"What the devil do you think? Tell fortunes. Read the past. Predict the future. Every Tom, Dick, and Harry laps up that stuff. We'll have two strings to our bow, and we'll put a picture of Tennie on the bottles, she being the best looker in the crowd."

Buck was a fireball when he roused himself. During the following days he ran around at a gallop, pursuing his schemes and wheedling credit, which was easier in a place where his reputation hadn't caught up with him yet.

He set Hebern to painting the sides of the cart barn red and its wheels bright yellow, colors, he considered, to give a glow of health and attract the customers. Then he ordered a sign for each side, decorated with flourishes and fancy lettering, reading, in one case, "MAGNETIC LIFE ELIXIR. Proprietor: *Dr. Reuben Buckman Claflin,*" and in the other, "AMAZING CHILD CLAIRVOYANTS. Manager: *Dr. Reuben Buckman Claflin.*"

He took Tennie off to a printshop, where the owner's wife sketched a picture, head and shoulders, to be etched in metal for the labels. Buck let himself go in composing the subject matter: "Miss Tennessee's Magnetic Life Elixir for Beautifying the Complexion and Cleansing the Blood. Warranted to be Perfectly Harmless and Purely Vegetable. Directions: A teaspoonful three times a day one half hour before each meal. Persons taking the Elixir should be careful in their Diet. Price $2.00 Per Bottle."

"Purely vegetable" was a lie. He said the best way to convince people they felt improved after swallowing a dose was to lace it with liquor, in this instance the yellow one, Tennessee, which he happened to have available. Anna stirred the cauldron that the landlady, Mrs. Hofmeister, lent him after he promised her a bottle, free. Anna sampled the mix he'd specified and thought to add more sugar. He ruled against that on grounds that his patients might conclude they were being shortchanged unless they tasted something ferocious. Her inclination was to include more lobelia, too, and his to increase the laudanum. He compromised on shaking in roughly the same amount of each.

He blarneyed a bookseller into letting him have a fat, leatherbound medical dictionary on approval. It listed every known disease from ringworm to ingrown toenails, with steel engravings underlining the prescribed treatments.

He boned up on the book during the evenings while there was still light in the barn, perched on the seat of the cart. Inside it was shaping up like a gypsy caravan under the sawing and hammering he and Hebern were doing. Frau Hofmeister had a shelf full of books in her parlor that she was willing for Victoria to dip into. Tennie met with Cinderella and Rumpelstiltskin while her sister dug into *The Universal Encyclopaedia; Organized Knowledge in Story and Picture.* She put her studying to use early on in picking a name for the horse, which Buck hadn't gotten to. She campaigned for "Rosinante," but he scorned that as too highfalutin. He wouldn't go further than "Rosy," which scarcely seemed fitting for a gelding.

The girls weren't sorry when everything was ready at last for the maiden outing. Anna had his pledge, for what it was worth, that he'd resist the thought of whipping either of them. He had pondered over the choice of place for their trial run and decided they should make for Lycoming, where a carnival was due, according to notices posted around town. They wouldn't be away more than a night, which would be convenient for Anna.

They wore their best clothes, which looked better for Mrs. Hofmeister's mending and laundering. He vowed to buy new as soon as the cash flowed in. They loaded the cart with food and blankets for themselves, oats for Rosy, a handbell, and three cases of Magnetic Life Elixir. Hebern climbed in, too, having a role to play in his father's plans.

They spent most of the journey rehearsing according to instruction after they set off that Saturday morning, planning to arrive by the advertised opening time. But he had misjudged the pace Rosy could maintain, whipped or not, and the fair was already under way when they paused on the road outside to drop off Hebern.

A brass band and a merry-go-round's pipe organ were blaring in competition, lungs and bass drum tackling "Home, Sweet Home" while the steam burped out "Oh, Susannah!" A throng of men and women, children and stray dogs circulated around the other attractions. One group of men was striving to shinny up a greasy pole while a second group ran in pursuit of an equally greasy pig. A sword-swallower with a turban on his head and tattooed dragons on his arms was thrusting a torch down his throat, ready to belch fire.

Buck reined in at a spot where traffic was steady and the music far enough away to talk without straining. He hobbled Rosy, who was drooling lather, and scrambled up onto the tailgate with his daughters bracketing him on either side. Victoria swung the hand-bell. Their ears were soon ringing, too, but it did draw an audience. He clutched a dark-brown bottle of the cure-all, which he brandished over their heads.

"Friends, and I call you friends because if you ain't at present you will be for the rest of your days once you've tried what I'm here to offer you. Looking down at your faces, I say to myself, 'How many of these fine people really enjoy to the full the abounding good health the Lord has entitled them to?' The years I've spent in medical practice in New York City, Cincinnati, Philadelphia, and elsewhere, they provide the answer. I observe symptoms of the pains and problems some of you are experiencing today or will do possibly no later than A.M. tomorrow. How many of you men are compelled to keep getting up nights to relieve yourselves or find difficulty tending the ladies? How many ladies are afflicted by obstruction, palpitations, and other female weaknesses? If you don't suffer them difficulties personally, turn to your wife, your husband, your children, your neighbor. See if you don't agree with me that they bear symptoms of trouble in need of curing—muddy complexion, inflammation of the eyeball, nervousness of disposition, warts, wens, and so forth and so on."

He had them spellbound, as was plain from the critical way they eyed each other. Bits of the patter that followed were lifted from the pages of the dictionary he'd packed in with the family supper. "Now in the profession I've dedicated myself to serving, we understand that the human body is formed and controlled, preserved and defended, and then, when afflicted, restored by the action of an invisible agent we know by the term 'the vital force.'"

He broke off to uncork the bottle and take a sniff. "Ah, the sheer, rejuvenating power of it! But to proceed. This vital force I'm talking about is magnetism, and as one of my distinguished colleagues has put it, 'Without magnetism there cannot be life.' Life is created and kept functioning by the influence of magnetism stirring the stomach lining, tissues, and digestive processes. Electrogalvanic potency;

negative working upon positive; acid upon alkali; action and reaction—that's the secret of everlasting vim and vigor, and that's the secret I'm extending to you in the bottle I hold here in my hand!"

Hebern had slunk up to the edge of the crowd. "Bottle in my hand" was his father's cue to him to start clapping, and a fair number in the gathering followed suit. "I appreciate your applause, but you mustn't accept my unsupported word for the miracles this medicine will work on you. I expect you to ask, 'Where's the proof, the irrefutable evidence?' Well, friends, it's right beside me, standing before you in the shape of these two dear daughters of mine, both of them, needless to say, my patients, too, since I wouldn't condone their being maintained in glowing health and beauty by no other hands."

Tennie and her sister performed on signal, first Tennie and then Victoria stepping forward to split their jaws with smiles and drop a curtsy. "This one's Miss Victoria. Give 'em your testimony, child."

"After Pa nursed me safe and sound through the smallpox owing to the medicine, of course, I was scared stiff my skin would always look a fright, but he kept up the dosing, and it didn't take more than one more bottle to fix me up without a blemish the way you can see for yourselves."

Buck's beam was as bright as a locomotive headlamp. "Before you hear from my second one, who's Miss Tennessee, I'd like to impart to you what happened to prompt me into giving her name to the Magnetic Life Elixir. My little sweetheart was born a cripple, and she grew into childhood incapable of toddling a single, tiny step. I confess, to my shame, that I let some other doctor, a surgeon he was, examine her. His recommendation was to operate, cutting down to the bone with a knife as sharp as a razor after the numbing poisons he prescribed had failed to ease her torment.

"The sight of her darling face all puckered up with fear roused me to my senses. I knew the impossibility of performing a surgical maneuver of any magnitude, slicing deep and violating the body, without risk of what's tantamount to actual murder. That's what drove me to experiment with the Elixir so I could stimulate and strengthen her vital force, substituting hope for anguish and science for butchery. I'm proud to admit it—she was the one I tested it on first. Cast your eyes on the result. Show 'em, Tennie!"

The directions he'd given in advance called only for a high kick and a brief sashay around the tailgate, which she didn't find demeaning when they gave her a cheer.

"What you've just witnessed, friends, is a stunner, ain't it? And I've got another surprise in store for you. Those down front there can read the price marked on this label. It says plain as a pikestaff, 'Two dollars.' But I'm not charging that much today, nor yet a buck and a half. You strike me as deserving, high-class people, so I'm offering each and every one of you a bottle of Miss Tennessee's Magnetic Life Elixir for precisely what it costs to produce in the manufactory—four bits, one dollar only, and it comes with a guarantee it'll work wonders for you as it's done for her."

Hebern had edged his way up close to the cart. It was his turn again. "I'll take three, Doc." Customers' arms were soon waving, and the Claflins on the tailgate were pushing bottles into the dupes' hands.

They put on a similar performance every half hour, taking time out to have a bite of food, washed down in Buck's case by a swig of raw whiskey. Trade was so brisk that he ruled against slowing down to tell fortunes, which could be saved for another day. Before the light faded they had sold out the stock. More than a few at the carnival were wavering on their feet by then. They hadn't been able to wait to get home before they sampled the physic.

The days of putting on medicine shows stretched into weeks, the weeks into months. He did some polishing of his spiel, though the gist of it was always the same. He abided by his warrant to buy new outfits for all and not lay into Victoria no matter what. He was apprehensive about covering the same ground twice without giving his clients an interval for recovery. They must rove farther and farther from Anna until winter set in and snow cooped them up at Mrs. Hofmeister's.

Nobody could tolerate such closeness for long, he least of all. Next thing the girls knew, he had sold the cart, along with Rosy, and they were retracing the trail back to Ohio, ready to open a new season in the spring.

They moved in, bag and baggage, to room with his eldest daughter, Margaret Ann Miles, whose husband, a druggist in Mount Gilead, was a peace-loving man hard-pressed to enjoy any now that he had a houseful of Claflins to badger him. Buck poured over Enos Miles's ledgers, which had doctors' prescriptions pasted onto the pages. He quizzed Enos about the diseases the various medicines were supposed to treat, extending his education by jotting down the answers in a notebook and stealing pages from the records for further study.

He bought a new horse and a spanking wagon rigged out with sleeping bunks and shelves to hold the brown bottles. He nailed his same painted signs to its sides, and Victoria christened the horse Rosy for old times' sake.

Victoria had concluded that she was a cut above common folk. She was also inclined to be broody, especially on days when the cramps seized her, which Anna's dosing failed to ease. Victoria went on contending in private that she was visited by spirits—no more angels, but Demos*thenes*—she rhymed it with "pennies"—whom she'd read about in Mrs. Hofmeister's set of the encyclopedia.

"What makes him so special?"

"He must have been the most wonderful man that ever lived, that's what. He used to make all kinds of speeches about freedom, telling how everybody ought to stand up and fight for their liberty. He trained himself by putting pebbles in his mouth and reeling off recitations as he climbed up mountains or stood down by the ocean, shouting until he drowned out the waves."

"Pebbles? You'd wonder he didn't swallow 'em."

"Don't butt in, Tennie; just listen. He shut himself up in a cell, too, with one side of his head shaved bald."

"Why'd he want to do that?"

"The encyclopedia said it was 'to guard himself against a longing for the haunts of men.' No amount of studying was too much for Demos*thenes*. He was a lawyer and a statesman and a warrior besides. Of course, it all happened a long time back—hundreds of years before Jesus."

"How'd he die—the Greek one, I mean?"

Her eyes opened wide. "He killed himself in front of enemy soldiers who'd driven him out of his own country. He hid poison on a pen and sucked it, fooling them he was writing a farewell letter. Mrs. Hofmeister's book said, 'He was one of the noblest characters in Greek history.' "

"And you reckon you've actually seen him?"

Her brown curls bobbed. "Once, twice, maybe more, Miss Nosey. He wears sandals with long laces and a linen shirt thing half down to his knees like in the picture. One night he tells me, 'You will know fame and riches,' and then another time, 'You will live in a mansion in a city surrounded by ships and shall become a ruler of your people.' I imagine that's the city I told you about once where I'll be after I'm married, the one that starts with a *C.*"

"You've got a long wait when you won't be fifteen till September. Polly's bound to be next on the list for a wedding."

The family was wrong about that—and wrong, too, in doubting the influence Demosthenes had over Victoria. Six years passed before Polly found a man to marry, though she did well, it seemed then, with Ross Burns, a local lawyer. But Victoria didn't last the season out with Buck's traveling show, and Demosthenes turned all the Claflins head over heels when his time came.

They rested on Sundays because Elixir sales were apt to be slow and the God-fearing were resentful if they worked on the Sabbath. The two sisters were out for a stroll one Sunday after church when a man scented with cologne stopped them to speak to Victoria. "Forgive me being so bold, but would you consent, if you are free, to come with me to the picnic?" This was a town attraction coming up on the Fourth of July. He announced himself as "Dr. Canning Woodhull," which they felt might or not be true; any man in those days could hang a shingle on his door and set himself up in practice without let, license, or hindrance.

Buck and Anna no longer fussed about the company she kept when she wasn't working, and Buck liked the thought of her being squired by a fellow professional. He canceled her performances on picnic day and nudged her into going to the picnic with Woodhull. When they got back, she was carrying a rag doll Woodhull had won for her in an egg-and-spoon race.

He'd have planted a kiss if she'd not pulled away. "Little puss, tell your parents I want you for a wife."

She didn't get the chance. Tennie had been hiding in the darkness of the hall. She cut in ahead and ran whooping into the kitchen, where Anna sat squinting at views of Washington, D.C., in Enos's stereopticon and Buck was totting up the day's take. "Victoria's out there with her beau, and he's bent on marrying her!"

Victoria would probably never have married Woodhull if her parents hadn't remained so calm about the prospect. It was Tennie that Anna fretted over most, saying how sorely she would miss her sister. Buck talked to him as though they were on an even keel in administering to the sick. He satisfied himself with questions about the essentials of his future son-in-law. Woodhull was a bona fide doctor, college trained, and a Freemason, too; born well-to-do in Rochester, New York, like the Fox sisters; based only temporarily in Mount Gilead, since he wanted a large family of children and was looking to move to a city where he'd gain income to provide for them.

Buck poured drinks. "Well, you can count on my blessing for a grand match, Doctor. Victoria girl, you've done us proud."

She looked more upset than pleased. She didn't like her job assisting Buck, but it was belittling to see him so ready to dispense with her and carry on with Tennie alone.

Tennie thought her sister married to spite their father. The gleam that lit up in Woodhull's eyes was never reflected in his young wife's. She blew hot and cold in the days before the wedding. Buck hounded her into going through with it, and he bought her shoes and a new dress. The ceremony was private, with the bridegroom the only Woodhull standing before the judge. She was still just short of fifteen, though they lied about that.

Three

The name on the envelopes was always Tennie's, for her to read the letters aloud to Anna, but Buck opened them first. Sure enough, Victoria was living in a city starting with a C—Chicago. Fame and fortune hadn't caught up with her yet at the little frame house in a section full of immigrants where the parlor served as Woodhull's surgery. Tennie wondered whether she had lost faith in Demosthenes, who wasn't mentioned at all because Victoria was wise to Buck's prying, and the subject of a dead Greek couldn't be counted on to gain his sympathy.

It struck Tennie and her mother as they talked about Victoria that she seemed worse off married than when she had been single. Woodhull had taken to drink, she wrote. "She's so mighty bullheaded she must have driven him to it," said Buck. She said her husband had turned out to be "unchaste." The meaning of that eluded them until Buck spelled it out: "He goes whoring." A baby was on the way already, which was no surprise; Anna had no spells or remedies to offer to ward off pregnancy.

Winter was on them by then. Anna fretted over Victoria as never before, wondering if she would remember to do what was necessary for a newborn. A baby had to be prodded into sneezing to free it from the power of goblins and restrained from glimpsing itself in mirrors lest its growth be stunted. Buck turned grumpy listening to her and seeing his money dribble away. He cast his eye in Tennie's direction one morning when she was grappling with the text of a story in a book Victoria had just sent her, "The Legend of Sleepy Hollow." He'd concluded, he said, that Tennie could advance herself in better ways than lolling around reading, now she was old enough to contribute tangible cash to the household more-or-less single-handed. What he proposed was clear when he removed the AMAZING CHILDREN CLAIRVOYANTS sign from the side of the wagon and nailed it beside the front door where it could be read from the sidewalk in its red, white, and blue.

Enos Miles was a bit taken aback when he walked home from work that evening, but he knew better than to complain or Margaret Ann would have been at him again. There was a boxroom off the upstairs landing that he was pressed into clearing. Margaret Ann had taught herself sewing after her firstborn, Euclid, arrived. She cut her wedding dress down to Tennie's size, and supplied her with a veil of gauze to cover her hair and half her face. She also contributed a drum table with cloth, three wooden chairs, and a set of crimson plush curtains long past their prime which Buck tacked up on the boxroom walls. He lettered a piece of cardboard to hang on the doorknob that said HAVE YOUR PAST READ AND FUTURE FORETOLD. FEE! $1. PAY ON ENTERING. At that point Margaret Ann announced that fifty cents of every dollar would be fitting compensation for her efforts. Buck objected, but not for long; in the matter of greed they were equals. The final furnishing was a crystal ball he had come across in a pawnshop window.

This was the plan of action he outlined: He would answer the doorbell if a quick look through the window disclosed likely customers. He'd ask some preliminary questions as he ushered them in, taking his time about conducting them upstairs to give time for Tennie to nip into the boxroom and get into costume. They'd be provided with a slip of paper to jot down a few facts about themselves—name, where they were from, etcetera—or he'd write it out for them if they hadn't skill with a pen. Then, while he went through the motions of sealing the information in an envelope, he'd switch the paper for a blank, palming the original for passing underhand to his daughter.

No college professor could have done a better job of coaching. Buck would be the only one shooting off questions during a sitting, and the questions would be a code, feeding in facts he'd pumped out of a customer beforehand so Tennie could frame suitable answers, even wearing a blindfold, which he wanted her to wear once in a while to make a good impression. He thought most people would come in search of something or somebody, and he shaped his queries accordingly. For instance, "What's he looking for?" signaled an item of jewelry; "*And* what's he looking for?" meant a missing sum of money. "What's she after?" signified a runaway husband or absent sweetheart. "What's her purpose?" intimated that the source of concern was some illness in the family and the customer was anxious for a dependable forecast about the outcome.

Buck undertook to render help in a number of other ways. If Tennie was snagged, she was to listen for his foot taps spelling out a letter of the alphabet, one through twenty-six. His coughs, one to four, would tell points of the compass, North, South, East, or West, and his sneezes the value of anything rounded off to the nearest hundred dollars' worth. If things got entirely out of hand, he'd feign convulsions as a distraction.

They took their first dollar off a fidgety woman whose otherwise pale face was marred by a lump on her jaw and bruises underlining both her eyes. Buck sat her down, somber as an owl, and collected her money, which he relayed to Tennie along with a sealed envelope. He also sneaked in the information slip their customer had filled in a minute or two earlier. The lamp was turned low, with a remaining glimmer of light focused on the woman as a precaution against her pinpointing what was happening only inches below her nose. Sliding the bill under the crystal ball, Tennie dropped the paper onto her lap, as her father had specified, gave it one quick glance, and was set to start. She made a show of rubbing the envelope to and fro across her forehead, taking in everything she could detect about the woman.

"Your name is Julia—Mrs. Julia Wigmore. You live on Elm Street."

"Why, yes, dear, that's correct. How do you—?"

Buck headed her off. "Don't address her direct, ma'am. It's apt to disturb the vibrations. And what's she looking for, child? What's she seeking?"

A gold band on a finger of her hands, which were twisting and writhing on the table top, had clarified one more point and the mouse under each of her eyes another. The girl quickly put two and two together. "You've come to ask about your husband . . . ."

She nodded. "Yes, he's——"

"Ma'am, I beg you say nothing to her. Let her tell you. Is he *good* to her, Miss Tennessee?"

This other secret message said, No, he wasn't; *fair* would have meant he was. Tennie shook her head, slow and solemn. "He's not with you any more. You had a bust-up. He beat you, then run off in a hurry."

She raised a finger to brush her tears away. "That's right. That's exactly what he did to me, and I'm so ashamed——"

"And the money; that went with him."

She launched into a fit of sobbing, shoulders shaking and head drooping close to the tablecloth. "No matter what he's done, I want him back. Help me, please. Bring him home to me."

Tennie couldn't help but feel sorry for her, but this was promptly checked. The girl had to keep her head clear, or else she'd be cornered. *Good husband?* "It's not easy to say, but he's with some other woman."

"Don't I know it! The trollop who lived across the street, that's the one; slipped off when he did and enticed him with her, the slut."

"Madam, madam, you're distressing the child. Can you perceive in the crystal where they're at, on behalf of the lady? Have *they traveled* far?" He coughed, just once.

The phrasing of the question and the cough delivered two clues: They'd quit Ohio to head north someplace. Tennie cupped her hands around the hunk of glass and pretended it was aswirl with information. "They've gone quite a ways. Up to Michigan, I think." He was signaling with a foot—four taps. *A, B, C, D*—"I see lots of buildings. It's a city. Detroit?"

This seemed to hit the nail on the head, leading her to regard the miraculous child as a fount of knowledge. "How in the world can she do it, Dr. Claflin?"

"A natural-born gift, ma'am, that her little heart compels her to employ for the benefit of humankind. Now, to ease your mind, I'll ask her to peer into what the future holds for you. You'll have discerned that the crystal is starting to lose its luster, due to the strain she's been subjecting it to. Science has learned there's some quality in the ink employed printing a dollar bill that restores the clarity. No obligation, of course, but if you feel inclined to contribute toward guaranteeing a sharp, clear inspection . . ."

She didn't need coaxing twice. "Grateful to you, ma'am. We're all set now to inquire: Will this good lady's husband be restored to her?"

Tennie was on her own, solitary, alone, with her father equally ignorant of the appropriate answer. She could think better with her eyes shut instead of goggling at the pawnshop relic that sat on the tablecloth. Everything grew still around and inside her. At first, nothing came into her head but flickering colors and lights darting like fireflies at dusk. Then suddenly there was a room like the high-class cabins in the steamboat, but bigger. A man and a woman lay snuggled up together on a bed, stripped down to their underwear, rumpling the spread with what they were doing to each other. Then the picture, distinct as slides in Enos Miles's stereopticon, disappeared, to be succeeded by one that was different.

She paused so long trying to decide what to say that Buck stirred in his chair, preparing to operate his plan of rescue. Reasoning that she'd better hurry before he threw himself onto the floor, she recalled what Victoria had said once about Henry Caldwell—that all he asked was a word of comfort.

She opened her eyes and found Mrs. Wigmore's gazing straight into them. "Yes, he will be back with you, sure enough. I've seen him packing his bag."

Mrs. Wigmore was so happy she looked tempted to dance a jig. She gave Buck one more dollar and Tennie a hug fit to crack her ribs. He said when she was gone that Tennie done well enough for him to change the sign and charge two dollars in advance from now on. But the next time Tennie saw Victoria she would tell her what she'd really seen at the end of the sitting: Mrs. Wigmore cramming her things into a trunk with the help of another woman who was about to take her to the poorhouse.

One way or another, money was made month by month, but she had no opportunity to explain exactly how to Victoria. From the style of Victoria's letters, the family concluded she was forging ahead with her reading and allowing her imagination a free, unfettered run. She told about bearing a son "in almost mortal agony, attended only by a half-tipsy husband." She named him Byron after the English blueblood who'd written poetry and been active in helping her precious Greeks.

By her account, Woodhull was turning out a bigger villain than she'd suspected. "He deserted me for one full month before I discovered he was living with a mistress at a fashionable boardinghouse under the title of wife. I went out on the wintry street in only a calico dress and India rubbers, entered the house, confronted the household as they sat at table, and related my story. It drew tears from all the company and brought confusion to Canning and his paramour, 'til by a common movement the listeners compelled her to pack her trunk and flee and shamed him into creeping back like a dog into the kennel."

Anna would have gone to her somehow, but Buck said a trip to Chicago wouldn't be worth the price in any event, since Victoria had always been one to stretch a point.

A month and more brought nothing further from her, but her father refused to soften. Then a letter arrived with a San Francisco postmark. She was there with Woodhull and the baby, working as a breadwinner, clad in high heels and a low-cut-down dress, selling cigars from a tray in a saloon on Portsmouth Square that stayed open around the clock, furnishing liquor and a selection of warm-blooded girls who were more than willing to hoist their skirts and climb the stairs. From what she wrote, San Francisco had it all over Chicago as a promising site for making a killing or getting killed and ending up nailed in a pine box, depending how the luck was running.

"The gold bug bites everybody. The best and the worst of men contend for wealth here, though it is principally the latter class that frequents the El Dorado, as the pinches administered to my bare

arms and other places testify. Prices for everything are so astronomical that half my wages go in rent on our miserable second-floor room where my feeble spouse does little else day or night other than tend to darling Byron. . . .

"I doubt whether my present employment will last much longer. The language of the customers is so crude it brings blushes to the cheeks. The proprietor is of the opinion that I am 'altogether too fine' for a cigar girl. But I must persist for Byron's sake."

Tennie would have taken off to join her if she'd had the cash. She had done enough traveling not to be fazed by any steamship ride around the Horn, which was the only means of reaching there—the Union Pacific tracks wouldn't finally be laid until a dozen years later. The Pony Express wasn't operating yet, so Victoria's news was three or four weeks out of date when it arrived; nevertheless, her next installment had a more cheerful ring:

"I have quit the El Dorado, but on friendly terms with the proprietor, Mr. Sullivan, who walked me home one night after there had been a shooting on the sidewalk outside. He recognized the masonic handshake, thumb rubbing thumb, that Woodhull greeted him with. Whereupon Mr. Sullivan presented us with a twenty-dollar gold piece, a whole double-eagle, for favors rendered, and dismissed me with his blessing.

"After I turned to the sewing needle for support—Margaret Ann knows how a baby's needs foster that skill—one of my customers chanced to be an actress by the name of Miss Anna Cogswell, who has brought her troupe here like many others of her profession, lured by gold abounding. She suggested that, instead of laboring as a seamstress, I had the looks needed for filling a vacancy in her company created by a girl who eloped with a black-jack dealer.

"The upshot is that I am the replacement, and have been for five weeks. Can you credit it, Tennie? Perhaps this is the long-awaited road toward achieving the things you and I used to talk about (remember D———es?) as well as my fond hopes for you, Ma. Next week we perform *The Corsican Brothers*, and I'm to be raised to $52. In the ballroom scene, I am to wear the prettiest dress you can imagine, pink silk and slippers to match. I wonder if I'll become a slave to fashion!

"I guess there's a dark side to most everything. In my case, it consists of the unwelcome attentions that certain male colleagues attempt to force on me, plus an accident Byron suffered last week. Woodhull, celebrating Mr. Sullivan's generosity over an outrageously expensive bottle of gin, failed to see our baby approach the open window of our room. The poor darling still seemed stunned from the fall when I got home from the evening performance. Byron is not yet his usual merry self, but it has had the effect of curbing his father's insobriety; he sits with him constantly now."

Tennie's dreams about her sister brightened after that, though the significance of the line about "a whole double-eagle for favors rendered" was a puzzle to her.

Buck had bought an armful of medical textbooks. Delving into them persuaded him the most profitable disease to tackle was cancer. It was no rarity among customers of his age and older, and half of those who weren't afflicted were scared it would strike them sooner or later.

He had one flaw of character which she fancied would have been overcome in the case of a real M.D.; he was squeamish about seeing any more blood than might come from a razor-nick in shaving. This was a blessing, not a handicap, in dealing with his average patient, who didn't relish submitting to a surgeon's scalpel. "Cancer cured without the Knife or Pain" said the handbills that Buck had a printer roll off for him.

As a precaution against disappointed patrons catching up with him after treatment, the notice that appeared in all advertisements was "Dr. Hebern Claflin, M.D., Specialist in Cancers, Tumors, and Malignant Growths of All Descriptions." Hebern was on the callow side to live up to his billing, but he was old enough to grow chin whiskers and a mousy moustache, which helped to age him to a degree.

The steady demand for Magnetic Life Elixir impressed Buck with the value of magnetism in separating customers from their cash. That was where Tennie came in. He worked himself to a lather on the subject. "Tennie, you are a footling, as your Ma puts it, which we know signifies you've power in your limbs to heal rheumatics, lumbago, and maybe more. Are you aware what the source of that power is? It's no secret to science. That power is magnetism, and it stands to reason that what you've got in the feet must accordingly flow through the hands and digits."

He was feeling his way into a gospel he'd use to good advantage when he started gulling the gullible. "Now by the simple act of laying on those hands, you can effect a cure once we get a patient into a receptive state of mind. Your fingers can't fail to inform you of the location of those dangerous growths arising within the human frame which we medical men describe as *cancer,* coming from the Greek word meaning *crab,* which we apply to the tumor because the enlarged veins around the swelling resemble the claws of the crustacean."

Anna threw up her hands. "*Ach!* I dislike to hear such talk."

"Then block your ears, woman! You mind what I'm saying, Tennie. Thanks to the miraculous and transcendental force of magnetism, those hands can soothe the torment of a sufferer far better than any habit-forming narcotic. Like they was hooked up to a regular army of storage batteries, they can radiate the very roots of the growth and untangle the fibrous framework that our microscopes customarily reveal enclosing the mass of malignant tissue. You, my girl, can be a genuine, certified magnetic healer, did you but know it. There's a fortune waiting for the reaping."

What could she answer? "I'll do my best, Pa. Leastways I can't poison 'em."

Nothing had been heard from San Francisco for months. Victoria had been gone so long, the worst pangs of missing her had passed, though she still haunted Tennie's thoughts. She had a feeling that her sister was in trouble, but Anna's anxiety was overwhelming. She inspected every clean bedsheet that Margaret Ann ironed, looking for a diamond-shaped fold, which Anna took to be a portent of evil. One morning, a robin flustered in through an open window, laying a panicky trail of blue eggs all over a rug, which to her was cast-iron proof that bad luck lay ahead.

Then Victoria turned up on the doorstep, Woodhull at her side and their son in her arms. When the hugging and the kissing was finished, Tennie got a good look at them. Victoria's face was the same washed-out color as the robin's eggs. Woodhull appeared no sturdier than a sparrow. As for the boy, it was clear from the way his head hung and his eyes wandered that he didn't know who he was with or where. (He never would.)

"I came just fast as I could, Tennie, but it was a terrible arduous trip in a Vanderbilt steamer down from Frisco to San Juan del Sur, with none of the crew lifting a hand to help us, not even Byron, and the weather never letting up. Then we were jostled in coaches and crazed by bugs clear across Nicaragua before we had another taste of Vanderbilt treatment sailing on up to New York. But it's wonderful to see you so much improved. I was in the middle of a show, the ballroom scene I wrote about, when this vision struck me of Ma beckoning and calling, 'Victoria, come home; Tennie's deathly sick!' Then I made you out lying on the floor in red-striped calico, pale as a ghost. Thank God you're better and looking so chipper! Has your strength completely returned, pet?"

Tennie was flummoxed. She was healthy and always had been; owned no striped calico and never had. She had been undecided about how much store should be set by the visions Victoria laid claim to, though she'd been persuasive concerning Demosthenes. But it seemed that in the matter of seeing things that weren't there, Tennie had the advantage. There was only one other possibility. She glanced at Anna. Had she got in touch somehow?

Tennie's arms went once more around her sister. "I'm fine now, and it's a tonic having you back. We can have lovely times together again." Neither then nor after did Anna tell whether she'd played a hand in bringing it about. Every time Tennie raised the question, the only answer was, "God works in His mysterious ways, His wonders to perform," which was part of a hymn she sang at camp meetings.

Space in the house was nearly as tight as it had been in Homer when the full tally of Claflins was in residence. Enos would have let them stay on; he took a liking to Woodhull and enjoyed conversing with him, which no one else bothered with much. But Margaret Ann's hints that it was time for change grew broader every day. It reached a point where she took back every stick of furniture from the boxroom and tore down the sign from the front door.

Buck caught on at last and mustered the original team of wayfarers to take to the road again: himself, Dr. Hebern, Tennie, and Victoria, who raised no objection to leaving Byron in his father's hands to afford her a taste of freedom. Margaret Ann said she'd be satisfied for the present with the arrangement, but she'd anticipate being paid room and board for everybody remaining under her roof apart from her own immediate family. The rest of them, she added, shouldn't feel they were neglecting her if they limited reunions to coincide with Thanksgiving and Christmas.

They didn't live cooped up in the wagon all the time, but drove from one town to another, pursuing business wherever Buck scented opportunity. In a town, they would lodge in a hotel and make the rooms a base for their activities, selling the Elixir and Hebern's cancer cure, telling fortunes, healing by magnetism, and communing with spirits by request.

They ranged over a considerable territory, covering Ohio, making it into Michigan, Illinois, and Iowa. They steered clear of Missouri, believing they'd feel uneasy with black slaves on every side, when they'd had no experience with them. Buck reckoned pickings would be slim across the Mississippi River, anyway, apart from the trouble and expense of getting a horse and wagon safely over when there wasn't a bridge anywhere along its length.

Kansas Territory was omitted from the visiting list for similar but more powerful reasons. It wasn't easy to keep up with the times when they spent such a measure of them rumbling along behind Rosy, with Buck forever complaining about hay and blacksmiths biting into the profits. But he picked up a newspaper whenever he could, so they stayed abreast of most events, including the trouble in Kansas Territory, where slavers and Abolitionists were settling accounts between themselves with Sharp's rifles.

A question that had been puzzling Tennie came up one night when the sisters were curled in a bed in some sleazy hotel room. "Something you once wrote in a letter when you were at that saloon in Frisco. You said about getting money from a man for 'favors rendered.' What did you mean by that?"

Victoria pressed her cheek against her sister's and drew her closer to start teasing. "You're still little Miss Nosey, aren't you? How am I to know you won't blab if I tell?"

Tennie pulled away. "I'm thirteen years old—a grown woman almost. Don't you trust me like you used to?"

"Don't get crabby! I trust you. Let's see if I can say it right. " 'Favors rendered' meant—well, I made myself be nice to him, and he appreciated it."

"Sounds like you egged him on, and you already married."

"Don't remind me about it! Married bliss is hogwash. Look at Ma and Pa. They're at each other all the time, and so's Margaret Ann at Enos Miles. Timmy Sullivan showed consideration at least, which Woodhull never did. Most men figure they're the only ones entitled to pleasure and it's a disgrace for a woman to have her share. I did egg Timmy Sullivan on, if you want to know. I needed the money because otherwise Byron would have starved."

"Did you let him—you know, take liberties?"

She laughed, but not loud, and a hand tousled Tennie's hair. "Yes, I did, and a tolerable lot of them, too."

"What's it like, to go with a man?"

"It depends who he is. The first time was wretched. I was tense as a fiddle string, and Woodhull was drunk. I'd have shied away if he'd been willing or I'd had the courage to disbelieve it was a bride's obligation. Things have changed between us, now, though. Sometimes, very occasionally, I feel sort of sorry for him because it's not all his fault. But there's no pleasure for me with him."

"Was this feller Sullivan any better, assuming he's the only other one you've been with?"

"He's the one and only so far. It was much better with him every time. All my life, I never felt so good, and if somebody else comes along that I fancy, I'll do it again. What do you say to that, puss?"

Tennie would have liked to ask more, like about the chance of another baby maybe not knowing who the father was, but that would have exercised Victoria's mind about Byron, which could only unsettle her. Tennie concluded the only sure way to save herself from misery over children was to avoid having any, then carried on talking. "Wouldn't that be sinful, fooling around with men?"

She had to wait for a reply. "When you come right down to the cold facts, a sin's a sin only if you think it is, and there's varieties of sinning. I call it sinful to compel a girl into marrying, and for a husband to force himself on his wife like a billy goat in rut any time he cares to. You sin against yourself if you don't struggle to be everything you can be and follow your own road regardless where it leads you. I hope that's what you'll do, Tennie."

"We ride in the same wagon, don't we? Maybe we always can."

Most of that time, though, Victoria and Hebern did more following than leading, when it was Tennie who was the apple of Buck's eye.

When Rosy finally wore herself out, he shunted her off to a glue factory and splurged on a team of horses and a brand new rig as roomy as a prairie schooner. They were looking forward to some rather taller living than they had met before.

Instead of gypsying here, there, and everywhere, he marked up a calendar and assembled a timetable so he'd be able to advertise appearances with notices sent ahead to the newspapers. This is what they read about Tennie in Ohio in the days when John Brown was declaring a personal war to free the slaves by raiding the arsenal at Harpers Ferry, Virginia, and winning himself a hanging for treason and murder:

A WONDERFUL CHILD! Miss Tennessee Claflin, Who is Only Fourteen Years of Age! This young lady has been traveling since she was eleven years old and has been endowed from her birth with a supernatural gift to such an astonishing degree that she convinces the most skeptical of her wonderful powers.

She gives information of absent friends, whether living or dead, together with all the past, present, and future events of life; also of lost money or property, identifying the person or persons concerned with so much certainty as scarcely to leave a doubt of their guilt.

She can see and point out the medicine to cure the most obstinate diseases—even those that for years baffled our best physicians, and can direct salves and liniment to be made and used that will cure cold sores, fever sores, cancers, sprains, weakness in the back and limbs, and other complaints.

She will point out to ladies and gentlemen their former, present, and future partners, telling exactly those that are dead and living, their treatment, disposition, and character in life; and when required will go into an unconscious state and travel to any part of the world, hunt up absent friends, whether dead or alive, and through her they will tell the inquiring friend their situation and whereabouts, with all the events of life since they last met.

She may be consulted at her room, United States Hotel, High Street, Columbus, from the hours of eight o'clock A.M. to nine o'clock P.M. Price of consultation, $2.00.

With Tennie the main attraction, he didn't object to Victoria fading off on her own when the mood came on her. During one visit back for a glimpse of Byron, she had a quarrel with Margaret Ann, which resulted in Victoria's stalking out the door with Woodhull and the boy. After that she preferred to go it alone—in the same trade but on a different trail from Buck's.

Over Christmas, spent in harness with the Mileses, Buck was happy because Lincoln had won hands down over the two leather-headed Democrats, Douglas and Breckinridge, who'd been set up against him, so now Abe would be heading for Washington in February. But Anna was upset to hear from Victoria that she was in New York City. In her mother's opinion, that place stank like a nest of dead vultures.

The next time Victoria put pen to paper the letter was intended for Tennie but never sent. She handed it over in person when she rejoined the traveling show the week after Stonewall Jackson had drubbed the Union Army at Bull Run and drove them in retreat to Washington, D.C. She had written this letter in April, while the new President was striving to raise the Northern militia and send them south for fear the Confederates were aiming to run him and his government out of town.

I have borne another baby, Zulu Maud, whose father is Woodhull beyond a shadow of doubt. This event occurred at Number 53 Bond Street, New York, April 23. He and I were at the time the only occupants of the house, the trial coming upon me while no nurse or servant or other human helper was under the roof. Zulu Maud entered the world at four o'clock in the morning, handled by the feverish and unsteady hands of her intoxicated father, who, only half in possession of his professional skill, cut the cord too near the flesh, laid the babe in my arms, left us asleep and alone, and then staggered out of the house. Nor did he remember to return.

Meanwhile, on waking, I was startled to find my head on the side next to hers in a pool of blood, her hair was soaked and clotted in a little red stream oozing drop by drop from her body. I reached a broken chair rung from the floor nearby and pounded against the wall to summon help from the next-door house. At intervals of several hours I continued this, no one answering until at length one of the neighbors who was attracted by the noise but unable to get in the front door, removed the grating of the basement and made her resolute way upstairs to the rescue.

On the third day after, sitting propped in bed and looking out the window, I caught sight of Woodhull staggering up the steps across the way, mistaking that house for his own. I can live no longer with him. I intend to apply for divorce at the earliest opportunity. Oh, Tennie, never, never let yourself be trapped this way! I could not bear to see you suffer as I have.

The principal effect the war had on them was to keep them busier than ever. There was no end to the procession of wives and mothers begging for bulletins to tell them whether a man of theirs remained alive, or, if they'd been notified otherwise, how he was faring in heaven.

Buck complained about the price of everything soaring, which called for raising their fees. He held out as long as he could to get paid in nothing but silver dollars, but when they dried up he settled for greenbacks like everybody else. Their traipsing around turned out well for Hebern when the Government introduced the draft, since there was no permanent address at which he could be tracked.

Tennie was delighted to have Victoria to talk with again after she had hired a nurse for the new baby and Byron, all lodged in Chicago, where a lawyer was making moves to free her from marriage.

She was having a hard time meeting expenses, which gave her the idea there was more money to be made, and quicker, too, by dealing in wholesale predictions instead of one at a time. What they should do, she said, was rent a hall and sell tickets for a seance or perhaps two every night for a week. Buck saw instant merit in the idea, but Tennie could spot a wide-open hole.

"How're we going to work it when we shan't know even their names and you won't be placed to provide clues? I can do without 'em sometimes, but it's fitful." One item she didn't raise was the hazy feeling she had about whether Sis could or couldn't achieve much in hobnobbing with spirits.

"Just leave it to me and your sister. We'll put our heads together, and then we'll all have some homework to do." Within the week, posters appeared all over town, announcing that in the ballroom of the Hotel Excelsior the world-famous spiritualistic mediums, Miss Tennessee Claflin and Mrs. Victoria Woodhull, of New York City, London, Paris, and elsewhere, consulted by kings and queens, would perform in a state of trance—give information of absent loved ones, whether living or dead—"Admission $1; small-change notes not accepted."

Buck and Hebern worked all day, fixing up a stage with dark drapes hung back and slides with a plush purple curtain in front and setting a row of dark lanterns for footlights. The stage itself was rigged up with a cubicle made from more curtains, a drum table with a tambourine, and a vase of wax lilies, and for the two girls an armchair apiece with a little surprise hidden in the upholstery of Victoria's.

That night the hall was filled with more women than men, some of them in widow's weeds. Hebern tended door, inviting them to use the back of the tickets they bought to jot down the name of anyone in particular they might care to contact in the hereafter, ready for collection by Dr. Reuben Buckman Claflin before the show got under way.

Victoria and Tennie slipped into their chairs after a peek through the main curtain, both of them shrouded in black, Victoria with a white rose pinned to her collar. She was serious and pale enough to attend a wake. Tennie was beyond caring. All well and good if they could pull off the stunts they'd been practicing; if they couldn't, well, the crowd looked too decent to do lasting harm to females.

Buck stood up before the curtain in a frock coat and button-up boots, spruce enough to qualify for a seat on the Supreme Court itself. "Good neighbors one and all, we meet here tonight in these times of stress to bring comfort to troubled minds and ease for sorrowing hearts. I warrant that the phenomena you are about to witness will lead you to conclude it's no longer a necessity to depend exclusively on church, clergy, or scripture for proof of the soul's immortality. There's more concrete evidence which you're going to marvel at, produced within these four walls. Two gorgeous young ladies are thrilling and willing to serve you—daughters of mine,

I'm proud to say. They will employ their unique faculties to enable you to speak with and possibly catch a glimpse of those cherished members of your families who you may have fallen into the sad habit of referring to as the departed."

Tennie leaned closer to whisper to her sister that he was "laying it on fearsome thick," but Victoria paid no attention to her.

"Some of you will exclaim, 'I never would have believed such things could be genuine until I saw them with my own two eyes.' Others may pipe up, 'It's got to be one of the good Lord Jesus' miracles, akin to the raising of Lazarus.' Nay, friends, these things are no miracle but a scientific manifestation of electromagnetism which I'll endeavor to explicate. My girls' armipotence derives in part from functions of the hypothalmus gland, which is the vestigial, primordial brain located at the base of the skull, and it's a regular voltage battery of potent powers. This gland has atrophied in the vast majority of ordinary individuals, but it can be restimulated by years of devoted practice, which is what's been accomplished by my daughters under my medical and metaphysical instruction. And now, without further ado, allow me to introduce to you—" He pulled aside the purple curtain.

The preliminaries had stretched on so long the girls were itching to get started. He had Hebern slide open the shutters of the footlights and lower the shades on the windows. Two women in the audience were cajoled into coming up to check out the girls for anything hidden in their clothing. This was done gingerly and in private inside the little hideaway. He gave warning against any spectator grabbing at any object that might materialize, citing an English medium who had been killed in this fashion in the middle of a trance. At last he explained that, to begin, he'd stand at the back of the hall and hold up half a dozen of the tickets one at a time. Tennie would seemingly read them though they'd be far out of range. It would be child's play for her when she would refer not to the tickets he was brandishing but to the six he'd palmed off to her while he was ushering the two women inspectors down off the platform.

The audience was so quiet that Tennie could hear Victoria breathing. He held up the first ticket. Tennie squeezed her eyelids shut and gripped the arms of her chair. Then she sang out, "Is the spirit present whose name is Isaac Webster?" Commotion broke out in the third row. She stole a peep at a white-haired woman up on her feet and sobbing. "That's him! My son. Sent off to fight at Rich Mountain and never a word since." Victoria seemed to have dozed off to sleep.

Tennie believed in telling people whatever they wished to hear —though that would change in the course of time. She pretended that poor Isaac was in heaven, keeping a lookout for his mother's eventual arrival there. That went down well with everybody, in particular with Mrs. Webster. The whole first act went smoothly even if Tennie had to backpaddle when it turned out a young man named Billy Fairchild was still alive but confined in Andersonville Prison.

Victoria roused herself for Act Two, an attempt at what Buck identified as materialization. He got four volunteers to step up and rope her into her chair, then slide the chair into the cubicle and draw the drapes. The rope, of course, was thick, and four pairs of fumbling fingers were better, from her point of view, than one. Sliding her hands out of the knots and back in again would be no test at all, and the upholstery hid what she needed.

Hebern dimmed the lanterns, and Buck begged for total silence, spelling out the danger of antagonizing the spirits at a moment as tense as this. In an instant a rock came flying out from behind the curtains; it was a plain, common, odd-shaped rock that Hebern had daubed with phosphorus paint to make it glow. Victoria, out of sight, was wailing as if she had lost her senses.

Buck raised a hullabaloo, urging two volunteers to pick up the rock while others satisfied themselves that the knots still held Victoria. A shriveled, bony little man with eyeglasses nipped across his nose got up, saying he was the new doctor in town. Might he have the privilege of examining what he called "the apport"? Buck couldn't instantaneously think why not, which set the doctor poring over the bit of rough stone. He declared it was "probably of extraterrestial origin" and he was going to ship it off to the Smithsonian Institution.

Father and daughter kept the ball rolling until the show was about over. He decoyed a score of people into linking hands to form "a magnetic circle" surrounding the hideaway in darkness. That brought about enough jostling between them for Tennie to crawl out unnoticed, double back with the vase of flowers, and toss it into their midst. The local M.D. hailed it as "a truly remarkable example of telekinesis."

Buck had advised the girls to raise an outcry if anyone closed in too near or became overtaken by curiosity. It was never necessary, not even when both Tennie's hands were held tight by a fresh set of dupes posted outside the curtains and she slipped off her shoes to rattle the tambourine with her feet.

Victoria had been sitting as still as a monument, eyes staring, scarcely breathing. What she did next wasn't listed anywhere in the program. She began swaying to and fro, then slumped in her chair, sinking into a sort of sleep with her chin squashing the rose at her collar and tears flooding her cheeks. Tennie heard the voice that had come out once before, when she was bluffing Henry Caldwell in his cabin aboard the riverboat.

"I walk in regions unknown to man where there is no sky above my head or ground beneath my feet. . . . I see circles of light and circles of darkness turning and twisting, coming forward and hastening away. . . . There's music flowing like raindrops over my wings, warm and gentle. . . . The circles swell and blossom into spheres of radiant gold so enormous the whole universe could fit inside. . . . Seven spheres joined by a spiral path patterned like a checkerboard with whitest marble and deepest jade. . . . All must tread the path as we leave the earthly state, to climb on and on ever higher until at last we enter the seventh sphere which is the mind of God." She lolled limp as a rag doll, mouth sagging open.

Everybody's head swung toward his neighbor, in several minds about whether to burst into a *Hallelujah!* give her three cheers, or take up a collection. Buck sensed there was no topping her performance. He quickly shut the curtains, thanked the audience for attending, and asked them to recommend the performance to their friends. Victoria came to as soon as the last of them had shuffled out, impressed by the wonders they had witnessed.

Tennie had a bone to pick with her. "What got into you, shoveling out all that missionary stuff?"

Buck chipped in. "Be damned, Tennie, they lapped it up like

fresh cream. Every performance from now on we'll make that the grand finale."

Victoria looked first at Tennie and then at him. "God's truth, that's what I saw clear as crystal. I can't swear it'll happen the same another time, though."

"What's that count for?" Buck got impatient. "Do it once, you can do it again. What's the difference if you just go on repeating youself? The greenhorns'll buy it like candy apples."

"I don't know as I care to."

In the old days, he would have whipped her for her cheek, but she was too old for that at twenty-five. For the rest of the time they put on their shows, they could never rely on her cooperating. Sometimes she'd rant on about the seven spheres, but mostly not. So they prepared a different finale, with Tennie behind the drapes of the cubicle with a stick, pushing out gauze cached in a chair. The way that gauze swooped and dipped in the shadows made converts by the score.

The attention the newspapers paid them built up a solid following, with the girls rated the equal of Cora Hatch, another onetime child marvel who'd gone through her first marriage and was in process of suing her husband for robbing and abusing her. The Claflins had rented a furnished house to winter in and perform in, too, on Mound Street in Cincinnati, when an account in the *Daily Commercial* brought a visitor to their door.

He wore a chin beard, and shreds of long gray side hair were combed across his otherwise bare skull. Gold-rimmed spectacles and a church-going suit hinted that he wasn't hard-pressed for funds. "The name's Jesse Grant. I'm a tanner of hides and manufacturer of leather goods in Georgetown, which lies twenty miles southeast of here. I'm prepared to make it worthwhile for you and your girls to come out to the house overnight. Mrs. Grant and I have some questions of a confidential nature to pose affecting the future of our son, and the trip is too far for her convenience." The looks the old man gave Tennie indicated that he had a different kind of question on his mind for her.

Buck accepted the offer of a dollar a mile each way for their trouble. They drove out with their caller in his buggy to a shingle-roofed saltbox where a wood stove burned in the kitchen fireplace. Mrs. Grant furnished salt pork and pickles for supper while he acquainted the Claflins with some history concerning the son.

"We baptized him Hiram Ulysses, and I always did have ambition for him. 'Twasn't till I secured a place for him at West Point that the congressman I was friendly with erred in allocating him the middle name of Simpson, which was what his mother was called before we were wed. He was only a little tad of a feller but strong and venturesome, you know, when he went there, and then, by golly, he sprouted up another half a foot. We're all aware of what he's achieved since, serving our nation against the Confederates, taking Vicksburg on the Mississippi River and then Chattanooga, Tennessee, to make up for the damage Longstreet did at Chickamauga Creek."

Jesse Grant turned out to have only two questions to put after the table was cleared and his wife took her apron off and installed everyone in the parlor. "I reckon Ulysses is duly qualified to take on command of all the armies of the Union. Is he to receive his just reward? That's number one. Number two is, and don't think we're being fanciful: Is there anything to hoping he'll be elected President of the re-United States?"

The Claflins had never heard such high-toned talk before. A glaze stole over Victoria's eyeballs. The greatest dream of her life took root that evening. Since she was so engrossed, it fell to Tennie to cope with the situation. The firelight gave a twinkle to the crystal Buck had brought in his valise. Finding the answers was a cinch.

"Yes, he's going to make it to chief general all right. I can see him here. He's in a big black hat, riding a horse, soldiers parading, holding something in his teeth. A bullet or a cigar maybe?"

"That's it! A cigar. He chews on 'em all the time. Go on! What else?"

"Hold on a minute. Here's another picture showing up. He's saying about peace, and now he's in a carriage by himself, driving through the streets of Washington. Everybody's cheering and, yep, he's bound for the White House."

The old woman clapped her hands, and the old man's chest swelled. He insisted on planting a ticklish kiss on Tennie as a just reward. With his wife around, he didn't request anything more personal, but he delivered a nip as he trailed Tennie up the stairs when Mrs. Grant led the way with a candle to store the sisters away for the night in the best spare bedroom.

Tennie's head had scarcely reached the pillow before a fancy she'd had long ago about Henry Caldwell returned to mind. He was fated to be shot down soon in a field there in Louisiana. The shooting would be done by a soldier in the dark-blue uniform of General Grant's army.

Four

Cincinnati was a fearsome place to live in. They hauled Anna and Victoria's two children out from Margaret Ann's place to Mount Gilead—Enos said he was sorry to see them go—and Victoria hired a German woman as nurse from a section of town known as "over the Rhine." At present all available members of the tribe were assembled again. Utica, copying a leaf from Victoria's book, was kicking up her heels as "an actress," according to a letter she wrote from San Francisco. Polly's first husband, Byrnes the lawyer, had used his professional know-how to divorce her when he found out she had a string of admirers on her visiting list. He planned on keeping Rosa, their daughter, out of her hands, but Polly took her with her into her new marriage to Benjamin Sparr.

Victoria's lawyer was slow on his feet, so she was still legally tied to Woodhull, though he had dropped out of view. The same was true of Malden, but Anna was the only one who cared about him.

The townspeople grumbled about the difficult time they had suffered last year, fearful that the Confederates were on the march to take them over. A fair proportion of them—those who denounced the city for harboring runaway slaves on their way to Canada—

would have had no objections to that. It would have improved nobody's health to speak up for Negroes in spite of Mr. Lincoln's declaration freeing them on the first day of January. The Claflins accordingly kept mum.

What appealed most to Victoria was standing by the river's edge, watching white packet boats, black coal barges, lighters ferrying sand or ice from Lake Erie, steamers and sailors cargoed with lumber, pork, whiskey, and beer, horns and whistles screaming to clear their courses.

"Doesn't it make you feel you're stuck with your feet in a hole, Tennie? It does me. I'm sick to death of milling around in these parts, just killing time, waiting for things to happen. If only I sensed how to bring 'em about." Victoria was always anxious to be moving on.

"I can't say it churns me up any," said Tennie. "Especially now I've got a new interest."

Her sister looked downcast. "Johnny Bartels, your fancy man? You must be a crackbrain if you let him chain you down."

"Who's talking about chains? He's my number one, anyways, and I aim to give him a try. He's no tosspot like yours was."

Johnny was a whiskey drummer who worked out of Chicago, and he had the passions of a gambling man. He had come in for a sitting with Tennie to tip him the winner in a race to be run the next afternoon. She joshed him about what a contrast there was between rendering small favors like that and the labor of summoning up the spirits. She made a blind guess at the answer he wanted and laid out a few dollars in stake money to add to his as a token of faith. She was too taken with his looks and diamond rings to pay much attention to what she was predicting.

The horse she singled out didn't even finish. Johnny returned the morning after, pretending he was there to complain, while he had in fact gone back to ask whether she would join him in supper at the Highland House, which stood on Mount Adams, with dining rooms, beer gardens, band concerts, and a promenade overlooking the river. Tennie leaped at the chance.

Pondering over Utica's manner of earning a living in San Francisco, it struck Tennie she was the only one of her sisters who'd never slept with at least one man and probably more. She had a theory about what it would be like, thanks to Victoria and the others, who kept no secrets concerning a woman's body or a partner they'd been to bed with. Victoria's general outlook made good sense to Tennie. She couldn't see why a girl need hang on waiting for a man to make the opening move. When the subject arose with Johnny, she said she had been a maiden long enough. He didn't hesitate to agree with her.

She didn't find the proceedings harsh at all. What developed in the room she shared with Victoria came not as a shock but a pleasure to her, something to look forward to after work when he was in town. Victoria was the only one in the family to ask questions. She soon quieted down when Tennie vowed her pleasure was on a par with his, and it beat reading books as a means of passing evenings at home.

When Johnny's head office faced him with a choice between moving on in pursuit of business elsewhere or losing his job, Tennie grew lonesome. She lost no time in embarking with other young sports she found appealing. She recognized later that this could have constituted an error on her part. Johnny and she took it for granted that what they did they both enjoyed. The question of money never entered into it. Some of the others said, when a bout was over, that they felt obliged to follow the normal rule in the circumstances, which meant depositing five or ten dollars under the mantel clock. Money didn't count as much with her as with Victoria. But there was no logic, said Tennie, to looking a gift horse in the teeth, much less a corralful of stallions.

Victoria sometimes tried to talk about the chances her sister was taking, but Tennie found no reason to worry about being pregnant. "I calculate," she said, "that I'm a lucky one, not cut out to bear babies." She thought she might have gone wrong in letting some of her regular callers bring in an extra girl or two. Buck said it didn't matter, provided there was cash in it.

Once or twice the neighbors went to the police, crying that the Claflins were running a panel house, but there was only one night when real trouble erupted. Two girls ended up in the Black Maria, but Buck vouched for Tennie. She had all her clothes back on by then, so the police took his word for it. She didn't mind missing an appointment with a judge, but it hardly seemed fair that the men in the party hadn't been included in the roundup.

The *Daily Commercial* printed only three or four lines about the evening, and Buck sought to square the account by composing a card which he signed "Elijah Backus" and the editor printed that, too, before the week was out.

Out of justice to *Miss Tennessee Claflin* (a natural-born clairvoyant) and a duty I owe myself and community I have thought proper to make the following statement:

On or about the 10th of November inst. I was informed that Mr. Bambrough, residing at No. 41 Sixth Street, was fast recovering from his perilous situation. He had been quite indisposed for some years, and within two or three months past had two paralytic strokes, the last of which nearly deprived him of the use of his limbs as well as that of his mind, and good physicians said his stay on earth was of short duration, and such was my opinion when I last saw him.

I heard he was recovering, and I went immediately to see him. Soon *Miss Tennessee Claflin* came in and commenced operating upon him with her hands and prescribing medicine, and I sat with astonishment and looked at him and her for some minutes, and he seemed to be so much better and in his right mind and can now visit among his old neighbors as usual. I put myself under her treatment as I considered myself in a dangerous condition also, and her operations and medicine gave me immediate relief. This young lady, who is only eighteen years of age, is now in residence at No. 25 Mound Street, where she may be consulted upon all matters pertaining to life and health.

Chester Bambrough did live on Sixth Street, in a house across the back alley from the Claflins. He would come in through the kitchen door on a regular timetable for an evening's entertainment, so he was prepared to testify to anything Buck asked of him.

The heat declined for a while, though not down to the point where the neighbors' hearts would have broken if the Claflins had bid them farewell. Eventually, of course, the bluenoses got together to hound them out. The deputation was made up of an assortment of leading lights—the landlord, a brace of clergymen, a dry-goods merchant, and a gentleman who said he represented Salmon Portland Chase, once governor of Ohio.

Buck conferred with them in the parlor, and Tennie eavesdropped outside. The ex-governor's spokesman believed that the place was being run as a "house of assignation." Buck, he said, was setting a poor example when he should have been encouraging young men to enlist with General Grant to preserve the Union instead of "dissipating themselves in wanton lewdness."

Buck would have blustered on longer if the merchant hadn't pointedly recalled the time when some sons of Cincinnati showed their feelings by burning out the printshop of a man named Birney because they didn't agree with his published opposition to the institution of slavery. The landlord threw in a hint of emphasis, saying he wouldn't be surprised if those same citizens hadn't retained their appetite for lynching. It was a persuasion Buck couldn't turn down. He would undertake, he said, to have the Claflins out of the Queen City of the West inside of twenty-four hours—forty-eight if it happened to rain.

He shook his head as he locked the door after them. "By Jesus, it's a good thing we weren't sheltering niggers, else they'd be planting us under by now." He wondered if it wouldn't be a solution for Tennie to be married to Johnny. She said she'd try it as soon as it was convenient. They loaded the wagon with their belongings and the best of the furniture the house had to offer, to set a course for the next port of call.

Their first choice was Chicago. That set well with Tennie because she could look up Johnny there. Victoria approved for a different reason: she clung to the fancy she'd somehow find that glory was spelled with a *C,* and she wanted to take another crack at it in a city where she knew her way around. To reach Chicago they had to work their way across Indiana—they lost count of the river crossings they had to make—then swing on north, pushing hard to be done with journeying ahead of the snow and bundled up in buffalo robes to fend off the increasing cold. But a blizzard began to blow when they were some eighty miles short of target. They recognized they'd have to bed down somewhere, perhaps to see the winter through if there was profit in staying put.

The last ferry of a freezing night took the wagon over the Fox River into Ottawa, Illinois, county seat of La Salle County—not to be dismissed as a one-horse town, but not much bigger than a hitch of four. Victoria regarded the whole turn of events as a good omen; this was the place where Mr. Lincoln had run his first rings around Douglas, debating him in '58—Stephen Douglas, that was, not Frederick Douglass, the runaway slave who campaigned for the Abolitionists. "Look," she said, "at the power of good that did Honest Abe."

They snugged down in rooms at the Fox River House, a hotel long past its prime. Tennie was exhausted from telling fortunes and raising spirits, and Victoria resented being eternally at her father's beck and call. "It's high time you got back working for a change, Pa. It would do you good to try something different from living off Tennie."

Tennie put a word in. "No use flashing fireballs at us, either. Sis is dead right. Go on; stir yourself!"

Most people's cheeks broaden when they smile; his only grew leaner. "So I've a pair of vixens, snarling and snapping at me, is that it? Well, you girls had best believe there's a card or two left up my sleeve." He gnawed on a pen for the evening, and the result appeared as a paid-for notice in the *Free Trader*.

> AMERICAN KING OF CANCERS. Dr. R.B. Claflin is stopping at the Fox River House. He is widely known and universally respected as the King of Cancers and all kinds of chronic diseases, fever sores, bone disease, scrofula, piles, sore eyes in the worst stages, heart and liver complaints, female weaknesses, consumption, inflammatory rheumatism, asthma, neuralgia, sick headache, dropsy in the chest, and fits in various forms.
>
> The doctor guarantees a cure in all cases where patients live up to directions.
>
> Cancers killed and extracted root and branch in from ten to forty-eight hours without instruments, pain, or the use of chloroform, simply by applying a mild salve of the doctor's own manufacture. The poor dealt with liberally. No appointment necessary.

Anna's face fell when Victoria read it to her. "Once again a *dummkopf!* Reuben, you bit off more than you can chew this time for sure! You heal cancers? Without my *liebchen* Tennie, you will be *kaput*."

Tennie was reenlisted without much protest. It would be an

improvement over moping about in a town full of strangers. The reason Buck bragged about shunning surgery and anesthesia was that he had nothing in either category apart from a jackknife and a supply of Tennessee whiskey. A week later, the *Free Trader* charged not a cent for printing the usual puffery about "the wonderful child who has astonished people with her amazing cures and mysterious revelations during her travels throughout the entire United States."

Either Ottawa was chockablock with gulls, she thought, or she was a nanny goat. A spell of bitter weather drove them in by the dozens. She would go through the mumbo jumbo of laying on hands or kneading their backbones; Buck would recommend a caseful of the elixir; and they'd go off feeling much improved until next week, including the poor, who paid up as gratefully and as fast as the rest. The Claflins raked in such a pile of greenbacks that Buck talked the graybeard who ran the hotel into renting them the entire place, attic to cellar. They opened up behind a sign announcing this to be "Dr. Claflin's Magnetic Infirmary." As things turned out, he did more to ravage Tennie's reputation than anything she could have conceived alone.

Victoria shied away from attaching herself to Buck in this latest venture. Besides having her hands full with Byron and Zulu Maud, she was eager for the rewards that Demosthenes had promised her, though it was a disappointing season for her in that respect. She also maintained a steady watch over the newspapers, pleased for Tennie's sake that General Grant had full charge of the Union Army now and was devastating the Confederacy.

The trouble that broke over the infirmary came unexpectedly. Buck set it off by sending to the newspapers a fake testimonial he had written, signed in the name of "Rebecca Howe." It was pure invention, not needed at all when on every floor except the top, which was reserved for family, he had patients paying for treatment plus room and board, which was meager, since Anna did the cooking. But when the real Mrs. Howe left the bed she had occupied, he had to make public his tale about the astounding cure Tennie had performed on her. In point of fact, she'd been carried out on a stretcher, and Buck calculated she wouldn't live long enough to dispute him.

Tennie was doing her morning rounds in her usual outfit of white when Victoria came clipping along in her wake. "Tennie, come on upstairs. I've something to show you. It's going to be hot for us again."

Up in her bedroom, Zulu Maud, her three-year-old, was down on the rug, trying to teach Byron how to pile wood blocks but making little progress. Victoria thrust out a copy of the morning's Ottawa *Republican,* folded so Tennie could instantly see the cause of her anxiety. The letter was signed at the bottom, "Rebecca Howe —witness, Margaret Ward." The first thing to strike Tennie was her own name, which received prominence throughout, heaviest in the closing paragraph.

> I deem it but an act of duty to say that I have been imposed upon by Miss Claflin's statements, which have proved to be wholly false and untrue. I am not only not cured, but much worse than I was when I first submitted to her treatment. Every step has been accompanied by extreme pain and aggravation of all the symptoms, and I have grown worse day by day. I make this statement realizing the fact that I have but a short time to live and that it is my wish to prevent, so far as I am able, the injury which might otherwise be inflicted upon innocent sufferers, who might be induced by the statement purporting to have come from me, to apply to Miss Claflin, whom I believe to be an imposter and more, and wholly unfit for the confidence of the community.

Tennie flung the paper into the empty fireplace. "Holy suffering Christ! We're skunked. Where'd she summon strength to carry on like this?"

"That's not the point. Nobody can curb Pa, but you've got to stop letting him prostitute your talents. He's got no right to, none in the world. You're a grown woman now, and you mustn't allow him or any man alive to trample all over you. You owe it to yourself. It's your moral duty. Don't you see that, Tennie, dear?"

"Don't sling a lecture at me, Sis. It's no time for talky-talk. Do you reckon we can brazen it out, Pa and me?"

"You'll have to wait and see, won't you?" Victoria gave her a good-luck kiss.

They weren't left in doubt longer than it took for twilight to fall that June evening. A carriage load of doctors, aroused by the letter, paid a call after they'd stopped first to determine how close to death Mrs. Howe had sunk already. They brought the police with them, too, according to Victoria, the only Claflin who hadn't retreated behind a locked door on the top floor.

She told the rest of the family how their visitors had inspected every room, appalled by the dirt and confusion. After a private conference, they had left, saying the Claflins would be hearing again from them, depending on how Mrs. Howe progressed.

Next morning, Buck and Tennie put brave faces on, telling the patients they all looked well enough to take themselves home. The only exception made was for four Tennie knew to be so riddled with sickness she doubted they'd survive a walk to the door. Buck was careful to collect cash in advance for the Elixir he urged on them to preserve their health in future.

It took two days to be rid of everybody except the four who were too far gone for dismissal. Buck paid a boy to loiter outside Mrs. Howe's house on Canal Street, watching for the shades to be drawn. In that event, he was to scurry back to give the Claflins fair warning. But she held on long enough for them all to decamp, next stop Chicago. "The hustling and bustling we're getting put to," Tennie grumbled, "is becoming downright monotonous."

The boy seemed honest, so he was left with a dollar to induce him to forward news of anything turning up in Ottawa to merit their attention. The first item to be delivered at Number 265 Wabash Avenue, their new Chicago address, was a clipping from the Ottawa *Free Trader*. The headline said SUDDEN DISAPPEAR-ANCE OF TENNESSEE CLAFLIN, and the end mentioned the four patients holed up in the infirmary: "These were cancer cases and were literally deserted, having no notice of her intentions to leave them. They were in the most horrible condition and were taken charge of by humane persons in the vicinity." Tennie didn't believe they'd be any worse off for that; possibly better, in fact, for being spared more of her mother's cooking.

Only one more clipping reached them and this from the *Free Trader,* too. It began:

State of Illinois, La Salle County, SS. —The people vs. Tennessee Claflin. Of the June term of the Circuit Court of La Salle County in the year of our Lord one thousand, eight hundred, and sixty four.

It went on to speak of "grand jurors chosen, selected, and sworn" and "divers quantities of deleterious and caustic drugs" until it got down to the crux of the matter.

Rebecca Howe died, and so the jurors upon their oaths aforesaid do say that the said Tennessee Claflin did kill and slay the said Rebecca Howe, contrary to the form of the statute in such case made and provided, and against the peace and dignity of the same people of the state of Illinois. . . .

They were after Tennie for manslaughter in La Salle County, but she was in Cook County now, and it would do no good to worry. She could have taken Johnny's name after she urged him to marry her, but she didn't feel comfortable being pronounced Mrs. Bartels after she'd been written up favorably so often before in the newspapers and drawn so much business as Miss Tennessee. On top of that, an army of customers swore to the benefits derived from her Elixir. Altering the labels would only confuse them.

Johnny didn't argue about that, nor did he contest her proposal that he should move in with her, not she with him. She couldn't picture herself slaving over a stove, making beds, and scrubbing floors. Telling fortunes and conjuring up spirits, which is what she fell back to doing at Wabash Avenue, gave her enough to do. She did not want to get burned again as she had been at the infirmary.

"Being wed," she told Victoria, "is a considerable convenience when the sap rises and sets you itching for a man to take to bed, which happens to me most every night of the week. Johnny can't always live up to expectations, making out he's wearied or claiming if you have too much of a good thing it plays hell with your constitution, but from my point of view, that's fiddle-faddle. Some days I get testy just waiting for him to come home."

Now old age was catching up with Buck. A year short of seventy, he looked increasingly like a turkey in molt. He was less concerned with doctoring than accumulating stocks and bonds. So Tennie talked her husband into quitting his job as a whiskey drummer to start peddling Elixir instead.

She was concerned that Victoria was aging as fast as their father. She was looking pinched in the cheeks, which Tennie thought could be put down to her not having a man to stir her. She had more time than Tennie for reading, but most of it only seemed to embitter her. There was one weekly, especially, to which she subscribed at two dollars a year, that invariably never failed to raise her hackles over the injustices it reported.

The Revolution was run by the same Susan Anthony that Buck had once derided for wearing bloomers instead of skirts. This brand-new publication expressed firm opinions on the rights of women and, more particularly, about the rights women were denied by the mulishness of men. Miss Anthony, Victoria said, was born a Massachusetts Quaker, though Tennie never would have guessed it from the attacks she wrote on Andrew Johnson and the Thirty-ninth Congress and what they were doing to give Negroes the vote.

"She's reason to be riled," Victoria said, "since she's been let down shamefully by Republicans, and Abolitionists, too, come to that."

"I always thought she was red-hot against slaving. How come they turned on her, then?"

"Of course, she fought slavery, and of course she favors donating blacks the vote—"

"You mean by stretching the Constitution so niggers can march to the polls—or find themselves marched there in the south if they're otherwise disposed to stay clear? Pa says he doesn't hold with meddling with the Constitution."

"Pa's a muttonhead like most all men. Blacks never could vote, but now the Fourteenth Amendment says, Yes, they can. Women never could vote, either, and Susan B. Anthony and Mrs. Stanton and the rest of them thought that same Amendment would say, *Yes, you can, too.* But it does no such thing, and that's why she's fuming. It only talks about 'male citizens.' Women have been fleeced."

"Well, it was men won the war, wasn't it? Women didn't have to go. Down there—where was it? New Orleans. Old Ben Butler had whole troops of niggers fighting for him. I reckon they deserve to make a start at voting."

"Women are plain chattels the way the law is now. We can't own things ourselves, only in the name of a husband. We're supposed to be meek and mild and surrender to anything he calls for, in bed or out. We're no freer than slaves, and nothing's going to change without we get the ballot."

"Maybe you were Woodhull's chattel once, but it's always been different with me and Johnny."

"Every woman isn't like you. Take a look at some of the poor creatures who come for help—cowed, trembling, black and blue with bruises, yet they still want the devils back to abuse them again because they don't know any better and the law doesn't lift a finger."

"Why don't Susie plead with the Republicans to give it another go-around?"

"Because she's not a fool. I can tell you in her own words what she thinks about politicians." Victoria lit on the fine print in a flash. "Here it is. 'Both the great political parties pretending to serve the country are only endeavoring to serve themselves. . . . In their hands, humanity has no hope. . . . The sooner their power is broken as parties, the better.' We can all say Hear! hear! to that."

"Know what, Sis? You'd be a dazzler if you was to take to the stump. I bet you'd have a crowd opening up quicker than clams in a steamer."

The idea tickled her. "Want to listen to me try?" A nod from Tennie had her on her feet, reciting Miss Anthony's opinions, philosophizing on them and doing it well. "The politicians preach reform, we preach revolution. We say disobey every unjust law . . ." She was in full swing when Buck tromped in.

"What's up with her? Sounds like she's running hysterical."

Victoria stopped short. "All right, Dr. Diabolical, it's time you knew you're a flathead, a gibbering dolt with no more brains between your ears than it takes to poison people with your physic and leech off Tennie. I've had it with you up to the hub, and I'm clearing out."

He shook his head as she flounced out the door. "Can't figure what's gotten into your sister. Case of hysteria would be my guess, misfortunately brought on by congestion of the female plumbing. A dose of lobelia ought to set her straight."

As Tennie saw it, there was more amiss than that. When Victoria debarked to fresh lodgings for herself, her two children and the German nurse, Tennie pledged her word that she would give serious thought to Victoria's viewpoint, so she sent off her own two dollars, wondering whether she would ever get to meet Miss Anthony in person.

Everything and everybody seemed to be on the move. Such droves of people were arriving in Chicago that the city was bursting at the seams. Most of them were immigrants whom only Anna could have chatted with in her German if she hadn't been too wrapped up in casting spells against them and brewing medicine in the backyard.

The squeeze grew tighter still in May, when the Republicans came swarming in to pick the man they wanted as next President. Tennie couldn't cross a street without being jostled by politicos parading in top hats, smelling of sweat, and staining the sidewalks with tobacco juice. Most of them were polite to her, but there wasn't one that captured her fancy. They looked so pleased with themselves, she thought, they'd expect a woman to sit up and beg like a dog mooching bones.

There was talk that Ben Butler might outdo Grant at leading the country, though Ben, at loggerheads with the general, didn't even appear in Chicago. "In no event," he told Grant, "would I be willing to hold personal intercourse with yourself or any member of your family." It didn't matter after Grant won the nomination hands down on the first ballot, which Tennie took as a testimonial to her powers.

The day that happened, an invitation came for her from Victoria. She was in a flurry. "Mark my word, Tennie, Grant's going to make it to the top just like you predicted to his pa. The Dems don't have a hope with that milksop Seymour. Oh, I get splitting mad seeing how smooth everything goes for a drunkard like Ulysses S. Grant. Do you realize how old I'm going to be come September? Thirty! And what do those years add up to for me? A blank. Nothing. Zero. And time's slipping through my fingers like an eel. Tennie, I've got to strike out on my own, and I want you and Hebern along with me—Johnny, too, if you like. We'll travel like we used to with Pa, only this go it'll be our money, money to use for ourselves."

"Supposing you can't make a go of it?"

Victoria turned white as chalk. "Then I'll give solemn thought to killing myself."

"Ah, get off it, Sis. You wouldn't know where to start."

"I would so. I'd do like they did in Rome—sit in a tub and slit my wrists."

Perhaps she would at that. "No consequence, anyway, because I'm coming; Johnny, too," Tennie said.

After they agreed in writing to his terms, Buck put up most of the stake, at 10 percent compound interest, repayable in full on demand if he decided to buy another bundle of railroad stock. They bought a Concord coach secondhand, and Hebern took to the paint pot again. They cast an eye over an atlas to lay out a trail to avoid such trouble spots as La Salle County and towns where Buck might have made work for gravediggers. But there was so much wide-open territory he'd never plowed, it was no wonder they scented opportunity ahead.

Johnny bustled around so much that Tennie doubted whether it was worth having him along for bedtime company. One night in Little Rock she enjoyed herself with a man who bragged about making a fortune in railway bonds, but Victoria and Hebern didn't breathe a word about it to her husband. Arkansas proved to be something of a gold mine, with carpetbaggers busy as bees in the cause of Reconstruction, while the two sisters tried to match them in piling up cash.

Tennie reminisced afterward, "They call Missouri the 'show me' state, which I was tempted into doing three or four times when I received a fitting approach from the right kind of customer, but it was in St. Louis that Victoria fell overboard hook, line, and sinker, and I couldn't have been happier for her, for I banked on it rendering her a world of good."

It was Victoria's turn to handle the sittings and Tennie's to tend door on the evening he paid his first visit, drawn by a notice in the papers placed by Hebern, who traveled a jump ahead of his sisters, priming the pump. Their caller was a restless little man, moustache attached to side-whiskers that he fidgeted with as he paced into the hotel room, back as straight as a poker.

"May I introduce myself? Colonel James Harvey Blood, formerly in command of the Sixth Missouri Regiment, currently City Auditor and President of the St. Louis Society of Spiritualists."

Tennie bobbed him half a curtsy. "Come on in. Make yourself at home." So many of them claimed to be colonels, it was a puzzle who'd ever done the fighting, but if his other credentials held water, she could see trouble looming again.

"You must be Miss Tennessee, but it is really Mrs. Woodhull I wish to consult, being acquainted with her resounding reputation." She hoped that let herself off the hook as she shooed him over to where Victoria sat at a mahogany table with a kerosene lamp burning on it against the far wall.

His chocolate-brown eyes lit up as he raised her hand to kiss it. This was reassuring, but Victoria was risking nothing with him until she'd taken more of his measure. Without a pause to dim the lamp, she let herself drop to the carpet in an apparent trance, eyes fluttering, fingers intertwined, pale lips trembling.

Her tone was smooth and soft. "I see your future linked with mine. Perhaps you are chained in a sundered marriage, which is a fate I share with you. But freedom from these bonds awaits us both. I vision our paths crossing. We are destined to find happiness in each other."

It worked like a charm of pure gold. Though tears were wetting his cheeks, he curbed himself from wiping them until she had composed herself. Then he covered her hands with kisses as he hauled her to her feet. Tennie hoped they were home and dry, and donned shawl and bonnet to take a stroll. "I reckoned it wouldn't be surprising if she was prompted by my personal example to revert to a pleasurable pastime."

Victoria was in bed but wide-awake and still bright as sunshine when Tennie returned. "Did anything interesting develop between you two?"

Victoria's bare arms branched up toward the ceiling. "Dearest sister, the colonel and I are betrothed. We're united already 'by the powers of the air,' he says. He was so tender and beautiful to me. I can't begin to explain, but I want you to share my happiness."

As she told it, the colonel was a man of parts, philosopher and anarchist rolled into one. He was gallant, idealistic, and furthermore broad-minded, which Tennie felt was undoubtedly true. He was prepared to take an oath declaring Victoria certain to have "a tremendous destiny," which settled it where she was concerned. Tennie couldn't squeeze in a word until her sister began to talk about the five bullet holes he bore in his torso as mementos of the war.

"I suppose you counted 'em for yourself?"

"What do you think, pet? Of course I did."

Johnny, who had charge of the cashbox, quizzed his wife one day about how she had come by ten dollars without his knowing it. That, she said, was none of his business. They launched into their fiercest quarrel to date. If he imagined she would be slapped down by any man, he had better think again.

After that, they brawled most of the time until Victoria agreed to take temporary leave of the colonel so the sisters might cover the final lap back to Chicago. She wanted to celebrate her good fortune in finding Jim Blood, and they had the money to make a splash—they'd been earning as much as a hundred dollars a day all summer.

Perched next to Tennie on the coach in a new purple gown with a white rose at her breast, Victoria sparkled like a circus queen waving at the crowd that was halted in its tracks by the blare of the marching band she hired to play through the streets to Wabash Avenue. It was the first parade the sisters were ever in. Victoria was in a state of ecstasy.

By then Tennie was tired of Johnny, and he maintained his distance. She gave him a share of the cash on the understanding he was to bother her no more. Since she hadn't taken his name, she didn't count herself married. It would have been throwing good money after bad to fuss with a lawyer to win a divorce.

Victoria stayed in Chicago barely long enough to change her clothes before she was off to St. Louis. Tennie promised to follow and bring the rest of the family, including Byron, Zulu Maud, and the nurse. For once there was no pressing need to skip out of town, so they took their time in packing. Then, when they had dawdled their way to the address Victoria had sent them, they found that she and the colonel had flown the coop. Just why, they didn't learn until later: the first and still legally the only Mrs. James H. Blood was on the warpath, with a pair of young Bloods flanking her.

Victoria related her travels with Jim after they had wandered back again to Chicago to make one big happy family with the rest of the Claflins. Victoria and the colonel had gone off in a covered van with a ball-fringed top, she said, working much the same route where Claflin pickings had proved easy before. But the two of them had been too wrapped up in each other's company to come close to cramming the cashbox as had been done in the past.

"It's like a miracle happens every time, Tennie. I hadn't recognized what it's like having a man worship you as if you were a princess and set your mind flaming simultaneous with your body."

"Sure as fate, you've got it bad, Sis."

"Jim says sex is a right and a rapture, and we're morally bound to abide by God's law when we're lucky enough to find a true mate whether or not there's a wedding ring. It's his belief every man and woman can be made over in the Lord's image, but they must start by considering loving each other as natural as breathing."

It struck Tennie that the two lovers were as close as Siamese twins in their habits of thinking and living. He said farewell to a salary when he left his auditing job. The St. Louis councilors weren't likely to miss him when he was a staunch Greenbacker, insisting that all debts ought to be payable in wartime paper money in place of gold, which was hard to come by. On their tour together he had taken over Hebern's role as advance man, trumpeting the impending arrival of Victoria, the amazing, supernatural clairvoyant. He also doubled as bookkeeper. To throw his wife off the scent, he called himself "James Harvey, Esquire." while Victoria was "Madame Harvey."

Anything he believed in, she did, too, and he believed in women's rights, with the exception of Mrs. Blood's; in governments of all nations joining hands; and in the souls of the dead returning to earth implanted in newborn babies. But what his heart was truly set on was free love.

This faith didn't falter even after he and Victoria sold the wagon and had been stripped of every cent they'd earned, to persuade Mrs.

Blood that she could get along without him. Tennie talked to him about that. "I used to think love should be handed out free, with no strings attached. But I don't see a thing wrong with accepting a price if it's tendered. Why should a woman put herself out for nothing?"

"Dear, mercenary little Tennie, you've grabbed hold of the wrong end of the stick. Those of us who advocate free love are not referring to the absence of a financial transaction or of red ink on a ledger page. We mean the liberating freedom to love, to participate in intercourse with a like-minded man or woman with whom we share spiritual affinity. Then the act of love in itself emerges as a force far mightier than gravity or magnetism."

How he did talk! "Does all of that figuring race through your head when you're with Sis? It's my experience there's too much going on for me to do more than join in and enjoy myself."

"We'll have you converted yet, never fear."

"Will you wager on it? And, hey, what about the plain ugly ones? Sis is still spry, considering her years, but would it be the same to you if she was some wore-out old biddy like Ma?"

"What matters is not the frail outer shell but the eternal inner spirit, the essence, the psyche. Love is not conditional upon mere physical factors."

"Want to double up on that bet?" No, he didn't; games of chance didn't fit in with his principles.

Yet he was so calm and collected compared with the Claflins that Tennie couldn't help but like him even when he sat around all day, nose in a book, contributing not a penny to the housekeeping. But Anna couldn't stand the sight of him. "That *schweinhund!*" she'd mutter. "I call heaven to witness the ruin of my daughter, and him with no bottom in his pockets!"

Buck's suspicions of him increased after the money his two daughters squirreled away was all spent and Victoria was forced to borrow from her father on IOU's he insisted that she sign. He was coming unstuck with his dabbling in Erie Railroad stock. Though Victoria had never backtracked from guaranteeing she'd always provide for her mother, Buck wasn't altogether convinced he was covered by the same warranty. He was worried when the yellow boys and silver cartwheels and all the other species of cash he'd been investing went floating down the drain, leaving him nothing to show for it but stock certificates engraved with Greek goddesses, Egyptian pyramids, steam engines, temples of commerce, and the Lord knew what else. On the present market, those bits of paper were good for no more than wrapping mackerel.

He laid the blame on those Wall Street sharks, Daniel Drew, Jay Gould, and Jim Fisk, who had cornered almost all the Erie stock. He left out of his reckoning Cornelius Vanderbilt, though better-informed investors would have rated the old Commodore more responsible than any of them for Buck's predicament. The way it came about was this:

Vanderbilt was the only man alive that Buck looked up to. He kidded himself that he, too, would have piled up a fortune if he'd had such advantages as owning a fleet of steamships and ten million miles of railroad track. When he heard that old Cornelius was buying all the Erie stock he could lay his hands on, Buck took the cue and did likewise, a mouse tailing a tiger. What neither of them knew was that Drew, Gould, and Fisk were running fresh stock certificates off the presses and selling them without allowing time for the ink to dry.

When the Commodore caught on and sicked the law on them, Fisk and Gould fled out of New York across the North River to a hotel in New Jersey with six million dollars packed in their suitcases. Fisk also took along his dear companion, the actress Josie Mansfield, as though things weren't heated enough without her. When Buck read about that, he concluded that the Erie's goose was cooked and his along with it.

Jim Blood had something to say on this point. "As I see it, there is only one way to restore your position, and that is for all of us to proceed to the scene of the crime—in other words, to New York. I am not inexperienced in monetary affairs, and Victoria shall be my pupil. I envisage a bright new chapter of life opening up for her there. It's undoubtedly the spot where there's money to be made and her reputation established as a national figure."

Buck was on him like a hawk. "What's in it for you?"

He was given a lofty answer. "When anyone can't understand me

well enough to know that I am working for the human race and not
for Colonel Blood, I don't care to have very much to do with them."

None of Buck's fuming could sway him. Wherever the colonel
went, Victoria would stick with him, and where she headed, Tennie
would go, too. And so it was that they steered east, with the two
sisters back at their trade and supporting the whole family.

The strain told on Victoria. She didn't relish returning to a city
where she'd fallen on her face before. She was worried about where
they would live and how long it might take to attract customers.
Then an idea took root in Tennie's head. She asked Hebern, who
was adept at such things, to write ahead to arrange for a furnished
rental to be waiting and never mind the expense. He was to keep it
a secret from everybody other than the two of them.

They had reached Pittsburgh before Tennie was ready to raise her
sister's spirits and the spirit of one other besides. What was called
the Steel City was shrouded in murk and grime. The marble-top
table by the window in the hotel bedroom Tennie was to share with
her parents bore a film of coal dust, which she saw as a bit of luck.
While Victoria and Jim were unpacking next door, Tennie used a
fingertip to scrawl the name on the marble, then draped it with a
cloth and refreshed her memory with a look at a letter from New
York that Hebern had collected at the desk downstairs.

She played on Jim Blood's weakness for probing "beyond the
boundaries of mind and matter," as he called it, by offering to slip
into a trance to see whether she could foresee what was in store. At
the family gathering held that evening in the parents' room, they
all took it for granted that Tennie could pull off this prescience
trick now and then.

At the marble-top table, she went through the usual abracadabra,
then pretended there was a house emerging into view and that she
was struggling to read the street sign and the number on the front
door. "Yep, now the mist is lifting. . . . It's coming crystal clear.
. . . It's Number Seventeen on Great Jones Street!" But she wasn't
done yet with surprises. She moaned that the spirit responsible for
this vision, dressed in a white tunic and laced-up sandals, had left
his name under the tablecloth. If anybody with a careful hand cared
to lift it . . .

When Victoria ventured to do so, she dropped to the floor. In the dust on the table, Tennie had lettered the name "Demosthenes."

Number 17 would have been a good choice if Buck had been tempted to tackle cancer again. There were rooms enough upstairs and down to put in at least two dozen cots, and a brass plate would have looked completely at home by the front door. The house and all its furnishings had an aura of respectability that the Claflins found unsettling until they grew accustomed to it.

Victoria took to the place from the moment they made their first inspection and spotted a library walled with old books in leather bindings. Ovid, Plutarch, Aristotle and, yes, there was a copy of *The Orations of Demosthenes,* which spelled fair sailing ahead to her.

Great Jones Street was a convenient thoroughfare, offering the choice, when they came down the front steps, between turning toward the Bowery and toward Broadway, depending on whether they were out for a bit of adventure or an hour of window shopping. Victoria mostly walked west toward A.T. Stewart's and James McCreery & Company, but sometimes Tennie would coax her in the opposite direction to see gin mills and concert halls and panel-houses, Dandy Dans in bell-bottom britches, harlots in short skirts and jaunty bonnets, and to hear the babble of tongues of all nations.

It wasn't hard for them to feel at home in New York City, except for Anna, who didn't give a tinker's damn for the finery on show in department stores and cursed everything about the Bowery as the deepest down pit of hell. She stayed holed up in the house, spatting with Jim Blood, who'd never be anything but a limb of Satan in her opinion.

It was evident they'd have to set their sights on a higher-class trade than they had attracted up to now. Everybody in New York City seemed either extravagantly rich or pitifully poor, with no one in between. A walk east beyond the Bowery would find so many foreigners that Tennie was sure the next boatload would burst the place apart. Going uptown, palaces fit for kings were rearing up like Jacob's ladders.

The condition of the streets disgusted her. The nonstop churning of wagons and drays, carts and carriages, splintered the wood planks underfoot and tore up the cobblestones faster than they could be set down again. It was a rare day she didn't come across a fallen horse with a shattered leg. There was no path to pick that wasn't choked with filth and peddlers' carts, and a sprinkle of rain turned even Broadway into a mudbath. New York streets stank with the reek of slaughterhouses, garbage, animal carcasses, and the gas works, compelling her to keep her nose buried in a handkerchief as soon as she stepped outside. What they needed was a carriage, but before they could afford one, she and Victoria would have to locate some paying clients.

Tennie didn't much care what line of work she followed so long as it showed a profit: spirits, the crystal, the Elixir, magnetic healing, or romance. The last item seemed to hold little promise in view of the heavy competition. The town was teeming with every type and stripe of girl, from maids fresh off the farm to worn-out drabs on a downhill gallop toward Potter's Field.

Jim Blood said it in a nutshell. "The traffic in female virtue is as much a regular business, carried on for gain, in this city as the trade in boots and shoes, dry goods, and groceries."

Victoria glowered. "For all that, they're free women compared with some poor downtrodden wives."

Tennie had a query to assess the strength of the competition. "Any idea how many are on the game, Jim? Not implying you've had time to count 'em, mind you."

"They say there are four hundred brothels within three miles of City Hall, if that's an answer, and they do an annual business of perhaps eight million dollars, with a share paid to the police for protection. The number of abandoned women involved is anyone's guess."

"Whew, that's a mountain of money, right enough."

Victoria brought up a different point. "They're always 'abandoned women,' but never 'abandoned men'! There must be ten times more of *them*. Eight million dollars to gratify their damnable lusts. Men reeking with the stink of fancy houses and streetwalkers they've bought at the price of their souls."

"I can tell," Tennie said, "without a judge summing it up that if anybody has to lay on her back to keep the wolf away from the doorstep at Number Seventeen, it's going to have to be me."

Another thing she hadn't counted on when they made their move

here was the admiration accorded horses in a metropolis where a
blade of grass was a rarity. Not the spavined wheelers that hauled
the carts nor the teams hitched to the brewers' drays, but the slab-
sided trotters she could watch every afternoon tittuping through the
traffic on their way up to Central Park, pulling a shiny sulky or a
curricle with some high-hat handling the ribbons. Buck started
talking about going back into horse-trading, but he was too rusty,
and he got no farther than taking himself up to the park to goggle
at the gentlemen in silk hats letting off steam in a trotting race
while he cross-examined the spectators about the identity of the
drivers and where their money came from.

Tennie went there with him once, and it *was* a sight to feast her
eyes on—bankers, builders, shipowners, actor-managers, reverends,
newspaper publishers, and merchants, all whipping along in a
storm of dust, scraping wheel against wheel to beat each other. She
judged the prince of the brotherhood to be a spry old fellow with a
cigar in his jaw, spruced up in a tight-buttoned black coat and
white cravat, who was urging on a pair of bays.

Her ribs felt Buck's bony elbow. "That's him! That's Cornelius
Vanderbilt, in person, and I've heard tell those two horses cost him
eight thousand dollars. He stables a dozen of 'em on Fourth Street
a block or two from our house and drives here every day. Let's you
and me give 'em the once-over tomorrow after he's finished his
airing and got in condition for his supper. It might render us a bit
of good, seeing as people say he's not stuck on himself and will
exchange a word with anybody. I've been doing some homework
with regard to the Commodore."

The sun was down and the lanterns were lit when father and
daughter arrived at the coach house behind Number 10 Washington
Place. A manservant stood there with a silver salver that held a
tumblerful of something—Buck guessed it would be gin with sugar
in it. Old Vanderbilt swung his curricle around the corner, lean
cheeks flushed pink, blue eyes sparkling, then reined in the horses,
and downed the toddy at a gulp.

Buck tipped his beaver hat. "A pair of spankers you've got there,
Commodore, and I know a thing or two about horseflesh, having
been in the trade myself."

The old man's voice was gruff as a bear's. "I appreciate your compliment, neighbor. This here's Mountain Boy, who's been clocked at two minutes and nineteen seconds over the measured mile, t'other's Post Boy, three seconds slower. I can lick any man alive with 'em, save Bonner, who runs the *Ledger,* I wager I'll best him one day, though he won't bet on it, 'cos gambling's against his grain." He snapped his fingers at the servant. "Give me a hand down. There's a crick in my groin just now."

The gaze was ten times more piercing than Buck's. "Who's this pretty foal? Your daughter?"

"That's it right on the nose. She's my Tennie, otherwise known as Miss Tennessee, the celebrated clairvoyant and magnetic healer to boot."

"The devil you say! I could stand a touch of healing myself. If I was to believe what the God-blasted quacks tell me, I'd never climb out of my bed."

"You'd be happy to oblige, wouldn't you, Tennie? She's a regular crackerjack at her calling, Mr. Vanderbilt."

"If she was plainer than a pikestaff, I'd be willing to try her out, but God's truth, she's winsomer than a ten percent dividend. Bring her around before breakfast tomorrow, seven o'clock sharp." The hand that clamped her chin for an instant was cold but strong.

That's how she trotted up to the starting post. The house inside was comfortable but plain for a man calculated to be the richest in the land, having won an extra fortune in the war on top of the millions made from ships and railroads. He'd lived there with nobody but household help since his wife Sophie had died six months ago while he was taking the cure and applying himself at five-point euchre at Saratoga Springs.

The butler led Buck into the billiard room and Tennie up a curved staircase to the bedroom, where the Commodore lay on top of the covers in a silk nightshirt, sipping Holland gin. The legs of the bed stood in saltcellars—insulators, he said later, to prevent his magnetism from seeping out into the Persian rug.

"I'm ready and waiting for you, little pigeon. Where d'you want to begin?"

She spun him the line about magnetism flowing through her limbs, positive on the right, negative on the left. She would give him a rubbing with both hands simultaneously, she said, to stimulate the current into coursing through his frame: "Is there any spot in particular like lungs, heart, kidneys, liver, or suchlike that's acting up this morning?"

"What I'm looking for is a general going over, in the nature of auditing the books, and I'll tolerate some juggling of figures if you've the competence to strike a trial balance."

She set off parting his locks of white hair to vigorate his scalp, which was flaked with dandruff. She proceeded to the nape of his scraggy neck before she had him undo the nightshirt so she could work on his fore and aft. By then he was sprawled out relaxed and cooing like a dove. Next, she asked him to roll over face down before she slipped off her shoes, hoisted her skirts, and clambered up onto the mattress to knead his back with her toes. In the middle of that procedure, he raised a hand around to catch an ankle, but she told him there was more and better to come. By the time she had completed the accounting down to the bottom line, he was fit to fly over the moon. "Balanced up a treat" were his words.

Knuckles tapped on the door, and a man's shaved face showed around it. "Breakfast is served, sir, and I've laid out your clo—"

The old man reached for the closest thing handy, which happened to be a shoe of Tennie's, and flung it straight at the servant's head. "Out, get out, you whoreson, and don't come back or I'll hang your hide on a tree!" After the door had been shut, the smile shone out again. "There's one other thing I'd admire your doing for me, but there ain't time right this minute. Now, you be sure to come back after supper, and we'll get to it then. Meantime, you can help me on with my clothes, and we'll take a bite of breakfast together."

Buck was included out of courtesy when they sat down in the dining room, but that was the last meal he ate on Washington Place. "I don't stuff," old Vanderbilt said, but nevertheless he put away the yolks—no whites—of three soft-boiled eggs, a thick lamb chop, lashings of toast, and a cup of black tea with a dozen lumps of sugar Tennie stirred in for him. She was as hungry as he was after all the exercise.

When they had finished eating, he packed Buck off home and took Tennie over to the coach house to meet his Hambletonian trotters, naming and cosseting them one by one and feeding them an apple apiece from a bagful stored with the tack. He asked her to call him "Corneel" as his family did, but "Com" struck her as better suited. He lingered longest by his stallions. "Ain't they a spectacle? I only wished I still retained their brand of youth and energy. Then I'd show you a run for your money. But I've got to be off." Her reward for the morning workout came to an even hundred dollars in gold.

She was curious about what the evening program held in store when she went back alone, carrying the crystal in a handbag and rustling as she walked in the new ombre-striped China silk dress she had spent part of the proceeds on at A.T. Stewart's. The butler smirked as he conducted her into the parlor, which stood empty, providing an interval she needed to study the portraits hanging framed on the walls, pride of place given to a sunny-faced old woman in an old-fashioned frilly cap who had to be his mother. Then she heard him roaring at somebody in a room close by about "the goddam Erie Railroad."

He bustled in with a fat, middle-aged man who sported a set of Dundreary whiskers on his jowls. "My boy Billy, who'll operate the Central for me when I'm gone, which won't be for a while yet, I promise you. I've been telling him how to bring them blowers Gould and Fisk to their knees by cutting rates. Not charge the present hundred-and-sixty-dollar tariff on a carload of cattle from Buffalo into my New York terminal, but lower it to forty. What d'you say to that? Billy, what are you lollygogging about? Get over there and greet the girl."

The whiskers tickled when he kissed Tennie's hand. "Father, is it, ah, safe to talk in front of, ah, this young woman?"

The Commodore let rip another bellow. "Safe, you blatherskite? I've got no secrets. Anyway, I've reason to trust my little pigeon, ain't I?" She got a slap on a thigh as testimony.

Billy's cow eyes held no secrets for her, either. The look in them said it might suit him for her to be available and serving to keep his father's hands off the housemaids. "What if the Erie plays the same game?"

"Then we cut again and go on cutting. I'll drop as low as a dollar a carload if I have to. I don't want to do 'em damage—just plain ruin 'em. But I didn't get Tennie here for railroad talk. You take your leave, Billy. She's going to get in touch with your grandmother for me. One last thing. Sell Hudson stock short when it's down to a hundred and ten."

It was amazing to her what a gull he was, this lonesome old man they treated like a king on Wall Street. He sobbed like a child when she pretended his mother, Phoebe, was floating around somewhere in the dark, recalling how she'd promised to lend him a hundred dollars to buy his first boat if he'd plow and plant eight acres of their farm on Staten Island by his seventeenth birthday, which left him no more than a month to do it. Tennie owed that knowledge to a keen memory, plus coaching from Buck.

Vanderbilt was in such a state of melancholy that she felt obliged to lay Phoebe to rest and call a temporary halt to give him chance to brighten up. When that was done, he threw in some extra details. "She figured she'd get the best of me on the deal, but I got some other lads to help me out, and we did the work, and did it well, too, for she wouldn't allow half measures. I claimed the money, bought the boat, hoisted sail, and there weren't a happier boy in the world."

"Bully for you! Well, what's next? Do you want me to try to raise your missus to see how she's faring up there?"

"She'll save for another time. Suppose you take a crack at telling what Hudson stock's about to do, rise or fall, bear market or bull?"

Tennie buffed up the crystal while she pondered that conundrum. She was too green then to realize a killing could be made either way on Wall Street. She imagined that a business needed to prosper before a share of it was worth much. Since she didn't care to cause him further grief, she predicted there was only one direction those shares could go, and that was up.

He was satisfied for her to shut up shop in the crystalware department after that. "Trading tomorrow will be proof you're right or wrong. There's better things to do here and now. Come on over here and let's have a squeeze."

The old man was only three years younger than Buck, yet he had the ardor of a bridegroom. He was considerate, too, of her feelings,

which grew cordial as the evening wore on. When he'd had his fill
of spooning with her laid across his lap in an armchair, he rang for
the butler to bring a decanter of gin, a pitcher of hot water, a sugar
bowl, and a deck of cards. They settled down for a gossip and some
hands of whist, Tennie with a fistful of dollars he supplied for
staking against his to spice the interest, anything she won to be hers
to keep.

The air grew blue from the smoke of his Havanas and bluer yet
with his curses if he lost a round, which wasn't often. He was always
apologizing for his language, "but it don't come easy to break
what's a habit of the waterfront."

"No call to say you're sorry to me. Christ Almighty, I don't give
a fart in hell what you come out with. I'll keep up with you, you
old muleskinner." That caught him on the funny bone, as she
calculated it would, and he laughed to split his sides, awarding her
a hug that threatened her ribs.

When he had simmered down, he brought up the subject of his
mother again. "She's been departed sixteen years come January,
which might make it tricky for you tracing her on a regular schedule. But if you can, it'd be a convenience. I've been forced to cross
on my brother Jake's ferries to Staten Island to consult a medium
name of Mrs. Tufts, who don't hold a candle to you in looks or
talents."

"You can count on me and save yourself the trouble, but I've got
a living to make, you know."

"I'll make it worth your while. There ain't a word of truth in
them claims I'm a skinflint. If it works out, I'll give you something
to prize above money."

"Which is what?"

He drew the ringlets aside off her right ear to whisper, "A lock
of my hair. There's terrible magic in hair, you appreciate that? It
don't take more than a snip of it in the wrong hands to give 'em
power to ruin your life."

It sounded like madness to her, but she was getting weary, so she
didn't pursue the question. "Com, old boy, it's time I took off to
hit the hay. Shall I come around sometime tomorrow?"

"You ain't going home. You'll stay here with me."

"But I've got no clothes."

"You'll do best without 'em. I'll send for all your gear in the morning."

She hadn't climbed into bed before with a man who'd never again see seventy. It was refreshing in some respects, though, not having to fend him off half the night, and peaceful, too, when all it took to please him was a snuggling to warm his old bones, followed by a little gentling to tame his heat. It came to her mind, as she fell asleep listening to his wheezing, that she had begun to take a fancy to him.

The dream centered not on him but on Jim Fisk, whose pork-chop face was familiar to her from engravings in the newspapers. The Com was blackguarding him and screaming, "You won't be-devil me much longer." The scene that came next told why. Some-body was going to shoot fat Fisk one of these days. She passed along the tale to the Commodore over breakfast. If that came about, he chuckled, it'd be the best thing that ever could happen for the benefit of the New York Central Railroad.

He bustled back into the house after the market closed that afternoon. She didn't object to his kissing her even though it was nothing to tuck away in a safe-deposit box. He said Hudson River Railroad was on the rebound, and he was buying more of it, but keeping the maneuver dark from Billy. He commissioned a gleam-ing maroon two-seater instead of the curricle for his daily spin and took her along with him, a silk scarf anchoring her bonnet.

It was a ride to remember. He wove the rig through the press of traffic on Fifth Avenue as deftly as a conjuror until they reached Central Park. A throng of people ripped out a cheer and got a wave of his whip in return. Then he flicked up the horses. Hooves pound-ing like mallets on a roof, they tore north to the entry onto Harlem Lane, which was renamed St. Nicholas Avenue some time later.

There was a string of low-class inns on either side, porches crammed full of gawkers out to eye the trotters and sulkies that swarmed up and down the lane. The yells rang out left and right. "Hey, Vanderbilt, you caught yourself a piece of dry goods there!" . . . "Who's your lady friend, Commodore?" . . . "My, ain't she a pretty peach!" A tickle of the whip under their tails set the team pumping away like pistons worked by a steam boiler.

The road cut through open fields for a mile or more on its way to

Macomb's Dam and then to Cate's Roadhouse at 162nd Street. That stretch was an enticement to him. His cheeks were pink as carnations, his eyes like blue diamonds. "Every man for himself—here we go!" He started cutting in and out and around the competition, forcing everybody to make way, yet doing it with such relish, not a curse was raised against him.

"There's Beecher ahead, the snot-nosed preachifier who's forever begging for his flock. We'll run him down, by God!" The old boy pressured the horses until they fairly flew, then teased them over to bring the wagon within a hair's breadth of a buggy that held a long-locked churchman in a back-to-front collar who lofted his plug hat with a smile. "'Pon my soul, it's Commodore Vanderbilt. Good day to you, sir!"

"Don't mealymouth me, you holy roller!" The whip sang again, and a twitch of the ribbons drew the Vanderbilt rig in so close that the brass hubs of two spiderweb wheels sideswiped each other, grating and squealing from the scraping. The Commodore pulled clear, and over her shoulder, she spotted Dr. Henry Ward Beecher muttering to himself as his horse shied. She would have taken an oath it wasn't a prayer he was offering up.

They followed a turn to carry them over the Harlem Railroad tracks, and there came an express hooting along toward the crossing. It didn't faze her Com. "Hold onto your hat, pigeon! We're going to beat her. Git up there, yah! yah!" The whip cracked like a Colt revolver.

It struck her that maybe the trotters were getting fagged. If they broke pace now as they neared the steel rails, she saw herself a candidate for a graveyard. The engineer had sighted them and the steam whistle was blasting to split her eardrums. The Com was braced up on his feet as the wheels jounced over the rails. She was clutching him around the waist, scared witless, but still staring spellbound at the business end of the engine. They'd barely cleared when the express clanged past, one yard short of their rear end, the wind of it kiting the Com's hat off his head.

He checked the horses to a walk to cool them for the trip home. "There ain't another man in New York who could do that."

"Well, I'm game to give it another go any time you are."

By the end of the week, he had bought seventeen thousand shares of Hudson, according to the tally he posted in the ledger, which was the only piece of equipment in his office desk. All the rest of his dealings were recorded in his head. Hudson climbed to 137. By her figuring, Billy's appearance at the house on Saturday was mostly to keep tabs on her, but the old man couldn't wait to badger him. "How far d'you go with Hudson? If you were dummy enough to sell short at a hundred and ten, you've lost twenty-seven dollars a share."

Billy was as calm as a ruminating cow. "I had ten thousand of 'em, that's all."

"Ain't that too bad!"

"Not so bad. I heard you were out to buy, so I bought, too—at a hundred and ten. I've cleared two hundred and seventy thousand."

In bed that night the Com rolled over away from her and spared a minute to himself. "Maybe Billy ain't the sucker I've been taking him to be. Maybe he does have his head screwed on level."

She was picking up a new box of tricks akin to those the bankers and brokers employed on Wall and Broad. The Com talked so much about his scheming that she felt it didn't take an act of genius to foretell the effects. Everything he did was done on such scale that it pushed the whole market up when he bought and knocked it down if he unloaded. Predicting the future was easy, in the circumstances, but by keeping Phoebe to a tight schedule and calling the shots on the market, Tennie was regarded by the Com as a miracle on two legs.

It wasn't her nature to be greedy, and she wanted Victoria to have a share in her luck, which was improving every week in the form of money stashed away. For all the schooling she was getting from Jim Blood, Victoria wasn't making much headway in proving Demosthenes anything but a liar with his prediction that some day she'd be rich and famous.

She blamed her poor progress on the fact of being born a woman. There were more of them in circulation than ever before after the losses of men in war. Yet the only place that seemed likely to give women the vote was Wyoming Territory, and this as a sort of door prize to tempt them into going there. "A girl," Tennie thought, "would have to be a certified crackpot to choose to live in a cabin at the end of the Oregon Trail and risk getting barbered by Shoshone."

To her way of thinking, it was easier to convert men one at a time to her individual point of view, but Victoria argued against that. She'd settle for nothing less, she said, than women and men being treated even: same vote, same jobs at the same wages, and almost everything else on a par. Jim Blood egged her on. Tennie couldn't decide whether to mark that in his favor or not. It made her so angry to see how shabbily most women were treated that she was given to brooding, though she had a steady flow of clients for the spiritualizing she engaged in.

Victoria's favorite reading was still *The Revolution*. The desire to set eyes on her idol, Miss Anthony, took her one day to a place called The Woman's Bureau, which was the paper's headquarters. From her telling, Tennie gathered the impression that the trip had jolted her sister to the marrow. She had expected to find a band of sisters poor as church mice working for the cause, but Number 49 East 23rd Street was a finer house than the Claflins, owned by a woman, Mrs. Elizabeth B. Phelps, a true believer with money to burn.

Susan was off making speeches somewhere along the trail, but Victoria made herself known to the editor of the paper, Mrs. Elizabeth Cady Stanton, a plump old lady with a lace cap nesting on a head of white curls, no more radical in her looks than Martha Washington.

Mrs. Stanton took to Victoria from the moment she gave her a report on Buck, the medical marvel, and his two equally talented daughters who were better known in Europe than here as healers, ambitious to relieve all human suffering—women's especially.

Mrs. Stanton's response was to confide some of her own family history, paying greater respect to the facts. She had grown up a firebrand, she said, because of her father, a judge given to telling her she should have been a boy when she was winning prizes at Greek and Latin as a scholar at Emma Willard's.

The fire didn't flare though, until she was in London at a meeting called to denounce slavery where the delegates proved unwilling to allow any woman a vote in the proceedings. This didn't suit her, nor did it suit another campaigner who was present, Mrs. Lucretia Mott, originally from Nantucket. So they set about forming a society of their own to try to win women their place—all of this a prelude to the rally at Seneca Falls that Buck had once found so droll.

This lay almost thirty years behind Mrs. Stanton, but she'd been fighting in the cause ever since, with seven children fathered by her lawyer husband. "My whole soul is in my work," she told Victoria, "but my hands belong to the family. I wonder how many men would marry if woman claimed the right to say when she would become a mother." Victoria remarked that Mrs. Stanton wasn't wearing bloomers to her office, but she replied that she still wore them when she was at home in Brooklyn, since they felt more comfortable than stays and tight lacing.

Victoria's call was made at the right moment to pitch Mrs. Stanton into a fresh attempt to change the United States Constitution for the second time within three years. The smoke was rising higher than it ever had over the Fourteenth Amendment, which spelled progress for blacks but not for women. The Fifteenth, not yet ratified, angered the suffragists by stipulating that white and black, born free or born slave, had equal rights, but again it did not apply to women. Ladies of Mrs. Stanton's mettle had good reason to resent it.

Miss Anthony, Mrs. Stanton, Mrs. Mott, and a host of others like them had rallied in Washington the past January to raise a rumpus—the first time women had ever stood up as a crowd to shout for the right to vote. They'd been united then, but today there was division among them. Miss Anthony and Mrs. Stanton foresaw that they would have to forget about being ladylike and start raising cain or there'd never be a vote for women in their lifetime. Mrs. Mott, who was only a year younger than the Commodore, did not agree. Neither did Mrs. Henry Blackwell, who clung to her maiden name of Miss Lucy Stone. They believed that votes for blacks were a long enough stride in the right direction for the present; women could sit back and bide their time.

So what they called "the Movement" was split down the middle. Of course, there was only one side that appealed to Victoria. Twiddling her thumbs while men had the upper hand didn't strike her as the best way in the world for a woman to achieve glory.

She said as much to Mrs. Stanton as she was asking her about the ins and outs of publishing a magazine, curious to know where the money came from when *The Revolution* sold for only two dollars a year. "Why, from the angels, Sister Woodhull. From those generous souls who believe in us—and from some who don't, yet nevertheless support us as a kind of novelty. If we could only increase our circulation to a hundred thousand copies, we should be more than capable of supporting ourselves."

"Where do you stand now, if I'm not being too bold?"

"I'm almost ashamed to tell you: a pitiful three thousand in the bank. It breaks Susan's heart. And we hear that Lucy Stone intends to bring out a new paper of her own in Boston, *Woman's Journal,* which could only be a blow to our ambition. Ah, me! I'm afraid we'll have to rely on manna from heaven and the likes of George Francis Train for a bit longer."

His name meant nothing to Victoria—nor to Tennie when she heard the story—but Mr. Train would bump along the same track with them a year or so from now. Mrs. Stanton mentioned him only as an angel who contributed to the paper in order to get his own articles into print. "He is what one might charitably describe as eccentric and a little, shall we say, conceited. He declares he will nominate himself for the Presidency of the United States; he would probably prove no worse than Ulysses Grant."

Two more seeds were planted in Victoria's loamy head. They sprouted in next to no time.

Tennie took her around to meet the Com, who enjoyed the attention of any woman as handsome as Mrs. Woodhull, particularly when she could take a hand with the massage and summon up Phoebe or anybody else he named in the great beyond. She left Tennie to go on with the bedtime chores, including clystering him by request, which he claimed soothed him to sleep better than a hot toddy.

The three of them hit it off together, even when he was in the thick of warring with Gould and Fisk, which sent his temper rising, then falling again, like a steam elevator. The two rogues had countered his price of forty dollars a carload of cattle by charging just a penny a head to bring the heads in on the Erie tracks on the west bank of the Hudson.

"They keep cutting down and cheating all the time. 'My God,' I says to 'em, 'When you get down low enough, stay there.' You'll see how soon they begin to holler."

But they didn't. His next move was to lower his rate to a dollar for carrying a carful into the city on the Central, which ran on the Hudson's east s de. Fisk bought six thousand head and shipped every one of them in by way of the Vanderbilt route. The Com came home that afternoon with his mouth rattrap tight, but a kiss or two soon soothed him.

"You'd best let Gould and Fisk strut on their own dunghill, while you stick to yours, old boy," said Tennie.

"Devil take 'em, I don't doubt you're right. From now on, sparrow, I'll let them blowers alone. But that dream of yours where Jim Fisk got shot—I've some curiosity about when that's going to come true."

Down on Wall Street, brokers' tongues were wagging over the trick Fisk had pulled, and the Com was concerned for the welfare of Central common when he'd taken such a pummeling. Victoria took a turn at prophesying and promised him the stock would bounce up twenty points at least, on grounds that, the fight being over, the losses he'd been suffering would be ended, too.

Central common chalked up a gain of 22 percent, and the Com took to delivering the same advice to anybody who came seeking a tip from him: "Consult the spirits like I do."

Victoria thought to add more bait to the hook by displaying faith in the old man. Tennie went along with that, and they handed over their few thousand dollars of savings for him to invest any way he saw fit. They couldn't have found a means to please him more until, a while later, Tennie gave him as a present an oil painting entitled "Aurora," bought in a gilded frame, which displayed a girl not unlike herself, large as life, clad in nothing more than a smile and half a yard of gauze. He hung that in the best parlor opposite the portrait of Phoebe.

There was no rhyme or reason Victoria could see for telling Mrs.

Stanton how life was lived on Washington Place or Great Jones Street. Elizabeth concluded that Victoria would benefit from being introduced to more high-minded people of her own kind. Now, working alongside of Mrs. Stanton on *The Revolution,* was Phoebe Cary, a lively woman who wrote hymns and poetry in her spare time. Phoebe shared an old house on East 20th Street with her sister Alice, who followed similar hobbies. By Mrs. Stanton's account, everybody who amounted to anything in the Movement showed up there on Sunday evenings, when tea was served along with generous helpings of conversation. Perhaps Sister Woodhull would care to join her there and bring along her young sister? Tennie was willing, though her taste in refreshments ran to something more fortifying than cups of tea.

The Carys' parlor, done up in red and green, was well supplied with sofas and armchairs that their male tenants found so comfortable they restrained themselves from getting up to make room for women to sit down. Tennie concluded that they had jumped the gun in freeing themselves from the bonds of common courtesy at about the same time half the women there had liberated themselves from corsets.

Her head was swimming, and so was her sister's. One gentleman hidden in spectacles and a thick fringe of whiskers was chatting with a tall woman as spare as a stick of rhubarb. "If you vote, are you ready to fight?" squeaked Mr. Horace Greeley. (They had said he was the celebrated editor of the *Tribune* and a heavyweight fighter for justice, though his voice sounded like chalk rubbing a slate.)

"Yes, Mr. Greeley," snapped Miss Susan B. Anthony, "just as you fought in the late war—at the point of a goose quill."

Victoria enjoyed hearing that. With her sister, she swished over to eavesdrop on what a pudgy old fellow with pockmarks on his cheeks had to say. "Mr. Phineas T. Barnum," Mrs. Stanton whispered.

"I've retired from business now, as you know, but I still retain connections with my old friend General Tom Thumb. I intend to join that celebrated dwarf in a fresh enterprise very shortly, proposing an exhibition tour of him and a party of twelve more in the show line with a complete outfit including ponies and a carriage, traveling entirely around the world. I shall also engage the well-known Siamese twins Chang and Eng and the giantess Anna Swan, sending them to Great Britain and there to hold levees to which royalty will be invited catering for that insatiate want of human nature, which is the love of amusement."

Victoria would have enlisted with him as an extra added attraction had he asked her to. The Claflin sisters crossed the hall to the library, which was paneled in oak and walled with books, to pick up cups and saucers and make the acquaintance of a man Tennie knew something about from listening to the Com. Mr. Robert Bonner sparked up when she asked about Dexter, which Vanderbilt had said was the fastest trotter alive, but Victoria's interest lay in his newspaper, not his stables.

"They say, sir, that the *Ledger* is read by a million people every day. How does one possibly achieve such success?"

"Well, a million people do read it, but only three hundred thousand buy it, though I don't complain about that. It's been done quite simply by spending money, as much as twenty-five thousand some weeks for advertising, one hundred dollars a column for a story I feel is going to sell my newspapers. Nobody in the country pays higher."

"Dare I ask whether you pay such fees to women?"

"I have no prejudice in that regard. Fanny Fern, for instance, who's back there in the parlor—she earns top dollar and five thousand a year besides to guarantee me exclusive rights to all she produces. I publish Henry Ward Beecher and his sister, Mrs. Stowe, Longfellow, Bryant—every one of them a winner in terms of circulation."

"Don't you find, sir, that more startling stories—of what transpires between the sexes, perhaps—would serve better there than sermons by Dr. Beecher?"

"Not a bit of it. We take care not to offend the most delicate susceptibilities. My editorial staff has a standing order. I tell them, 'Take the most pious old lady in a Presbyterian church, and any word or phrase, innuendo or expression that she would want to skip if she were reading a *Ledger* story to her grandchild, strike out!' "

Victoria expressed her thanks, but her brow knitted as the two women turned away, tea untouched. "That might do for Robert Bonner, but I'll bet there's no shortage of people who'd welcome more spice on a page. I know what I'd do if I was putting out a paper."

By and large, the house was aswirl with everybody gossiping and cutting in on one another's conversations. Whatever else this crowd might be, it was loaded with radicals. Not one of them had a kind word for Ulysses Grant or banks or Wall Street or John D. Rockefeller's Standard Oil Company, or any other business. They didn't approve of railroads' raising prices or the Government's letting Western Union monopolize the telegraph lines. There was a lot of talk, too, about how poorly the blacks were still treated and how it would help everybody if debts could be paid off in greenbacks in place of gold, which would be one way of curbing the bankers. They spoke about emancipating women and saving democracy from the trusts to the point where Tennie had the desire to nip back to Washington Place for a drink.

But Victoria hung onto everything she heard, even when a lull was called for Alice Cary to recite her latest poem, which had to do with her early days on the family farm in Ohio. They gave her a round of applause for that, and then Mrs. Stanton took the floor. She opened by saying, "Marriage in many cases is mere legalized prostitution, a condition in which women have no respect for themselves and their husbands none for them."

After Mrs. Stanton sat down on a chair that Barnum graciously gave up for her, Tennie was hoping to leave, but her sister had been cornered by a newcomer with circles under his dark eyes and a moth-eaten beard, a man about sixty years old, she judged.

Stephen Pearl Andrews was one who couldn't be turned off once he got started, and he fascinated Victoria. He announced that he spoke Latin, Spanish, French, and Chinese, and had written a book, *Basic Outline of Universology,* which ran not a paragraph longer than nine hundred pages. Victoria said she was sure it made fascinating reading, and he said he happened to have a copy at home that he'd be delighted to lend her.

She pried some more details out of him. He had taught in a seminary in Louisiana while he studied and preached Abolition.

Since his reception down there couldn't be termed friendly, he'd made tracks for Houston to have a try at freeing slaves in Texas, which he might have known in advance wouldn't be a land flowing with milk and honey for his kind, either. But he seemed to have prospered just the same. His second wife, the current one, was a qualified doctor, so nothing would do but for him to study for a New York medical degree.

He'd invented what he termed "phonography," a method of writing that used signs in place of normal letters, which weren't enough of a challenge for him. He was urging that this be taught in schools as a time-saving practice. As if he couldn't speak in more languages than a head waiter, he had concocted one of his own, which he called "Alweto"; he planned on everybody on earth's learning it as soon as he took over. And domination was his target: he counted on running the world in the name of what he figured was the greatest thing on earth, which was free love. "Oh, Andrews," Tennie told herself, "is a positive, pearl-handled beaut!"

She couldn't tear her sister away until Victoria had twisted a promise from him that he'd bring the copy of his book around for her bedtime reading on Great Jones Street. While they waited for a cab, she gushed about his genius. "That man's got more knowledge in his little finger than Jim has in his whole head, and don't think I'm putting down Jim when I say that. Isn't Stephen Andrews inspiring, Tennie? I could just feel my mind take off and fly as he spoke."

"If you could make out what he was cracking on about most times, you had the edge on me."

"I'd like to hold a soirée every night of the week, to have him there with his friends, teaching me, feeling myself grow, learning all the time, making everything come true."

"You mean old Demosthenes saying how you can bet on being famous?"

Two patches the shade of red roses flushed Victoria's cheeks, and her eyes glimmered like fireflies. A nod did for an answer.

"It'd be a tight fit squeezing a soirée in with you and Ma and Pa and Hebern," Tennie exclaimed. "There wouldn't be room left to swing a cat."

"Then I'll find a bigger, more imposing place. All it takes is money, and we're not short of that, you especially."

Tennie caught the hint. "I'll do what I can to wangle something with the Com." In private she knew she'd be making herself scarce every time Andrews came over the horizon.

She was nestled together with Cornelius on the sofa that afforded the best view of "Aurora" when she raised the subject. His response was unexpected. "There'd be no call to ask for cash if you was married to me. I'd give you all you asked—set you up for life. What do you say to that, little sparrow?"

"I don't hold with marrying. I tried it once, but it turned my stomach."

"Ain't you willing for one more try? Make a honest woman of yourself?"

"I guess I'm honest enough without it. How it is now, we're more like equal partners. If you tire of me, you can throw me out. If I tire of you, I can shove off any time."

"It ain't likely you'll tire me, I promise. What are you telling me, anyway? That you're one of them emancipated women, as they term 'em?"

"Not by a damned sight! Sis is, though, and we don't quarrel over that. She's ambitious for herself, and I'm not, but I'll help her out all I can."

"You ain't contemplating walking out on me, are you?"

"Walk out? I don't think! I'm not crazy for you, Com, but I wouldn't harm a single hair that's left in your old gray head."

He laughed until he choked for breath. "You'll do for me, gal." His hand fell hard on her rump under the Mother Hubbard she wore around the house to the exclusion of everything else. "I'll see you don't run short. But I want you to think the proposition over. You'd be a stunner as Mrs. Cornelius Vanderbilt."

"You'd best check what Billy says before we go through all that poop again."

That put a stop to talk of marriage. Billy didn't picture Tennie as a stepmother. For once his brother Cornelius Jeremiah and their nine sisters went along with his judgment. Billy reminded his father of his wish to hold the family fortune together for the long run by willing it into only one set of hands—Billy's—and guessed if Tennie were Widow Vanderbilt with a wedding ring on her finger, she'd fall into a good share of it. But so long as the Com wasn't tied in a marriage, there was danger of him smiling into trouble, so Billy played matchmaker and whistled up a bride who would keep the money in the family.

Miss Frank Crawford came up with her mother from Mobile, Alabama, to take the summer waters at Saratoga Spa and look in on Cousin Cornelius. Miss Crawford, a great-granddaughter of Phoebe's brother Sam, was thin as a rail, her mother a widow as plump as a Strasbourg goose. When Tennie caught the way the tide was flowing, she twitted the Com about marrying the mother.

"Not on your nelly! If I marry her, Frank would go off and get spliced to some other man. Now I'll have 'em both, and Billy says the old lady keeps a mighty good table."

He eloped with Frank aboard a Central special that took them across the border to New London, Ontario, December marrying April or maybe May—he was seventy-five, while she admitted to thirty, though Tennie added a few years in her personal calculating. Before they left, he had his lawyers draw up an agreement, delivering Frank five hundred thousand dollars in first mortgage bonds of the New York & Harlem.

Tennie didn't fret, for he was a good old geezer at heart. In any event, she promised to be on call whenever he felt inclined for a touch of healing. The first time she went, he grabbed a kiss from her in full view of his bride. "You might have been Mrs. Vanderbilt, sparrow," he said to keep things clear. He also put up the cash for the Claflins to move to East 38th Street and furnish the place in the style of a high-class bawdyhouse. And to crown it all, he set the two Claflin sisters up as Wall Street stockbrokers.

Five

They earned their keep from him before they'd even opened shop as Woodhull, Claflin & Company, Bankers and Brokers, the "Company" being Jim Blood. This came about in consequence of Gould and Fisk's contriving to buy every ounce of gold they could find on the market. They'd started trying to corner gold that spring of '69, when the price stood at 132. Now it was near the end of September, and by the Com's tally they had accumulated forty millions' worth of the stuff, about twice as much, he said, as was usually in circulation. They were confident that President Grant wouldn't order the minting of any more, since they'd bribed a brother-in-law of his, Abel Corbin, and Corbin seemingly carried influence with Ulysses.

Jolly Jim Fisk was making the rounds of Wall Street and the Gold Room of the Stock Exchange, dropping hints about the killing the gold bugs would be bound to make when the figure hit 200. The high rollers flocked after him as if he were a Judas sheep. Tennie was tempted to take a flyer herself, and so was Victoria, but the Com declined to let go of their nest egg.

"I don't trust that pair of blowers any further than I could fling 'em. They've had me once, and that's once too often. I'm going to hold onto your money until it's turned into a solid something for you girls—a tidy $250,000 let's say."

September 24—Black Friday—went down as a liability in everybody's ledger. Gold opened that morning at 160. The Com picked up the two sisters with his carriage and coachman to take them down to the Exchange, where they could sit in the gallery and watch the bedlam on the floor downstairs as part of their training. He'd be at the Bank of New York all day, he said. They had both been around by invitation to Washington Place the night before, Tennie to render a rubdown, Victoria to conjure up a vision. The old man was feeling ragged about the gold bugs churning the market, and he wanted simultaneous soothing and heartening. Tennie spotted that "Aurora" had disappeared from the parlor wall, and he said that was his bride's doing; Frank was fonder of chanting hymns than paying attention to works of art.

Victoria obliged with a trance, but she was playing it foxy; all she really did was whisper about seeing "mountains of gold." He had such faith in the sisters, though, that he took this as a tip that Ulysses Grant was due to put down the bottle and open up the United States Mint.

That Friday morning, the floor of the Exchange looked like a beehive that'd been kicked over. Everybody was clamoring for gold, but nobody was offering to sell. Western Union telegraph boys were darting in and out of their booth, waving the latest tidings off the Edison stock tickers, and the figures on the blackboards lasted no more than a second before they had to be recalculated. When gold reached 162, top hats soared up toward the chandelier, then were trampled underfoot. Tennie wondered how many of those men boiling in the cooker down there would set about pummeling each other out of aggravation as railroad stocks and everything else began to slide.

Just before the bells of Trinity Church started to chime the hour of noon, gold dropped two points. A rumor spread like smoke that Gould was unloading. When the echo of the bells faded out, the price was down to 138, with three more points to fall before they called it a day. There was panic in the mob beneath their feet. Some turned pale as winding sheets, others stampeded out the doors. One man wandered across the floor, moaning, "People have threatened to shoot me. Here I am now. Shoot, for God's sake, shoot!"

Central had lost twenty points, but the Com was seizing an opportunity. His dealers moved forward, yelling, "It's time to go for Central," which brought about a measure of recovery. Someone in the row behind the Claflins found a word of praise for him: "The old rat never forgets his friends. If he hadn't come to the rescue today, I don't know what would have befell the Street."

As the sisters headed for home through the hubbub outside, riding in a street car, since the throng was too thick for walking, Victoria evaluated the performance they'd seen: "Men! What sapheads most of them are! Lords of the earth when things go right and puking like babes when they get hurt. If we can't do better in business than them, you and I don't deserve to be women."

The Com considered a check for $7,000 was fitting reward for their Thursday evening services. Tennie bore it off to open an account for Woodhull, Claflin & Company at Clews' Bank. Mr. Henry Clews himself was on hand, not entirely certain whether to treat her as a princess or a scullery maid. Three or four days later, she went back to ask him to spend it all on buying a thousand shares of Central, since the Com had let her know he was about to declare an extra dividend to celebrate his railroad's having survived Black Friday when ten thousand other firms had been bankrupted from the Barbary Coast to Broadway.

Clews smelled a rat, believing the Commodore was using her to bait the bank into following suit and risk getting loaded with the stock, which Vanderbilt might then be tempted to drive down some to crack the market. The banker made the excuse to her that their account wasn't of a size to interest him. He rang for the cashier to close it out.

Tennie didn't take to that brand of treatment, but she simpered at him and cut off to the Fourth National to deposit his check there before giving him another call. "Mr. Clews, our new bank wishes to have me identified. Would you do me the courtesy?" He couldn't refuse such a favor, so he sent a clerk around to vouch for her. It had the precise effect she'd planned on: now the Fourth National was convinced Henry Clews, as well as Vanderbilt, was backing Woodhull, Claflin.

They splurged on a suite of rooms in the Hoffman House, a deluxe hotel with a marble front standing on Madison Square. They badgered the manager into fixing up half their space like a ladies' drawing room with a grand piano, statues, and oil paintings, including a portrait of the Commodore flanked by an embroidered sampler that read "Simply to Thy cross I cling." The other half of the quarters held a desk apiece for them and bookshelves filled with the tools of the trade, bought second hand, to make the business look solidly established.

They devoted considerable attention to the appearance they would present as the first two of their sex to run a brokerage house. Neither of them fancied flapping around in layers of skirts and petticoats, and bloomers had gone out of style. What they did was to cut each other's hair about as short as a man's, have a tailor make them wool suits with skirt hems reaching no lower than the tops of their button-up boots, and buy men's striped shirts and neckties from A.T. Stewart's.

They took the plunge by strolling through the January slush on Wall Street, trailed by a rented carriage that carried them on the final lap to the hotel. Next morning, a piece in the *New York Herald* told them they'd struck oil. Victoria pasted the story on the first page of the new scrapbook she kept in the office.

> The general routine of business in Wall Street was somewhat varied today by the mingling in its scenes of two fashionably dressed ladies as speculators. Who they were few seemed to know, except that they were from the Hoffman House. Where they obtained their knowledge of stocks was a puzzling conjecture with those whom they met. After investing to the extent of several thousand shares in some of our principal stocks and selling others, and announcing their intention to become regular habituées of Wall Street, they departed, the observed of all observers.

She still had paste on her fingers when the drawing-room doorbell rang under the thumb of a *Herald* reporter. Tennie went out and played him like a fish on a line, affording him a flash of ankle as well as a piece of her mind when they had settled themselves on a sofa.

"It's a novel sight to see a woman on Wall Street as a stock operator. I presume you find it rather awkward?"

"Awkward? If I were to notice what's said by what they call society, I couldn't leave home except in some fantastic walking dress or a ballroom costume. But I despise what squeamy, crying girls or powdered, counter-jumping dandies say of me. I think a woman is just as capable of making a living as any man, and I've seen men so vain and effeminate I'd be sorry to compare their intellects with mine. I don't care what society thinks. I don't go to balls or theaters. My mind is my business, and I attend to that. We have the counsel of those who have more experience than we have, and we're endorsed by the best backers in the city." She was starting to talk like her sister.

With that off her chest, she poured drinks for two. He wrote a gem of a story: "A continuous smile plays upon her countenance. She is the firm foe of the 'girl of the period' creation, whom she describes as a 'sickly, squeaming nondescript.' She was the prototype of a business woman—keen, shrewd, whole-souled."

The truth got some varnishing from Victoria when her turn came, with him staring at the diamond ring on her thumb and the white tea rose pinned in her haircut. She told him there was a plan in the works for mining silver in Nevada. "And the firm has been in business for three years and has made seven hundred thousand dollars, but what do present profits amount to when it costs us over twenty-five thousand dollars a month to live?"

This was pure invention, although Claflins had flocked in from most points of the compass to help themselves to a slice of the new pie. Sister Polly turned up from Cincinnati with Benjamin Sparr and two sets of children, calling herself "an electric magnetic doctor" but without a patient to show for it—and Sparr wasn't known to carry more than five dollars to his name. Margaret Ann brought her clutch of four from Mount Gilead, but they had no father with them; that marriage had cracked up, she said, after trampled-on Enos Miles had gone hunting for her at a neighborly widower's house one night with a butcher knife in his hand. Utica was another prodigal, also lacking a husband; Mrs. Thomas Brooker, as she had been once, was so wrapped up in a stock company in St. Louis that she dug her heels in and wouldn't quit when he left for Illinois. Now she was finding consolation by gulping down anything she could lay a hand on, without improving her looks in the process.

Victoria, contrary to being short of a husband, had a surplus of them when Woodhull arrived on the doorstep one night, seedy, shabby, and desperate for a drink or a needle of morphine after his family had thrown him out as past redeeming. Jim Blood was still the ace of lovers to Victoria, of course, but she wasn't vindictive: she provided for Woodhull, principally so he'd give his time to Zulu Maud and to Byron, who was kept out of sight because his presence was unsettling. Buck and Anna made up a total score of seventeen. Anna declined to part either with her old habits or her old clothes, while he strutted about like a tailor's dummy in the new finery he bought on his daughters' money. Hebern had taken off on his own as a medical man, "putting on such airs," Tennie declared, "you'd fancy he was Dr. Joseph Lister in the living flesh."

She was happy to be out of the house all day, calling on clients and going home mainly to change clothes before passing the evenings with one or the other of two new beaus—Johnnie Green, who was city editor of the *Sun,* and Dick Maxwell, another broker, who felt so relaxed in her company that on one encounter he gave her seven hundred dollars fished out of a pocket of his pants as they hung over a chair.

Woodhull, Claflin & Company would have stayed on longer at the Hoffman House but for a showdown with the manager over a woman's right to the downstairs bar. By every man's telling, it served the best free lunch in town—a full-course meal for the price of a drink plus two bits for the waiter. It wasn't the food that caught Tennie's fancy but a painting by the Frenchman Bougereau that was framed behind the mahogany counter. From what she'd heard, the picture put "Aurora" in the shade in number of nymphs and flimsiness of their drapery. She wanted to see it for herself with Victoria as her partner, though when it came to downing even a schooner of beer, Sis was Lemonade Lucy.

After laying their customary noontime bet with the bookie who operated around the corner, they tackled the bar, where men, and only men, had trod so far. They strode in over the pile carpet, noses aimed at the ceiling, but they had caught no more than a glimpse of the scene when a flunky in a tailcoat popped out of the woodwork. "Come, come, ladies, you must be aware you're not welcome here."

Victoria's stare would have stopped a train in its tracks. "And who says so? Women are forbidden to go where male customers are encouraged? We have rooms in this hotel, and we wish to enter your bar."

"I beg your pardon, madam, but it's always been the rule of the management—"

"And it is a denial of our right." The clink of glasses and clatter of dishes died down. Though every whiskery face was turned toward them, the place was hushed as quiet as a tomb.

"Madam, please. You're embarrassing the gentlemen—"

It was Tennie's turn. "A shakeup might do 'em good. Or are they scared we'll bite?"

Victoria didn't raise her voice, but it had a sting to it. "Bring the manager to me. We'll settle this nonsense here and now. We shall wait for him."

Trade across the bar was still slow when the factotum came back with the manager. "Ah, Mrs. Woodhull! Good day to you. If you and your sister would kindly step out the door with me, the gentlemen will no doubt imagine you came in by mistake, looking for me. That will solve our little problem."

Tennie perked up again. "It's not our headache but yours, old boy. We're perky as larks."

The barflies were restless and giving out catcalls. *Damn radical shemales . . . throw 'em out of here. . . . Who do those hinnies think they are? . . . . Bed's the place for that pair, not the Hoffman Bar.*

Victoria's cheeks burned red and her tone was bitter. "We pity you for your ignorance, gallant gentlemen. We are not strangers to abuse, and it will not deter us. I promise you have not heard the last of us." She swung around to the manager. "As for you, my friend, you may make up our bill."

Every bank and brokerage house sent somebody nosing around when the sisters held a levee to open their new offices at Number 44 Broad Street, south of Wall. The lobby floor covered with Oriental rugs, black marble countertops, black walnut furniture, magnums of champagne in silver coolers, and Marvin wall safes big enough to house a horse contributed a touch of stability.

With the Commodore's tips to help in their finagling, they were coining money. The newspapers were full of stories about "the queens of finance," "the fascinating financiers," and "the bewitching brokers," all snipped out by Victoria and pasted into scrapbooks that were laid out for inspection on the counters.

The *Sun,* thanks to Johnnie Green, city editor, allowed that Tennie had "the impulsive gaiety of a gypsy" and was "all verve and vivacity, full of imagination and excitability." Her eyes "flashed with magnetic fire." The *Herald* sent a reporter around for another interview, then published some further jewels of Tennie's. "I have at least one financial opinion, and that says gold is cash, and to have plenty of it is to be pretty nearly independent of everything and everybody, even that terrible personage, public opinion, and that very interesting individual, Madam Grundy."

Victoria won equal attention. "Mrs. Woodhull could talk a blue streak from here to Christmas," as one interviewer put it. "She is apt to call things by their right names, speaks out boldly what she thinks, and we should infer that she had adopted as her own the motto of the Knight of the Garter." She checked out that remark with Jim Blood, who instantly caught the drift of it. *Honi soi qui mal y pense* fitted her to a tee, he said.

There was usually a throng of people watching from the sidewalk when they rode to work at ten o'clock sharp in a new clarence, a team of two white horses between the shafts, a coachman in scarlet on the box. Ladykillers would burst out whistling or la-de-laying a ditty popular at the time, "Oh, that Ten-Ten-Tennessee," which Miss Claflin didn't find displeasing.

Most mornings they had to squeeze through the cluster of men waiting on the stairs who rated them an attraction on a par with Barnum's Jumbo. Women who stopped by in hope of multiplying their savings had a back entrance that led into the private parlor. Victoria didn't respect them for using it, but they had to be accommodated somehow because she wanted all the business she could get.

Tennie welcomed Susan B. Anthony when she paid a call and made her entrance through the front door. She'd aimed at seeing Victoria, who was out, but she settled for interviewing Tennie for *The Revolution* and collecting a check for an advertisement for Woodhull, Claflin to run in its pages.

Johnnie Green's term for Susan was "a brave old maid." She'd just passed the half-century mark and was back from a tour, drumming up subscriptions and delivering lectures at seventy-five dollars apiece in an endeavor to pay off the debts accumulated by her paper, which was ten thousand dollars in the red. Tennie felt outright sorry for her, for her stringy brown hair foxed with gray, her sunken cheeks, and her mangy squirrel cape.

"What I retain faith in doing is teaching the young girls that to be true to *principle*—to live an idea, though an unpopular one—that to live single without any man's name may be *honorable.*"

Tennie mentioned she felt much the same way herself, without going into details about Bartels, and tried to cheer her by saying she'd enjoyed reading what *The Revolution* had printed about Albert Richardson, who had worked for the *Tribune* and ended up in the office there with a bullet in him, fired by Daniel McFarland because Richardson had been going around with the former Mrs. McFarland, now granted a divorce on grounds of her husband's brutality to her.

When Richardson was only an inch away from dying, he was carried to the altar to marry her, with Dr. Beecher of Plymouth Church, Brooklyn, doing the honors and Horace Greeley a witness. Yet most newspapers pictured her as a double-dyed Jezebel. *The Revolution* had sided with her, though, stating, "I rejoice over every slave that escapes from a discordant marriage. With the education and elevation of women, we shall have a mighty sundering of the unholy ties that hold men and women together who loathe and despise each other."

When the judge let McFarland off scot-free, Miss Anthony had summoned a meeting of two thousand people, then spread the news of it in her paper. She upset so many readers that she lost them to the rival *Woman's Journal,* proprietor Lucy Stone, with Julia Ward Howe as a partner. Julia, whose eyes had seen the glory of the coming of the Lord, remained blind to the need to secure more rights for women.

Tennie questioned Miss Anthony as to whether reporting the McFarland and Richardson affair had done anything to improve sales. Only for a week or two, she said, but Tennie found that interesting and told Victoria so when she gave her an account of the call. Neither of them could foresee *The Revolution*'s having a long life ahead when Susan had stated before leaving, "It's impossible for me to lay a straw in the way of anyone who personally wrongs me. They may try to hinder my success but I never theirs."

Victoria said anybody wronging *her* wouldn't get off so lightly, and maybe if *The Revolution* was at its last gasp, they should try at filling the gap at a profit one day, supplying subscribers with some warmer reading. She had the chance to spread herself in the pages of the *Herald* when James Bennett, who ran it for his old father, paid her to write regular pieces once a week under the heading "The Petticoat Politician." Jim Blood and Stephen Pearl Andrews concocted the pieces for her to sign.

Not every woman who came along was as easy to deal with as Miss Anthony. One woman styled herself "the Princess Editha Gilbert Montez," claiming to be the King of Bavaria's bastard by Lola Montez. She took her case against the sisters to court, wanting the judge to order the return of a ring with three diamonds that she said the two sisters had accepted for deposit to her account—she was penniless, and the Astor House was intent on evicting her for neglecting to settle her bill.

Victoria stood in the witness stand to square the account. "I know the lady. She came to my office. She never gave me any jewels or money. I gave her five dollars to pay her board, to keep her, as she said, from a house of prostitution. She was entirely lost to truth and, I thought, likely to involve me and my friends. I think the girl never had a diamond or knew what a diamond was. She asked me to get her before a New York audience to have her claim as the daughter of Lola Montez supported. In this I assisted her. I warned her against making statements about her mother being poisoned by a gentleman at Flushing and his retaining her diamonds."

The judge was satisfied, the case dismissed, and one more young woman handed over to the Commission of Charities and Corrections. "It didn't count for much, anyway," Tennie reflected, since Lola Montez had jigged herself off the stage nine years ago into a grave in Greenwood Cemetery under her christened name of Elizabeth Gilbert, and Sis could afford any number of diamond rings at that time without snitching other people's.

Since *Honi soit* covered Victoria's having two husbands living in the same house, it could be stretched a point further when another admirer moved in. Andrews kept his word about lending her one book, and then added a shelf-ful more, the message of all of them about as clear as pea soup, as far as Tennie could make out. After he'd been punctual in sitting at the dining-room table on East 38th Street for a month, Victoria decided it was time to have him stay on the premises. She had such respect for the twaddle he dealt in that she thought the sun rose and set around his shaggy head. To make room for him, Polly and Ben and every little Sparr had to find fresh lodgings, which blew up a storm until Victoria paid Polly off. Anna, as might be expected, treated Andrews like a mangy dog, just as she did Jim Blood. Her idea was to see her two girls go back to telling fortunes, taking her on tour with them. The neighbors muttered, as usual, about the din that broke out some nights, but the Claflins were used to that kind of reception.

Jim Blood and Andrews hit it off together, but there was a streak of business sense in Jim that a microscope couldn't have traced in Andrews. Once or twice Tennie got trapped into an evening of listening to Andrews' plans for curing the world's troubles, so she felt she was in a position to judge.

People of his sort clung like limpets on a rock to the fancy there was a remedy for everything on the list from loan-sharking to lechery. Miss Anthony was one of a host who fancied cold-water bathing was a defense against sickness. Horace Greeley preached that Dr. Graham's crumbly crackers and a diet of vegetables did more for the human frame than a ten-course dinner. Communists swore by Karl Marx, who had written for the *Tribune* that the route to heaven on earth lay in workingmen seizing the reins from the President, the Congress, and the Supreme Court, while the Anarchists attributed the trouble to laws in general, saying that when the slate was wiped clean of them, then everybody could live as one happy family.

Andrews had so many dreams swirling in his head that one could never tell ahead of time which would seize him next. Stirpiculture, which meant breeding people like pedigree cattle to strengthen the blood lines in mind and muscle, was one of his favorites.

"The existence of domesticated species has undoubtedly influenced the uneven civilization of the world. Europe and Asia were well supplied, but North America, at the time of its discovery, had none except the dog. The domestication of cattle in the early history of man made a settled life possible for him, with an assured food supply and the acquisition of property—the identity of cattle and property in early times being illustrated in the word 'pecunious,' from the Latin *pecus* or cattle. Today, we are in an era of development where the domestication of mankind by application of eugenic principles can carry us to a more elevated plateau of civilization."

"Men like you," Tennie said, "all mouth and no guts, are always spouting about your ever-loving principles without sticking your necks out to do anything about it. Woodhull and Claflin's is a horse of another breed. We're doing more for women's rights by carrying on our own business than ten years of speechifying and windbagging." Victoria kicked her under the table.

Tennie reckoned the queen bee in his skep was something he called "the Pantarchy," his program for spreading the gospel according to Saint Andrews and taking over the world by easy stages. The Pantarch, naturally, was Stephen Pearl himself: Accept no imitations; use only as directed.

"Social arrangements resulting from the principles [*he was at it again!*] of individualism and competition are essentially imperfect and immoral. I propose to substitute principles of cooperation, of united effort. Society as a whole must be organized on the lines requisite to give full scope to the harmonious evolution of human nature.

"I observe a fundamental harmony in the four great departments of being, of *esse*—society, animal life, organic life, and the material universe. But the full, free development of *homo sapiens* is thwarted by the unnatural restraints imposed by society on the gratification of desire, which are the root cause of all misery and vice. What the Pantarchy will practice is the unrestrained indulgence of human passion as the only possible way to virtue and happiness."

Tennie dipped her oar in. "In other words, the motto is, 'Screw yourself to paradise!' Is that what you're saying?"

"Tennie, don't interrupt! Please go on, Stephen."

He said Charles Fourier, a French writer he'd read as a student, had the right idea for dividing everybody into *phalanges* of roughly

1,600 people who would all live together in a *phalanstère,* which sounded akin to an army barracks, and farm the land they'd be given, dividing up the crops between themselves so nobody would go hungry. "They'd raise families, of course," said Tennie, "and live as happy as bastards, which was what the children are bound to be, because as you put it, 'The institution of marriage is of necessity abolished.' "Am I right?"

"Substantially so."

"Take it from one that knows, it'd never work. Most girls keep their legs crossed till there's a ring on their finger. I don't favor that myself, but I'm what you might term a rarity."

Victoria jumped on her. "Only fools and the dead never change their minds."

His smile as he looked at Tennie was no warmer than a snowball. "You are in error, Miss Claflin, child. A *phalange,* or a close approximation to one, was established at West Rosbury, Massachusetts, in the year of 1841 by the Reverend George Ripley, a former Unitarian minister, aided by his wife, Sophia, a woman of wide culture and academic experience. Their desire at Brook Farm was to combine the thinker and the worker; to guarantee the highest mental freedom; to prepare a society of liberal, intelligent, and cultivated persons whose relations with each other would permit a more wholesome life than could be led amidst the pressure of competitive institutions."

"Never heard of it. How come it didn't last?"

"Alas, while they celebrated with a dance the completion of a large central structure to be known as the Phalanstery, a *phalanstère,* the alarm was given that the building was on fire, and it burned to the ground."

"Sparked by the flame of passion, I guess? Well, so long, you two. I'm about ready for some shut-eye."

He could knead Victoria like dough. His brainstorms and her money opened up a house on 23rd Street where free love was on tap to rally recruits for the Pantarchy. Victoria would have been just as happy if they'd let her into the New York Sorosis, but the women there looked down their noses at her. The Claflins weren't high-minded enough to be considered *ladies.* But she reigned like an empress behind the curtains of the Psyche Club, which Andrews had named for another Greek. "And a rum choice it is, too, in Jim Blood's estimate," Tennie scoffed, "when the original was a virgin, untouched by hand."

Compared with Andrews, Jim was as straitlaced as a bishop, though Jim could still raise his sights whereas the Pantarch was long past his prime—in Tennie's guess, "no perkier than a shucked clam." The way she saw it, the club was a convenience if you wanted to let your hair down along with anything else you had in mind, and free meant *free,* and no mistake. "After you'd paid your annual dues, which I never did, you did as you liked, two by two or any arithmetic you fancied so long as there were others willing to take a turn, and no calls for cash afterward. It mightn't have contributed much toward peace on earth, but it did bring a lot of goodwill to men and put a temporary dent in the panelhouse trade."

It also advanced Victoria's education in some respects and sent Tennie back to studying with her. The course was spelled out in a batch of notes and sketchings by Andrews, and they were rumpled from previous handling. The material was written in Hindu originally, he said, which was a language he had learned. It was a handbook for brides, titled *The Kama Sutra of Vatsyayana.*

Tennie reminisced about it. "It was a good job and Sis and I were pretty broad-minded, for those pages were real eye-openers once you skipped over the dull bits about the Lord of Beings and Holy Writ and such like and got down to the lingams and yonis and jaghanas, which struck us as outlandish ways of referring to commonplace human parts. We'd never appreciated there were so many different methods for tonguing and kissing and rolling around in bed. It took a while to get used to the meaning of *congress* and stop picturing a throng of Washington politicians having a frolic together.

"Victoria took it all so thundering seriously she had us both submitting to the bending and stretching that was supposed to put you in shape to tie yourself in knots, which was a plain necessity in some cases if Andrews' drawings could be believed. We were something to see, rolling about in our pelts on her bedroom floor, panting, groaning, aching inside and out. She wouldn't venture a guess about the good it was inflicting on our jaghanas, but we got a cruel backache."

If Victoria felt the proceedings dragging, she would read extracts aloud. "Here's something for you, Tennie: 'She should make every endeavor to unite herself with prosperous and well-to-do people and with those whom it is dangerous to avoid or to slight in any way. Even at some cost to herself, she should become acquainted with energetic and liberal-minded men, who when pleased would give her a large sum of money, even for very little services, or for some small things.' "

"Liberal-minded and *energetic?* If old Andrews fancies that applies to him, he must be off his rocker."

Victoria let that pass. "And listen to this: 'Thus if men and women act according to each other's liking, their love for each other will not be lessened even in one hundred years.' There's sound sense in that."

Tennie rose, creaking, off the rug. "Love, now? What do you reckon that is, Sis? It's a stranger to me."

Victoria put down the tattered book and focused her stare on her sister. "Love's something you give even if you've no hope of getting anything back in return, but when it's given, it comes back, anyway, sometimes much more of it than you give or expect."

"Like saying, 'I'll scratch your back, and you scratch mine'?"

"Don't poke fun at me. It's more important to me than anything else in the world. If I don't feel loved, I'm just drained dry, lost and hopeless, better off dead."

"Have you loved every man you've gone with?"

"Of course not, but that's not the point at all. I can give my body away without loving the man, but there's no corruption in that when I'm my own mistress, controlling myself, picking and choosing whom I might favor for an hour or a week or maybe a lifetime."

"So you figure sex is all right without love, but what about love minus the sex?"

"Tennie, there's so many different kinds of love—you and me, me and Jim—"

"You and Andrews?"

She nodded. "Respect can be part of it, too. If I can teach people to love one another, then I'll have done what I was put here on earth for, which is to do God's work."

"How can you love God when nobody's met Him and you never set foot in a church?"

"I keep on striving. Truth is love, and love is truth, which is what Stephen's always saying. We all grow in the search for them, but the searching never can end. If it did, and we found what we were looking for, then we'd know God, you see."

"Wouldn't that be a shocker!" You had to take what Sis said with a sprinkle of salt when she fell into this particular mood, but Tennie was used to it from the days she used to go on about angels showing up in the attic.

The time came when they had gone about as far as they could with the *Kama Sutra,* and they qualified themselves as experts. Victoria's proposal was for them to pay a call at the club to try out a sampling of the members. "I was powerful curious to see how they could possibly carry on there without greasing the palms of the police," Tennie recalled, "so we dropped in together one evening."

The first order of business, chalked up on a blackboard inside the front door, was a lecture by Andrews, "The Nature of Love," to be presented in the front parlor. The room had been stripped down to bare walls with rows of folding chairs set up, facing a baize-covered desk holding a vaseful of red roses, a pair of candles in brass sticks, and a lithograph of Jesus framed in seashells. The congregation was as sanctimonious as if in a church, men in black Sunday suits and shiny boots, women topped with flowery bonnets, all as pious and prosperous as Nantucket Quakers. It wasn't hard to tell the regulars, who made themselves at home the moment they came in, from the recruits, who twisted and turned in their seats, wondering at what time the more serious entertainment began and whether they'd have the nerve to join in.

Andrews shuffled in, scruffy as ever, set his sermon down on the desk, then raised a hand and closed his eyes as if expecting an early call from the Almighty. When he opened his mouth, he sounded so quivery Tennie had to strain to hear him. "And God said, Let there be light; and there was light. *Amen.* In this house of love, let us bow our heads and join together in meditation."

She took a peek to see if a piano or any hymn books were around, but the answer was no. That was consoling, since she had never cared much for hymns. Beside her, Victoria was engaged in brooding. He gave a cough to signal the start. "The Nature of Love" was peppered with so many remarks borrowed from other people that

Tennie thought anybody could do as well, if not better, when all he did was copy things out instead of making them up for himself.

He threw in bits from the Bible and admitted it, which she considered was to his credit: "Though I speak with the tongues of men and of angels, and have not love, I am become as sounding brass or a tinkling cymbal." He went on to add a quote from Saint Francis of Assisi, wherever that might be: "Where hate rules, let us bring love; where sorrow, joy," and all of us ought "to love each other more than to be loved."

Victoria clung to every word as though they were straws and she were drowning. But most of the others were getting jaded after half an hour of such talk. Tennie whispered, "He's got about as much spark as a pan of dirty dishwater, and he keeps going around in circles every time he puts in a thought of his own." She sat up for a moment when a queen of Poland, Jadgiva by name, cropped up along with opinions she held on the subject, but that was another letdown. There wasn't a mention of performances in the royal bedchamber, only one more quotation: "Nor can that endure which has not its foundations upon love. . . . And those who invoke its aid will find peace and safety, and have no fear of future ill."

That was his concluding remark. When the clapping became thin, Victoria hurried up the aisle. "Brothers and sisters, let us not sit mute and mournful but rise up in joy and reverence for the principles for which we stand." When she had them on their feet, she sang out like a bell: "We dedicate ourselves to truth and love of humankind. We believe in knowledge, for we shall not suffer ignorance; in reason, for without it we are the victims of falsehood and prejudice; in community, for not one of us can endure alone. And above all we believe in love, free, glorious, unfettered love, for it is the creative force, the secret, the magnetic power of living." They gave her a round of hurrahs for that.

Andrews pumped her hand, babbling about "inspiration" and "fortitude." They left together, arm in arm, heads close, as the crowd sidled out into the hall. Tennie was baffled by the number that did no more than saunter off into the music room, where there was a spread of tea and cakes, remarking on what a stirring evening they were having. But as soon as Victoria appeared again, a sport with a red carnation in his buttonhole tackled her. "Sister Wood-hull, you were magnificent, most impressive, positively provoking, if I may say so. Will you allow me?"

He raised her fingers for a kiss. "I sense in you, Sister, a spirit akin to mine. As the poet says, 'That I should love a bright particular star and think to wed it.' Perhaps we might spend a few precious moments together?"

Though he was well set up and scrubbed clean, Tennie couldn't believe her sister would fall for his hogwash. Yet they lit off up the stairs side by side. She told Tennie later she had met him before and admired him for the faith he expressed in the Pantarchy, which deserved encouraging, and besides she wanted to put the *Kama Sutra* to practical test, which it seemingly survived with flying colors.

Tennie didn't succumb so readily. "I was too benumbed after all the talky-talk to take on any of the three or four fellers who closed in with the old Adam in their eyes, but I went back once or twice after that and found Sis wasn't lying about the value of our home-instruction course. We got bushwhacked into playing threesomes one evening, but never again; I liked to be sure whose hand was doing the exploring. Eventually, a squad from the local precinct house padlocked the club for good, and half a dozen members who got caught in the act had a free ride in the Black Maria, which was a pity, because it could have been avoided if Sis and Andrews had raised the dues so they could pay for police protection like everybody else in the catering trade."

By then they had bigger fish to fry, a barrel of them, thanks in the main to the efforts of Andrews. He'd frittered half his life away trying to win favor for his schemes and getting less general attention than a dog scratching fleas. The way Victoria had dazzled that gathering of free lovers set the wheels spinning in his brain, though most of them were missing a cog here and there. Victoria asked Tennie and Jim Blood to make a point of being with her the evening he was ready to reveal what he was aiming for next.

He stationed himself on the hearthrug in what she called the salon, which used to be a common parlor. "I will commence by stating that after due deliberation I envisage myself in the role of

Pygmalion—I am confident that there is no necessity to refresh your mind, Victoria, as to his identity."

"Oh, none at all, Stephen. He was the Greek, the sculptor who grew so disgusted with women that he refused to marry, and then he—"

"Yes, yes, memory serves you well. Pygmalion, son of Cilix, grandson of Agenor, who was king of Cyprus; brother of Dido, sometimes called Elissa, the reputed founder of Carthage, whose husband was slain by—"

Tennie had had her fill of dead Greeks. "Get on with it."

"What? Eh? Well, yes. As I was endeavoring to explain, Aphrodite, as a punishment for Pygmalion's stubbornness, decreed that he should become enamored of a statue which he had fashioned out of ivory—"

Jim took a hand at pushing the pace. "That would be Galatea, of course."

"No, no, no! There *is* a popular misconception that Galatea was the name applied, but I find no authority in antiquity for the introduction of that appellation. However, to proceed. Aphrodite in an act of compassion responded to his supplications by granting life to the image, and nymph and sculptor were united in wedlock."

Tennie wondered, "Are you saying you want Sis to be your bride?"

His yellow skin turned pink. "Please. You misinterpret me. You are permitting imagination to take wing. No, I speak of Pygmalion because I conclude that I, too, in my humble way have fashioned an image in Sister Victoria. She has sundered the bonds of restraint upon her intellect under my tutelage, and now she is prepared to fulfill her appointed destiny as an Amazon, so to speak, of the Pantarchy."

There *was* a change in Victoria. She was approaching thirty-two, yet she'd kept the body of a girl, and a complexion to match. She carried herself like royalty, and the tone of her voice gave the same impression. If the main things in life were love and money, she'd developed a close acquaintance with both.

Jim was peeved; after the time and attention he himself had expended on her, here was Andrews taking over. "What do you have in mind for her to do, then?"

Andrews provided some sheets of paper covered with his spidery scrawl and started reading: "First Pronunciamento . . ." When he had finished, Tennie felt as if the roof had fallen in and flattened her. She hadn't breath left for more than "Hell sweat!"

The First Pronunciamento, after Jim had trimmed it into shape, was printed over her signature in the *Herald* on April 2—twenty-four hours after All Fools' Day. Since Andrews rambled over hill and dale whenever he opened his mouth or picked up a pen, his handiwork ran to most of a full column, but the crux of it was this:

> While others of my sex devoted themselves to a crusade against the laws that shackle the women of the country, I asserted my individual independence. While others prayed for the good time coming, I worked for it. While others argued the equality of woman with man, I proved it by successfully engaging in business. While others sought to show that there was no valid reason why women should be treated, socially and politically, as being inferior to man, I boldly entered the arena of business and exercised the rights I already possessed.
>
> I therefore claim the right to speak for the unenfranchised women of the country, and believing as I do that the prejudices which still exist in the popular mind against women in public life will soon disappear, I now announce myself as candidate for the Presidency.
>
> This is an epoch of sudden changes and startling surprises. The Blacks were cattle in 1860; a Negro now sits in Jeff Davis' seat in the United States Senate. Political preachers paw the air; there is no live issue up for discussions. The platform that is to succeed in the coming election must enunciate the general principles of enlightened justice and economy.
>
> I anticipate criticism, but however unfavorable the comment this letter may evoke, I trust that my sincerity will not be called in question. I have deliberately and of my own accord placed myself before the people as a candidate for the Presidency of the United States, and having the means, courage, energy, and strength necessary for the race, intend to contest it to the close.

"We've got better hope of witnessing the Second Coming," Tennie said, "than seeing you at the winning post, Sis, when not a vote in the land can be cast by a woman, but I back you to the hilt for spunk." She tried envisaging what lay in store for them. "All I can get is a discouraging picture of us doing time together in the jug."

Still, there were two more years left to go before the election, and it was her practice to look on the sunny side.

Jim Blood had a practical question to raise: how did Victoria and Andrews plan on getting their message across to more people than would fit in the Psyche Club even if she worked double shifts six days a week and three on Sundays? Jim supplied his own answer and took off to confer with the men at the *Herald,* who praised her in print for "the merits of novelty, entertainment, courage, and determination. . . . Now for victory for Victoria in 1872!"

He learned that they'd had a message over the Atlantic cable from Jamie Bennett, who lived in Paris, saying they might give her a free hand so long as it helped sell copies of the *Herald.* They thought it was worth a test, and Andrews was soon chewing his pen writing pieces for her under the heading "The Tendencies of Government."

Even after Jim had cut them in half, they were as dry as dust, but the *Herald* took them anyway, tempting readers' appetites with ponderous references to ancient Egypt, ancient Greece, and ancient Rome before they got to the main course, which Andrews had been serving for years: America could run the world single-handedly if everybody would take the trouble to tackle Alweto and practice living on love.

In Washington, D.C., Ulysses Grant showed no sign of concern over this new competition. The news of the day there was that the Fifteenth Amendment was finally ratified. All citizens now enjoyed equal rights—"citizens," however, still didn't mean women. The Claflin sisters heard nothing from Miss Anthony or any of the other suffragists; they were too occupied with crying "foul" because another round had gone against them.

After the *Herald* discontinued "The Tendencies of Government," the editor wrote an assessment of Victoria's chances, which she pasted in the scrapbooks once she'd retrieved her copy of the newspaper from the fireplace.

> Mrs. Woodhull offers herself in apparent good faith as a candidate and perhaps has a remote impression, or rather hope, that she may be elected. The public mind is not yet educated to the pitch of universal women's rights. At present, man in his affection for and kindness toward the weaker sex is disposed to accord her any reason-

able number of privileges. Beyond that stage, he pauses because there seems to him to be something which is unnatural in permitting her to share the turmoil, the excitement, the risks of competition for the glory of governing.

"Now here we are," thought Tennie, "stumped again over how to keep the pot on the boil so Sis can go on ladling out opinions cooked up for her by Andrews and Jim. Without we find a means of giving voters a taste of her recipes, we might just as well douse the fire and take up knitting."

Victoria's luck changed for the better. Word arrived at the office that Susan Anthony was turning over *The Revolution* to one of her followers, Laura Curtis Bullard, and she would have help from Theodore Tilton, who was a public advocate of the rights of women, as well as a bosom friend and disciple of Henry Ward Beecher. Susan was taking it hard, saying, "It was like signing my own death warrant," and she insisted on paying off every cent of the debts she'd incurred while she ran the paper.

Victoria sized up the situation in a flash. *"The Revolution* can't be anything but a dead duck without her. It's a chance we can't afford to miss. We'll bring out a paper ourselves. We've got enough cash in the bank to swing it, and if we should run short, you, Tennie, have always got old Vanderbilt to fall back on. What do you say, Stephen?"

"I shall be happy to become your principal contributor."

"Tennie?"

"Count me in—you'll need a bit of spice if you want to make a go of it."

Woodhull & Claflin's Weekly was a sellout when it went on the streets in the middle of May.

Six

"Generally speaking," said Tennie, "when you put your best foot forward, it's not likely you'll get caught with your drawers down, and that's the rule we're going to follow." They picked the most promising address in town as a publishing office. Number 21 Park Row stood only a few brisk steps away from the *World* Building, the *Herald,* the *Tribune,* the *Times,* City Hall, and Tammany's new wigwam. They divided the chores among themselves in accordance with one of Andrews's borrowed war cries: "From each according to his ability, to each according to his need." When they got down to details, this meant putting him on salary and Tennie doing the rounds of the banks, brokerage houses, and insurance companies, drumming up advertising at $2.50 a line, cash on the barrelhead, to print on their front page. She'd throw a flash of ankle as a bonus if a customer needed prompting.

She had sold every available inch before the plunge was taken, including space bought by Henry Clews and August Belmont, the Rothschilds' man in New York. Jay Cooke, the richest banker in the land after cleaning up on Union war bonds, was another advertiser, though Cornelius figured Cooke was going in above his head these days buying Northern Pacific stock. "Building railroads from nowhere to nowhere ain't legitimate business," was the Com's opinion.

Tennie likewise paid regular calls on liquor dealers, wine merchants, and pool-hall keepers, but their notices were hidden on inside pages, and Victoria drew the line at soliciting madams and abortionists, which was something the *Herald* indulged in. For old times' sake, the sisters took announcements from quacks like Dr. C.A. Barnes of the Healing Institute of Chicago, who peddled a book called *The Sexual Question and Money Power,* and Professor J.M. Comins, "Cancer Cured Without the Knife or Pain." Tennie also had a standing order from the Wakefield Earth Closet Company at Number 36 Dey Street—"Abolish that nuisance in your back yard, $16–$25."

The sale of the *Weekly* soon was up to twenty thousand copies at a nickel a copy. "Upward and Onward!" was the first slogan carried under the title, but when Victoria got into her stride she changed that for "Progress! Free Thought! Untrammeled Lives!"

The arrangement called for Andrews to supply virtually everything Victoria wanted in the way of words. "He's the Comstock Lode in breeches in that regard," Tennie jeered. "We print enough missionarying about the benefits of the Pantarchy to turn anybody into a headhunting cannibal."

Of course, the main object was to get Victoria elected, as was clear from an announcement made plain in the first issue; "It will support Victoria C. Woodhull for president with its whole strength; otherwise it will be untrammeled [*"untrammeled" was becoming as popular with her as "principles"*] by party or personal considerations, free from all affiliation with political or social creeds, and will advocate suffrage without distinction of sex."

Sex, strictly speaking, was Tennie's department, with Jim Blood plying the pen, managing both businesses, and minding the store at Woodhull, Claflin & Company when the Claflins were busy on Park Row. She was glad he could set down a sentence that could be understood without consulting a row of encyclopedias. For a sample:

At present, the profession of prostitute is illegal. If seen to stop and speak to a man, to prevent arrest she gives the patrolman $3 to $10 a week and the privilege of visiting her gratis. She pays $15 for board, and for every visitor an additional tax of from 50¢ to $2 to the landlord. Police captains and police sergeants demand $20 to $30 when these officers need money. Wine is furnished them when wanted, and they are accorded the privilege of frequenting without charge such inmates as they may select.

Tennie knew what she was talking about; she had done her homework on the Bowery.

They didn't believe in being mealymouthed when scandal and sex sold papers, and they wondered why nobody but Jamie Bennett had hit on the same conclusion. The *Herald's* review of their opening effort gave Victoria one more clipping for her scrapbooks: "The example of Woodhull and Claflin is a highly commendable one, as they do more and talk less than any two divisions of female agitators put together."

There was no real competition from either of the two divisions. The Boston group—the American Woman's Suffrage Association, whose president was Dr. Henry Ward Beecher—had *Woman's Journal*. The local ladies—the National Woman Suffrage Association, president Elizabeth Cady Stanton—had a failure on their hands in *The Revolution* in spite of Theodore Tilton's contributions. The two old friends, Beecher and Tilton, were walking different sides of the street by now for reasons that will be obvious later.

Victoria guessed that the trouble with both flocks, Boston and New York alike, was that they let too many of their own sort have a hand in publishing. "We won't have our paper spoiled by women," she said, and they took on only men to help them. There was too many prudes in the Movement. Victoria didn't want to waste time arguing with them about what she planned to print.

It was a point of pride as well as profit to put a sizzle into every issue. The *Weekly* was strong for easy divorce (a personal interest of Victoria's) and the right of a wife to walk out on a husband who battered her or their children. Spiritualism, labor unions, free love, and votes for women—they were all grist for this new Claflin mill.

Prostitutes were another surefire subject for raising eyebrows and sales together. "The infamy of punishing the victim and letting the wrongdoer go free is apparent to all but helpless blockheads," thundered the *Weekly*. "Tax vice and provide means of reformation! Give women access to all honest employment and pay her family—that lays the axe to the root of the tree!"

They knew they were well launched when the *Tribune* denounced Victoria for favoring harlotry over marriage, while another of the dailies snapped that "her social theories are most revolting and find but few endorsers, for their adoption would sap the foundations of domestic life and bring man down to the level of brute creation."

"It's always *man* not *woman,* always *him* not *her,*" Tennie cried, "but what else can you expect when God Almighty's supposed to be an old geezer with white whiskers and every angel a male under his skirts even though he gets along without shaving?"

Jim had an idea for padding the take by offering pictures of the two sisters through the pages of the *Weekly* for a dollar a head. Victoria agreed to that, but insisted that his portrait go on sale, too. Letters from her followers began to pour in. She printed them to keep the ball rolling. "As I was looking at Sister Victoria's picture," wrote one devotee, "I involuntarily exclaimed, 'Who can look into that sad, thoughtful, tender but firm face and not see love, truth, and purity enstamped upon every lineament of the countenance?' " Tennie had an answer for that. "Some days, Sis, you'd make a first-class saint, but you're a hellion if anybody crosses you."

Since the professional suffragists, New York or Boston variety, had done them no favors, Victoria didn't see why they shouldn't take a shot at Mrs. Stanton, who was giving talks "for ladies only." Victoria put her in her place by writing, "It is a pity for women to set the example of discourtesy," which brought a visit from Miss Anthony, feathers ruffled by what she claimed was a slur on her best friend.

Susan lectured them about what a wonder Mrs. Stanton was and how high she stood in Susan's estimation: "I have very weak moments and long to lay my weary head somewhere and nestle my soul to that of another in full sympathy." Victoria ran out of patience. It was a pity, she said, that Mrs. Stanton and her kind weren't showing more steam about liberating women. That riled Miss Anthony. Victoria, she replied, was "obviously a lady quite declassée in any society which calls itself polite." She left more disgruntled than when she'd come in. It was plain that Victoria would be an idiot to look for support from the National Women. If a bandwagon was to roll, she'd have to get it started herself.

Andrews made the going harder by having her tack his colors to the top of every editorial page as "Fundamental Propositions: A United States of the World—the Pantarchy. The Universal Church. Universal Home. Universal Science, based on the Nature of Things and the Philosophy of Integration. The Universal Language—Alweto. A Universal Canon of Art. Reconciliation—Harmony of the Race through the Cooperation of the Spirit World and the Inauguration of the Millennium." If this was the plank Victoria hoped would carry her into the White House, it seemed to Tennie that her sister would fare better preaching the benefits voters would gain from sudden death and higher taxes.

The day came when Jim totted up the printers' bills and the wages that had fallen due, then added in the Claflins' upkeep, two husbands, and assorted freeloaders on East 34th Street, and he gave warning that money was getting scarce. Washington Place would be the best source of supply. The next morning Tennie went off to see the Com.

The smirk returned to the butler's face when he left her to cool her heels in the front hall. An organ was wheezing somewhere in the house, and two voices, tenor and soprano, were raised in "Yet in my dreams I'd be nearer, my God, to Thee, nearer to Thee." When the hymn was done with, out came the new Mrs. Cornelius Vanderbilt, trailed by a chubby clergyman who was introduced as Bishop McTyeire. Tennie suspected what he was up to—he was another one out to pick grapes in the Commodore's vineyard.

She was most terribly sorry, said young Mrs. Vanderbilt, but the Commodore was indisposed and had been committed to bed, making a special request for some uplifting music, which she and the bishop were in the midst of providing. Otherwise, Miss Claflin would be welcome to stay for a warming cup of cocoa.

A bell jangled on the second floor of the four-story house. The voice that sounded was weak, but Tennie knew it in no time. "Can't I get attention up aloft? I crave more hymning. Who the devil is it you're gabbing with down there?"

"One of your well-wishers stopped by, Cornelius, but she's afraid she has to leave."

"What's the handle on her?"

"It's that Claflin girl."

"Then clear the tracks and shoot her up here. And you can scupper the next hymn."

The bishop applied a consoling pat to Mrs. Vanderbilt's shoulder as she heaved a sigh, and Tennie followed them up the stairs. The Com's room was new to her—he'd been moved down a flight so the others in his household might catch a night's sleep. She had hoped to find him alone. Instead, he was attended by a slew of medics and clerics, relatives and nurses.

A woman whose uniform from apron to cap creaked with starch was cajoling him. "Come along, Commodore. We'll snug ourselves down in the wheelchair so we can sun ourselves in the library. We mustn't plague ourselves with bed sores, and the exercise will do us a world of good."

"Leave me lay in my bed of pain and bear down on the hereafter." He swiveled his rheumy eyes onto his eldest son, who was perched on a chair by his father's side. "Billy, set them working to enlarge the mausoleum, and don't count the cost. That'll be my next port of call."

The bishop edged up, murmuring what Tennie assumed was a text from holy writ. "And now, behold, I go bound in the spirit unto Jerusalem, not knowing the things that shall befall me."

A grimace twisted the Com's sunken cheeks. "I'm bound for New Dorp, Staten Island, not the spot you've made reference to."

The clerical smile was tolerably tolerant. "I was quoting Paul, sir. Acts, chapter twenty, verse twenty-two."

"I don't give a damn for that blower." He sighted Tennie, though his wife was endeavoring to screen her from his view. "God almighty, it's my little pigeon! Must have been a fair wind blew you in. Come over here so I can clasp your hand." His fingers in hers were as cold as his charity had once been to all but her.

"How you faring, Com? Looks like you could do with a tot of grog."

"I've sworn off. I ain't taking anything likely to diminish my

powers of reason. Take a drop too much, and I might come out with
something they'd use to prejudice my drawn will and testament.
Frank, scuttle off and fetch Miss Tennie some fluid refreshment.
And Billy, you can cut off along with your stepmother."

Tennie rubbed his skinny wrists. "Is that all you're going to offer
me? Or is the traffic too thick around here to suit your purpose?"

"You'd collect a kiss off me if I was to get bolstered up."

She waved away the nurse who bustled forward. "No need to
concern yourself. I'm familiar with the case. I've had long experience." He was no heavier than a baby when she propped him against
three pillows and wet his dried-out lips with hers. "That should
hold you until it's time for the next dose. What's up with you,
anyway?"

He groaned, which was another novelty coming from him. "It's
a briefer tally to tell you what's down."

"Well, let's hear it so we can figure if there's a cure."

"They've been into me with a knife to slice the stones out of my
bladder. That proved such a fierce undertaking I wished they'd cut
my throat. My belly keeps swelling up, so they lay cracked ice
across it, which don't compare with the comfort I've had from you.
It's a challenge to breathe sometimes, and there's a rupture in my
gut that dangles half to my knees. All that aside, I remain in the
pink."

"Poor old bugger. I'm buggered myself if I don't feel a touch of
sympathy for you."

The bishop led a general advance toward the bed. The Com's
glowering drove them into rapid retreat. "Back off, you, and the
harpies, too! When's that drink due in for my little pigeon?"

One of them scurried forward again with a cup and saucer in her
clutch. "I heard you say 'drink,' Mr. Vanderbilt. I've brought your
beef tea." Tennie stood back while the nurse raised the cup to his
mouth. He flickered an eyeball at Tennie as he took a gulp, then
spat a warm brown flow across the lace counterpane. "There's my
judgment of that slop." The woman flurried back to the group at
the far end of the room.

A hint of the old wolf grin showed on his lips. "Sympathy's not
my need from you. What about a touch of a more confidential
nature? I'll get shot of the audience in quick time."

That was the point at which Billy and his stepmother again came through the door, she carrying a mug of cocoa and a folded damask napkin on a little silver tray. Tennie knew her time was running out. She planted one more kiss on the old man's scaly brow. "I'll be back to give you the rites of passage."

"Pledge your word."

"Cross my heart."

She felt Billy's hand firm on her arm. He drew her aside. "Get it through your skull that I'm in charge now. If you've come to beg, you're out of luck."

His stepmother still held onto the tray and the cocoa. She was muttering to herself, "He has to die soon. I can't stand the torment."

Tennie hitched her shawl around her shoulders and threw her a smile. "Do the best you can then. Don't ring for the flunky. I know my ins and outs around this place. It's been real jolly meeting you and your ever-loving son."

Jim Blood found the words Tennie wanted for next week's issue.

When Vanderbilt and Fisk get to work and make sport for the people, how we simple ones laugh! We are told first how Mr. Fisk, most daring of speculators, cornered that profound calculator, the Commodore, on grain transportation at ridiculously low rates; the grain turned out to be cattle, carried over the Central at prices that won't pay for car grease. Meanwhile flour and bread are no cheaper; somebody is making money, and sure it is that when Behemoth and Leviathan make up their difference, which they surely will, the public will have to pay for the sport.

She let a day or two pass after that issue went on sale before she beat a path back to Washington Place. She'd spent hours by then patrolling the streets around the Claflins' house until she came across an Italian organ-grinder with a suit of green velveteen on his back, rings through both ears, and a monkey dressed just like him on the end of a leather leash. She pushed two dollars into the ape's grubby paw to seal the bargain she struck with his master. He'd be waiting outside for her when she set out to call on the Com again. If there was one thing the old man couldn't abide, it was the din from a hurdy-gurdy.

Her heels sank in the straw laid thick to keep down the patter of feet on the sidewalks and the clatter of wheels on the cobbles. The medical men who served the street's most eminent and demanding invalid prescribed peace and quiet for him for lack of knowing what else to do. She picked an hour when Billy and his brothers were sure to be off at work. Their grasping sisters, every one of them nagging their father to leave them a fortune, weren't likely to have arrived for the usual evening of badgering him.

His bride was the main problem, but she was in the habit of ordering up a carriage to take her on a morning jaunt around the department stores. Tennie stationed herself across the street, popping peanuts to the monkey from a bag she'd brought along. She'd bide her time until Mrs. Commodore disappeared from the scene.

Then up came the horses and the coach in its coat of sparkling maroon. Down the front steps trotted Frank Vanderbilt, looking worn to a frazzle but stylish in a beaver wrap. Tennie hung on for five more minutes before she nudged the little man beside her. "Thank your stars the Com's sick or he'd be at his window with a bead drawn on your head. Give that handle of yours a crank." She nipped across the street to hide herself on the stairway leading down to the servants' quarters next to the front door.

The hurdy-gurdy began to churn, and the monkey pranced around its master. She hummed to herself as the jangle echoed off the wall above her. "A life on the ocean wave,/A home on the rolling deep;/Where the scattered waters rave,/And the winds their revels keep!" Somebody else would be raving in a minute, she thought.

The front door opened again, and the foxy-faced butler bounced out with a five-dollar bill in his fist. As soon as he'd started across the cobblestones, Tennie was up the steps and into the hall, bolting the door behind her. She took the first flight at a canter, then smoothed down her dress before she went into the Com's room.

She strolled sedately past the trio of nurses who had been installed behind a Chinese screen to shield them from the hot-water bottles and assorted sickroom items that Vanderbilt hurled at them whenever he was feeling particularly out of sorts. "Top of the morning to you, old horse." The life on the ocean wave came to a sudden end.

He pried open his eyes, which were seen to be rolling in his head. "Pigeon, my little love. I was fancying you'd skipped out on me." "I wouldn't do that. I've come to give you a magnetizing rub up and a shake down to follow. Are you primed?"

"Provided they're delivered in the sequence mentioned."

"Then move over and make room for me." She put her bonnet and shawl on the bedside table and slipped off her shoes. The bell was clanging outside the front door. A face peered out from behind the screen. "Belay there, you bunch of grannies!" cried the Com. She curled up on the counterpane and cradled his head against her breasts.

"You've got scurf crusting your scalp. Needs scraping."

"Take your hand to it later."

"What mischief have you gotten yourself into lately?"

"Had difficulty passing my water."

"A spot of massage down there might relieve you. Want me to try?"

"It'd be a blessing, I reckon."

She made up her story in the course of obliging him. "I had a dream about you the other night. You were wallowing there at the bottom of the briny, trapped in some kind of net, and sharks swimming in expectation of making you their dinner. Then somehow I exercised my will and called in one of your steamboats. It was a hell of a haul, but you got out of it with a rope thrown overboard and you spouting water out of every hole in your frame. Is that making you feel better?"

"You've kept your touch, my darling."

"So we'll move on to the dessert. What do you reckon as the size of the bill you're running up with these quacks that are leeching onto you?"

"That'd have to be a question to pose to Billy."

"Fair enough. What would you say to my coming in twice a week—oftener if you like—to render a treatment, paid for in advance?"

"I'd be obliged if you would, pigeon."

"Then we're on. I don't suppose you've got a crock of gold stashed away under your pillow, so I'll take an IOU. Just apply your John

Hancock to this bit of paper. I've got another dream to tell you next time I see you."

When she had what she was after, which was a promissory note for five thousand dollars, she was dressed again, down the stairs, and out on the street within a count of minutes. She wouldn't risk a return visit before the family put up the shutters against her. But she thought the old boy deserved what appeared in the *Weekly*'s following issue about "that indomitable, self-shrouded Commodore Vanderbilt, who stands alone in his sphere, the envy of little minds, and the gigantic scoffer at the impudent malice of his enemies."

Though a flick of the whip hadn't worked on Billy, it was worth applying to others of his kind. The *Weekly* emitted a sudden odor of cowhide.

> We discovered frauds contemplated by petroleum and shoddy bankers who like scum had risen to the surface in boilings of the dishonest cauldrons of the war. We have employed the ablest detective talent, and we are prepared with the names of each party, the description and extent of the frauds perpetrated, the amount of bonds and shares in many cases which gratuitously and dishonestly went to each banker, Congressman and State legislator. We shall not hesitate to give names, acts, transactions.

Andrews was fearful that they'd find the front page stripped of advertisements when the bankers and brokers ran for cover. Victoria argued they dare not pull out; it would be an admission of their guilt if they did. She proved to be right; they didn't lose one line of advertising. Everyone but Andrews knew they were on safe ground. There was enough scandal to be sniffed out on Wall Street, at City Hall, and in Washington City to keep them in business until hell froze over.

The only puzzle was deciding where to start. Jim said that Oakes Ames of Massachusetts was doling out bribes in both houses of Congress to keep Federal funds gushing into Credit Mobilier, which was making millions laying track for the Union Pacific Railroad. Jesse Grant was aswim in the Whisky Ring with his accomplice, Ulysses's private secretary, Orville Babcock, and they were all cheating the Government of revenue due in stamps they omitted to apply to the liquor they distilled. New York had a "Ring" of its own, named for Boss William Marcy Tweed. *Harper's Weekly* was raking Tweed and his cronies for lining their pockets with city bonds and taxes. But when the big boss himself dropped in on the Claflin women, as he did before they'd printed a word about him, nobody had done much more than complain. By Jim's account, Tweed was still Grand Sachem of Tammany Hall, who handpicked the mayor and the governor in Albany, where the Boss sat in the Senate and served as lawyer and swagman to anybody who made it worth his while, including Vanderbilt and Jim Fisk.

He puffed in, scaling perhaps three hundred pounds in his boots, piggy blue eyes sharp as needles and divided by a long, thin nose. He helped himself into an armchair without so much as an if-you-please. "So you're the queens of Broad Street, and you must be Mrs. Woodhull, our forthcoming President. Howdy do, ladies!"

Victoria did the honors. "Good morning to you, Mr. Tweed."

" 'Bill' to my friends, ma'am, and there's a legion of 'em inside and outside the Democratic Party, but I took it upon myself to come over from Duane Street to see two beautiful females in person, since one of my slogans is 'Do it now.' I just happened to have read this week's paper, finding it fascinating, as per usual."

Tennie thought that whatever he was getting at, the old hog could be winsome, his voice booming like a steeple bell. Victoria still did the talking. "You flatter us, sir, and I'd be happy to add you to our free list if—"

A hand pawed the air. "Thank you, but I'll decline the offer, gracious as it is. I buy your paper and twenty-six more of 'em published in the city, and I always insist on paying my way and the other feller's, too, should the occasion arise."

"What is it they say—every man has his price? You must be kept busy."

"As to your second point, I'll allow without risk of boasting that I'm always at work, never wearied out, stirring from morn till midnight. As to your first, another of my slogans says, 'Something for everyone.' The small fry would eat the paint off a house if I didn't hold them in check."

"Does 'small fry' cover the Board of Aldermen?"

"There never was a time you couldn't buy *them*."

The pig eyes twinkled, and the sisters laughed along with him. "Well, you're frank about it if not totally respectable."

"Respectable men are only a nuisance in politics, but I challenge any politician in New York to point out one instance where I've broken my word. Though I pride myself on being a good Party man, I'm a firm believer in justice for one and all, prince or pauper, friend or foe, and that doesn't exclude you good ladies, of course."

"Even when we have no vote to cast on Election Day?"

He wagged his rusty whiskers. "Ladies may lack the ballot, but they've the influence, you especially, with the power of the press at your disposal."

Tennie made a different offer. "Glass of bubbly, Mr. Tweed?" It's the real McCoy—imported."

"I never take a drink nor yet smoke a cigar. I'm not much of a bargainer, either, contrary to some opinion."

Victoria picked up the thread. "Is there anything to bargain about?"

From his look she might have fancied that butter wouldn't melt in his mouth. "Bargaining's out of place in the present situation. I've noticed you've support for your paper from a number of banks, but one of 'em's missing up to now. I've a small interest in the Tenth National. Perhaps you'd allow me to have a word there to see whether they'd like to advertise with you on a regular basis?"

"We'd take that as a courtesy."

"There's only one thing they might be tempted to ask in return."

"Which is?"

"Like any other respectable business—let's say Commodore Vanderbilt's as an example—they don't relish being rubbed the wrong way."

That struck Tennie as funny. "You're right about the Com, leastways."

He took hold of Victoria's hand to seal the deal, hanging on long enough to signal he wouldn't object to a share in her favors. He said he'd count it a pleasure if they met him at Tammany Hall on the night of October 27 when there'd be a torchlight procession as a warmup for the election. After he'd left, Jim reported that the

Tenth National was Tweed's personal bank; it was there that the loot was deposited. (They didn't know the scale of the Ring's operations until after the Boss was jailed, when the *Times* came up with a guess of $200,000,000. "I reckon," said Tennie to her sister, "we let him buy us off cheaper than a fire sale when you called off naming the cheaters on grounds it'd eat up space in the *Weekly* that had to be spent winning votes for you.")

They were both bathed in limelight as a result of the dailies' prying into where they had come from and what they had been up to beforehand, though still not a whisper was heard about the cancer clinic. But Victoria opened her mouth too wide concerning Demosthenes to one reporter, which brought her a snippy note from Mrs. Stanton. "Dear Mrs. Woodhull: Will you ask Demosthenes if there is any new argument not yet made on the Fourteenth and Fifteenth Amendments that he will bring out through some of us at the coming convention?" The National Women would be holding their annual convention in Washington City in the New Year, but Victoria would be no more welcome there than an attack of pneumonia.

She was getting nowhere the night they drove through storming rain to Tammany Hall. The city had a strange feel to it. Grant had sent his soldiers into New York, making the harbor forts their barracks, and there was one warship anchored in the Hudson, another in the East River. The general was a Republican, Boss Tweed a Democrat, and Ulysses had sent the Army to mount guard over the polling stations and prevent any trickery on Election Day, which would be here in less than two weeks.

"Sis, how do you figure Tweed's chances, with the *Times* slinging mud at him every day?" Those Park Row neighbors were branding him every kind of thief and digging up facts to prove it.

"If it isn't already in the bag, he'll steal it the way he always does."

"With the Army on his neck?"

"He'll see to it there's no call for them. It'd be a surprise to me if he hasn't already told his supporters, 'No violence, no disturbances, no burning the boxes.' He's a smart politician, though he lacks my respect."

"How do you figure your own chances?"

Her eyes were dreamy. "I am different. I am set apart for a high and sacred duty, and I shall perform it without fear or favor." The trouble was that she meant it.

It was said afterward that fifty thousand men marched in the procession, ignoring the drenching that made rags of their bright red shirts and set the torches they carried sizzling like damp firecrackers. Every one of them wore red and carried a burning light that gave the glow of sunset to the biggest turnout the city had ever seen. Red was Tweed's color from his days as a firehouse volunteer, picking a tiger as the badge of his engine company, and tiger heads snarled from the placards the marchers joggled as they sloshed through the streets. But they behaved themselves; Tweed was too smart to allow anything rowdy.

On the platform inside the hall, diamond stuck in his shirt front, he sat between August Belmont and Jim Fisk. "See, Tennie? The *Times* says they're all in it together." There was a swarm of other men up there, too, but not a woman in sight. Tennie was fearful she'd be deaf for life from the cheers that went up when Tweed stomped to the lectern.

He claimed to be shy. "I can't talk without stammering before a throng of good, loyal people like you, and I know it." It only took him four or five minutes to get it over with. "We know and feel that although an aggressive hand is upon us, yet we must, by a judicious exercise of law and order, which is our only protection, show that it is a law-abiding and, as all the world knows, a well-governed city."

The Claflins thought they'd never reach the head of the line to shake his hand, he spent so long with everybody ahead of them, but when they did, he had a word for them as well. "I'm counting on you ladies' support, remember, and as for votes for women—if you're ever in Washington, give Ben Butler a call. You might find him willing to listen."

Ben Butler. They hadn't met him, but they knew his reputation. His father had been a privateer who'd died dancing at a rope's end strung from a ship's yardarm off Cadiz; his mother a boardinghouse keeper in Lowell, Massachusetts. He was a lawyer who'd never been caught out in a crime. He'd been a Democrat and a Lincoln Republican in turn after Honest Abe had his eye on him as a running mate in '64.

By then, Ben had made his mark as a Northern general. He put runaway blacks to work on Fortress Monroe, saying he was detaining them "as contraband of the war," and he ruled New Orleans with a heavy hand in '62. Southern women plastered pictures of him to the bottom of their chamberpots and sewed the Stars and Bars across their bosoms, which they'd peel back their shawls to expose. His answer was to have his men stitch the same flag to the seats of their britches, and they'd counter the women by hoisting their coattails.

Southerners hated him more than anybody except Sherman. They called him "Beast Butler," an outlaw who'd be strung up on sight if ever they caught him. Today he was a Congressman, radical Republican, credited with possessing one of the keenest minds in Washington City. Tennie told her sister, "How much persuading he'll need to come out for you I can't judge, but whatever he asks for we'll provide, you or me or maybe the two of us."

They postponed going down to see him until the election was over. They wanted a look at how voting was handled in the city, hoping to pick up pointers for the day Sis's name would go on the ballot. On the Tuesday morning, they toured around polling stations. Tweed had put the lid on tight. Everything was calm as a church picnic, with not a soldier in sight. They talked their way into one place by saying they'd like to write some inspiring paragraphs for the *Weekly* about democracy at work, including the full names and addresses of the marshals who were doing their noble duty as supervisors.

They ran into an enlightening experience. The first man to show up after they'd been let in told the hunchback who sat at a table with a fistful of voting lists that his name was Michael Murray. The checker pushed a pinch of snuff up his nostrils while he went up, down and through every line of the lists. "There's no Michael Murray, only Michael Murphy."

"Hold on now, chief, hold on!" The anxious voter rummaged through his pockets for a scrap of paper, which he slitted his eyes to read. "Sure, and it's Michael Murphy. That's what it says right here." Off he went to make his cross and earn his five dollars. A lot of these men of conscience had trouble getting a word out in English, and their clothes still reeked of carbolic acid, vomit, and close quarters under battened-down hatches on the crossing to Castle Garden, where the ships from Europe docked. When the two women had had their fill at the polling station, they followed one of them—he had a tangle of whiskers and mop of black curls—to a barbershop around the corner. They marveled to peek around the door and see what a quick shave and a haircut along with a change of hat and coat could do for a repeater.

The Democrats romped home again, of course; Tweed's governor, John T. Hoffman, went back to Albany; and his mayor, elegant Oakey Hall, won two more years in City Hall. The Boss himself wasn't up for reelection until next time, and a host of people were glad of that when it turned out to be a cruel winter, sidewalks covered in ice, and ragamuffin boys taking turns sleeping over Park Row gratings where the steam rose up to warm them. He earmarked $50,000 then on food baskets for the poor.

It was nowhere near so cold in Washington City when they took the train down in December, but a glance through the windows was enough to tell them there was more poverty in these parts than in New York. Alongside the tracks they saw scrubby fields that had a scattering of frame shanties bare of paint and held up by coats of whitewash; ponds of slimy water; geese, hogs, and droves of children varying in tint from coal black to unwashed gray.

Coming out of Union Station, they gawked at avenues a furlong wide leading off straight as arrows to nowhere, streets a mile long with nobody about on them, stretches of cheap little brick houses interrupted here and there by large white buildings that seemed to have been put up just last week, waiting for a landlord's FOR RENT to be tacked up on the walls. The Washington Monument towered up out of a waste of mud like a factory chimney with its top lopped off.

Mud was the word wherever they walked, forcing them to wonder why the city fathers didn't pour on more water and convert the streets into canals. A gondola would have given the two of them a smoother ride than the broken-down growler that rattled them to their hotel, which was nothing but a row of houses knocked together and opening in back on a yard where two hound dogs and a pig wallowed together, "As matey," Tennie noted, "as councilmen in caucus." From the front there was a distant view of more houses, one with a sign outside saying CITY LUNCH, another with kegs of oysters in the bay window, a third with a blackboard propped up on the stoop—PANTS FIXED TO ORDER. Victoria sent off a messenger to the Capitol with a note for General Butler before they were reminded of what it was like to bed down with fleas in the blankets.

His reply was waiting down at the desk when they took a chance on breakfast: he'd be delighted to have them stop by in the ladies' reception room on the House side of the Capitol any time between 10 and 11 A.M. Victoria figured they'd be wiser to wear their new Lord & Taylor dresses instead of mannish serge, since soft women might be his fancy. They didn't stint on the French perfume, either. "Washington's supposed to be the wickedest place in the land, wide open for lechers, tosspots, plungers, and every other brand of voters' idols floating around with time to kill," said Tennie. "We'd look out of joint in our regular working gear."

They turned up early at the Capitol, built on Corinthian lines, Victoria explained, which was why it looked like a mountain-sized Greek temple. They took a stroll through the rotunda, taking in paintings of George Washington, Christopher Columbus, and a gallery of others, along with more statues than could be found in the average cemetery, including a figure of Justice, which the guide-book said had been planned to display more of her flesh, but "the public sentiment in this country would not admit of it." So Justice was wrapped up in enough marble coverings to ward off frostbite.

When they finally reached the ladies' reception room, it was easy for them to see why it was called "the Cattery." There was standing room only, with every inch of chair and sofa taken, and such a clatter of voices everybody had to shout to be heard, and nobody bothered with listening.

"Feeding time at the zoo can't hold a candle to this place," Tennie whispered. "There's more fur on their backs than you'd sight in a menagerie." There were red-fox muffs and black-bear boas, possum collars and beaver mittens, sealskin sacques and nutria dol-mans. "Rigging this crowd out must have called for shooting off as much ammunition as Custer fighting Sitting Bull."

Some of the faces were of the same honest cut as Susan Anthony's, and these women wore her sort of homely clothing. But most of them followed a different calling, if furs, feathers and jewels as fine as any high-class whore's were any indication.

After they announced themselves to a factotum at the door, in a matter of minutes they were shown into the quarters of a little bald man with a Roman nose and the shoulders of a bull, who waddled out from behind his desk about as tall as when he'd been sitting down. First thing that struck Tennie was that Ben Butler didn't see things the way most people do because his eyes were crossed, and second, that he wore carpet slippers with his toes pushing through them.

He rolled a fresh cigar east and west in his jaw as he talked. "And what is your opinion of the Cattery?"

Victoria's answer came sweet but firm: "A demonstration of what women are driven to in seeking man's attention, since he persists in treating them as his inferiors."

The cigar kept traveling. "Agreed. Lobbying, job hunting, and prostitution have something in common, and there's no difference between a he- and a she-adder in their venom. I am immune both to lobbyists and prostitutes. On the other hand, I have some interest in the rights of women, unlike the gentlemen drones who loll in their easy chairs on the Hill. I am quite willing to take issue with them at any time."

Tennie couldn't decide which of them he was looking at, so she left the talking to her sister. "You might well be regarded as something of a hero for that."

"Not by Mrs. Butler. No man is a hero to his wife. She sees too much of him in his unheroic moods. And you must never believe anything you read of me in the newspapers. Good or bad, either will be false.

"The record indicates as much from the time I was a young lawyer, working eighteen hours a day, my first clients the mill girls of Lowell whose absentee employers did not see fit to pay them a living wage or work them less than seventy-two hours a week. When I first stumped the Commonwealth of Massachusetts, signs were posted in those mills: 'Whoever employed by this corporation votes the Ben Butler ten-hour ticket on Monday next will be discharged.' "

"Then you have more than interest—you have faith in our cause."

"I have no faith in any cause. I have hung better men than some of our self-styled true believers. But I have a reputation for getting things done. What can I do for you?"

Victoria floundered for a moment, puzzling over where to sink the hook. She started telling him about herself, but there was no need to do so—he knew as much as had been printed.

"What it boils down to is that at present you are shouting down a well. I am not concluding you would make a less successful President than Grant, who after staggering into the White House proves to be stupidly dull and ignorant, no more comprehending his duty or power under the Constitution than a dog, but how do you propose to harvest votes when you are scarcely recognized outside the pages of your newspaper and the streets of New York City?"

"Have you any suggestion to offer, General? You are a man of great education—"

"What education I have has been by reading a few good books, not by writing poor ones like one of your associates." Tennie liked hearing that, being partial to Andrews's getting his lumps delivered from any corner of the ring. "Your immediate need is to gain attention, make yourself known as a champion, and the place to begin is right here on Capitol Hill. What you must do is memorialize the Congress."

This was something new. "You mean learn all their names in case Sis bumps into 'em at a party?" Tennie asked.

A smile didn't help a face as lumpy as his. "I invite you, Mrs. Woodhull, to prepare a statement of facts together with a petition that something be done to improve the situation. You will then submit your documents to both Houses. That is what is known as a 'memorial.' You may be jeered at, but you will be remembered, and nothing was ever greatly gained without something greatly risked."

She turned to Tennie. "I believe Stephen would know how to write—"

Butler's left eye swiveled toward her. "I would not recommend it, being reasonably well acquainted with his doubtful abilities. You shall have my help. As a citizen of the United States, women have the same, equal right of suffrage as the Negro, in my opinion, and

I have been doing my share for Negroes from the day the Corps d'Afrique of runaways was mustered into the Union Army. Some of them say of me, 'He has a white face but a black heart.' " The death's-head grin showed up again. "I am ready to risk members of your sex saying, 'He has a man's face but a woman's heart.' "

"What fee might you charge for your services, General?"

He puffed out his cheeks like a bugle boy's, then slowly let the air out. "How much are you worth?"

He had her flustered all over again. "I cannot say exactly. Our bookkeeper could supply the figure if it is needed. But expenses are high. Why, it costs us over twenty-five thousand a month to live —"

"I have counseled three Presidents, commencing with Lincoln, whom I managed to dissuade from using all our naval vessels and all the merchant marine in a plan to transport American Negroes to the Spanish-speaking island of Santo Domingo; Johnson, whose impeachment I subsequently conducted; and Grant, who nevertheless still flirts with the purchase of Santo Domingo as a dubious haven for the blacks. What is my help worth to you?"

Her stare hung on him forever, it seemed. "Whatever you ask of me."

"I ask nothing, which you are not to consider in any sense a slight. You are a handsome woman, and you have sand in your craw, but I have greater respect for Mrs. Butler."

Here was something for Tennie to be thankful for. She wasn't sure about Sis, but there were limits to what she was willing to donate to the cause. They settled down after that to settle the details. He'd draw up the memorial and have it printed for her to present to John Spafford Harris of Louisiana in the Senate and George Washington Julian of Indiana in the House. Then Butler would arrange for it to get pushed along to the Judiciary Committee, which was his special realm, and he'd set up a hearing for Victoria to attend in person, making her the first woman to address the Congress since the dawn of time. Tennie wondered what Susan and her friends would say to that.

They skipped down the steps of the Capitol as frisky as hares, with only one more thing left to do before they took the train for home. They wanted to inspect the White House. Victoria was so borne up by Butler's plotting that she felt convinced her next address was destined to be the mansion on Pennsylvania Avenue.

She had a card from him to work the trick, handed over with a parting word: "This country has more vitality than any other on earth if it can stand this sort of Administration for another two years."

There was a tide of people, carriages, streetcars, horseback riders, and railroad trains flowing along the avenue, the trains flagged down from time to time to give pedestrians a chance to cross the tracks without fear of suffering more damage than cinders in their eyes. Reaching the entrance meant elbowing a way through a throng of loiterers and peddlers who had placed their stalls on both sides of the iron gates and were doing a brisk trade in balloons, candy, and Stars and Stripes in assorted sizes. The gravel walks and the gardens had the same new-laid look as the Government buildings, which Victoria attributed to the fact that Washington City had been the next best thing to an army camp during the war, with banks of earth flung up to slow down the Confederate Army, hospital wards full of wounded, huts and tents everywhere, and the local citizens piling up money received from soldiers hungering for home-baked pies, tobacco, and contraband liquor.

Butler's card got them into the front hall without a fuss. It was no problem, either, to find a bell push designed to bring a Negro servant trotting up. When nothing happened after two or three tries, they helped themselves to a tour of the first floor. The rooms all held a fair turnout of callers, mostly men with hats firm on their heads and hands deep in their pockets, and only a scattering of women. There were two distinct varieties of people—the tiptoers who went around as if in a church, exclaiming over the rugs and paintings and fixtures, and the loungers sprawling on sofas, making themselves at home and surveying everything that wasn't nailed down as if they were looking for souvenirs. Victoria talked like a housewife about how the place could be improved by new curtains and a reshuffle of the furniture, already counting the days to being elected.

A Negro in a suit to match his color went by, whispering to those strollers he seemed to be familiar with. When Victoria showed him Butler's card, he said the general was such a hero it would be a shame if they left without a glimpse of Mr. President himself. He was on the point of receiving in his upstairs study; perhaps they'd care to join in. Victoria didn't want to miss an opportunity to size up her competition, so off they went with a handful of others.

His room was barracks-bare and foggy with cigar smoke. As they walked in, his wife, Julia, a plump little woman with a squint, was leaving, having deposited a tray and coffeepot on his empty desk. "My afternoon refreshment—not exactly what some gentlemen of the press would lead you to expect." His voice was a rusty saw, his jaw a steel trap.

No matter what she'd read, it was a wonder to Tennie to see a man she had already envisioned as President before he had even been made General of the Army. For once in her life, she had nothing in mind to say, and neither had her sister. They kept their mouths shut and their ears open. He allowed he was downcast by the Democrats' victory in New York, "but give them enough rope, and you'll witness the usual consequences." Somebody mentioned Tweed. "You might as well try to spoil a rotten egg as damage his character," Grant said. He confessed to being tone-deaf: "I know only two tunes. One is 'Yankee Doodle,' the other isn't."

Victoria had to put one question to him. "What are your present views on woman's suffrage, sir?"

"The answer will rest in the hands of the Supreme Court." At ease! Tennie told herself. Platoon, dis*miss!*

Victoria muttered, "God help us if we've no other refuge."

Ben Butler stuck to his word and the timetable, too. Three days before Christmas, they were back in Washington to collect "The Memorial of Victoria C. Woodhull" and pass it on for presentation on the Hill. The *Weekly* had continued plugging away about votes for women, yet still nothing had been heard from the ladies of Boston, though New Yorkers were busy preparing to come down to Washington for their annual convention on January 11. With Susan off lecturing again and Mrs. Stanton overladen with more desk work, the job of organizing the meeting landed on Isabella Beecher Hooker, who was Dr. Beecher's half-sister but no great admirer of his exhortations from the pulpit. The latest president of the National Women was Theodore Tilton, who'd done no better than Miss Anthony in sparking up *The Revolution*, but he was mystifying the faithful by declining to show up at their convention. The Claflin sisters soon learned why.

Cutting through the verbiage, Victoria's petition came down to an argument that since the Fourteenth Amendment made everyone born or naturalized in the country a citizen of the United States and the Fifteenth stipulated that *every* citizen had the right to vote, how was it that women weren't included? It was high time, Ben Butler wrote, for the Congress to pass fresh laws with teeth in them to make sure women weren't robbed of a right they already had, though most men wouldn't admit to it.

His two tame Congressmen asked for the memorial to be referred to the Judiciary Committee, according to schedule. "No objection was made, and it was so ordered," the *Congressional Record* said. The next order of business was to give Victoria a hearing in front of that committee.

Butler was no admirer of the veterans in the Movement. When he heard Isabella Hooker was in town as a guest of Sam Pomeroy, Senator from Kansas, and the National Women were filling the hotels for their January 11 gathering in Lincoln Hall, he named that the day Mrs. Woodhull would have her say in the Capitol. "They've treated you and me like dirt," Tennie said to her sister. "It's your turn to rub their noses in it."

The National Women protested that Victoria was a notorious free lover with one husband too many and a habit of pursuing any man who took her fancy. Susan was the first one to show a grain of sense, suggesting they should postpone their morning opening and present themselves in the committee room to hear what the free lover had to say. Isabella still objected until Sam Pomeroy explained, "That is not politics. Men could never work as a party if they stopped to investigate each member's antecedents and associates."

The whole tribe—Miss Anthony, Mrs. Stanton, Isabella, and dozens more—came rustling in that morning, looking as if they expected to find a pair of gypsy fortunetellers banging tambourines. Instead, Victoria outdid them in refinement—plain dark walking dress, velvet neckband, brown curls topped with an alpine hat, her only ornament a white rose—and Tennie was a match for her except for the rose. At the head of the table, Ben Butler threw the sisters a Dutch-uncle nod.

Victoria turned so pale Tennie thought she was about to topple over, and her voice cracked when she started talking. Then her cheeks flushed, her blue eyes flashed, her throat cleared, and she was off and flying. This was Victoria Woodhull, who'd never tackled any such challenge before. The reporters started scribbling in their notebooks. Though it was a case of standing room only, there wasn't so much as a cough to interrupt her.

What she wound up saying was this: "Women, all women, white and black, are members of the human race, which comprises everybody, male and female. The Constitution decrees that the color of a citizen's skin has no bearing on the right to vote. Neither must sex be allowed as the reason for denying us that same Constitutional right."

Tennie had a mind to cheer when she was through, but Butler's rolling eyes quelled her. He was the first, though, to shake her hand, and then the ladies swarmed around, covered in smiles, bonnets bobbing with approval, for all the world as though she'd been their favorite from the beginning. She took it in good part, but Tennie admitted to feeling squeamish.

The National Women took the two of them to lunch, then bore them off to Lincoln Hall for Victoria to repeat her performance. The platform was filled with bigwigs of both sexes, Senators Nye of Nevada, Warner of Utah, Wilson of Massachusetts; Congressmen; suffragists; and black, bushy-topped Frederick Douglass, who'd soon be tapped by Grant for a Presidential commission to Santo Domingo. Susan and Isabella led the sisters up to the platform, and when the time came, Isabella had Victoria's hand in hers as she led Sister Woodhull forward to be introduced.

Victoria had another fit of tremors before she recited her memorial again, then repeated much of what she'd told the Butler committee, saying that those gentlemen of Congress had "promised that the heart of every man in the Congress is in the Movement." If they had gone that far, Tennie had missed hearing them say so. Victoria also pledged that she and her sister would beard Grant in his den again to win him around. But that engagement was forgotten in the dither everybody was caught up in during the days ahead. So was her promise to donate $10,000 to the National Woman war chest.

But she got enough notice in the morning papers to fill a new scrapbook. The New York *Times* said, "The cry of the suffragans was anthems to Woodhull." The Philadelphia *Press:* "General Grant might learn a lesson in silence from the pale, sad face of this unflinching woman. She reminds one of the forces in nature behind the storm, or of a small splinter of the indestructible." *The Commercial Advertiser:* "This is the bravest and best movement that the women have yet made." And the *Star:* "The National Woman Suffrage Association Convention has had the wind completely taken out of its sails by that lively little yacht, Mrs. Woodhull!"

They tore up the program for the rest of their convention so they could chew over the Woodhull memorial and apply a nudge of their own to Congress. Instead of seeking yet another Amendment, they decided to call on women everywhere to do their duty by registering to vote and sue in court if their rights were denied. "They figured it'd be a shoo-in after Victoria's dosing the Butler committee with electromagnetism," Tennie said later—but they couldn't have been further off the mark.

Ben Butler was one of a minority of two concluding "that the right of suffrage is one of the inalienable rights of citizens of the United States, subject to regulations by the States through equal and just laws." But it was the rest of his committee that had the final say. "Resolved: That the prayer of the petitioner be not granted, that the memorial be laid on the table, and that the Committee of the Judiciary be discharged from further consideration of the subject."

In the long run, though, it wasn't the speeches Victoria made in Washington that upset the Claflins' apple cart but the chance remark of a stranger, a man they never met. When Isabella was ranting about wicked Mrs. Woodhull while they were still trying to freeze her out, he had warned her, "It would ill become these women, especially a Beecher, to talk of antecedents or cast any smirch upon Mrs. Woodhull, for I am reliably informed that Henry

Ward Beecher preaches to at least twenty of his mistresses every Sunday."

After Tennie and Victoria heard this nibble of gossip, it went into storage in case the day came when they had to go back to living on scraps from richer people's tables.

Seven

———❦———

"You can't put a foot wrong among those women," Tennie told Victoria. "They treat you like you was Joan of Arc and the Queen of Sheba rolled into one and deserving a monument set up in your honor in the middle of Central Park." Victoria was the National Women's treasure, their new pride and joy. Out of all the tender messages they sent her, Isabella's took the prize for flattery—"My darling Queen"—but another ran a close second: "Bravo, my dear Woodhull! Go ahead, bright, glorious, young and strong spirit, and believe in the best love and hope and faith of S. B. Anthony."

Of course, the women of Boston reacted in the spirit of sisterhood and denounced the National Women for taking up with a free lover, but Mrs. Stanton had some stones of her own to cast in return.

"When the men who make laws for us in Washington can stand forth and declare themselves pure and unspotted from all the sins mentioned in the Decalogue, then we will demand that every woman who makes a Constitutional argument on our platform shall be as chaste as Diana. We have had enough women sacrificed to this sentimental, hypocritical prating about purity. This is one of men's most effective engines for our division and subjugation. He creates the public sentiment, builds the gallows, and then makes us hang-men for our sex. Women have sacrificed the Mary Wollstonecrafts, the Fanny Wrights, the George Sands, the Fanny Kembles of all ages. Let us end this ignoble record and henceforth stand by wom-anhood. If Victoria Woodhull must be crucified, let men drive the spikes and plait the crown of thorns."

Pauline Wright Davis, another National Woman, wore French gowns to prove a suffragist needn't be a frump. She wrote to Victo-ria: "I believe that you are raised up of God to do a wonderful work, and I believe that you will unmask the hypocrisy of a class that none others dare touch."

Such blandishments had a powerful appeal for Victoria, but they went to her head, which was not surprising. Before very long, she truly believed she was chosen by the Lord to perform miracles. She sounded off to one reporter, "I am a prophetess, I am an evangel, I am a Savior if you would but see it; but I, too, come not to bring peace but a sword."

Tennie quizzed her. "About the holy, holy, holy stuff you're serving. Do you reckon you're fooling anybody?"

She was stunned. "I am not trying to. Whatever else may be said, I am a truthful woman—"

"Come off your high horse, Sis. We've both been known to tell a few stretchers in our time. What's changed?"

"I have. I am doing what I was born for, what I am impelled to do. If there is one thing I have learned in the process, it is to bury the dead—there's nothing else for it."

"Like Mrs. Whatsit in Ottawa? Or do you figure on resurrecting her?"

"She was a goner, anyway. And I felt like a corpse myself, once, if there's any meaning to the word, but I have been resurrected. Do you envy me, little Miss Tennessee?"

"Could be." Next morning, Tennessee had a Claflin memorial drawn up that echoed Victoria's, except it was Andrews's doing, not Butler's, and aimed at the State Legislature, not the Congress of the United States. Tennie thought it wasn't worth a train ride up to Albany to hand it in, so she saved herself seeing it filed away to pick up dust.

Victoria went back to Washington to share a platform with Isabella, and the Washington *Chronicle* called it "a triumph." The spellbinding advanced a step further when she talked at Cooper Union in New York under a banner reading "Only Criminals, Idiots and Insane May be Deprived of the Ballot—There Are No Free Women," and the newspapers reported that she was "literally covered with bouquets as she made her exit."

Lecturing had an advantage over and above the bouquets—the fees came in useful at the *Weekly,* which was going hammer and tongs now singing her praises. She was ready to make a speech about anything Andrews put her up to. "Wherever I find a social carbuncle, I shall plunge my surgical knife into it up to the hilt." That was Victoria talking to another Park Row scribbler. Andrews's hand lay heavy on a gem he called "The Relations of Capital to Labor," which advocated taxing the rich to help the poor, so next time out the subject of her lecture was "The Great Political Issue of Constitutional Equality," giving her the chance to throw in some tidbits about sex and how women suffered in childbirth, which always raised a crowd's eyebrows.

It was easy to see how she did it: reading sensationalism in the *Weekly*'s cold print was nowhere near as inflammatory as hearing it from her in person. She was never in better form than when she was goaded. If spoilsports hissed her, as they did now and then, her eyes flashed sparks. She'd forget about Andrews and sail on under her own steam, shooting down the critics who'd ventured across her bow. Admirers put her in the same class of public speakers as Abraham Lincoln, Dr. Beecher, and Demosthenes himself. Tennie failed to see how anybody living could pretend to be a judge of *his* performance.

The invitations and cash rolled in together, taking her to Philadelphia, Syracuse, and Brooklyn, which was Beecher country—Plymouth Church there overflowed every Sunday when he climbed into the pulpit to turn on the tears.

The Claflins were getting to know more about the Bible-punching reverend than was healthy for him, Pauline Wright Davis being a principal source of information. Until Victoria took over, Pauline's dearest friend had been Elizabeth (Mrs. Theodore) Tilton, who taught Sunday school in Beecher's tabernacle. Mr. and Mrs. Tilton and four little Tiltons lived in a house on Brooklyn Heights with a sign over the front door saying, "And whatsoever house ye enter, ye shall first say, 'Peace to this house.' " Pauline considered this a beautiful thought for everyone to live up to—though it didn't apply to any place a Claflin ever rented.

It didn't suit the Tiltons' home, either, once Beecher got his foot in the door, remarking on what a pretty place it was and "I wished I lived here." Mrs. Tilton took that as the next best thing to a blessing direct from heaven. The reverend was soon making himself at home with her when Theodore wasn't around.

Tilton had set Beecher up on a pedestal and thought he was the good Lord's personal representative on earth. He'd have continued wearing blinders if Elizabeth hadn't concluded that she was a sinner and blabbed out the truth to him. In Tennie's philosophy, one reason for taking things with a grain of salt was that it saved you from hurt when you found you've been cheated. But Tilton felt the ceiling had fallen in on him. He'd made his wife sign a confession, which he tucked up his sleeve to play as an ace later on in the game.

So far, so good—but then, as Pauline related it, the plot grew thicker than molasses. Tilton worked in part for Henry Bowen, who'd been in the dry-goods business before he spotted bigger killings waiting to be made by publishing a daily and a weekly newspaper, and investing in a promising piece of tax-free property called Plymouth Church. It was Bowen who'd brought in Beecher in the first place, and Bowen, as a bond holder, enjoyed a guaranteed slice of the pie when the plate was passed every Sunday. He engaged Beecher to write an uplifting essay every week for Bowen's magazine, the *Independent*. Beecher had repaid him by seducing Mrs. Bowen, who was so overcome by shame that it drove her to her grave, or so her husband decided.

As a result, the two men of faith had a falling-out, and Beecher started up a rival weekly, the *Christian Union*, which rang with even more piety than the *Independent* or Bowen's daily, the *Brooklyn Union*. Tennie summed up the situation. "You've got three marvels of manhood smelling no sweeter than skunks to me: Bowen, who blackguards Beecher behind his back, yet won't tolerate anything that might shrink the church collections; Beecher, whose bowels will cut loose when he hears about the signed confession; Tilton, who after swallowing his wife's promise to be pure as snow again, and saying he was saint enough to forgive Beecher, is having second thoughts about it." In the *Independent,* Tilton was moaning, "Love departs, marriage ceases, and divorce begins. This is the essence of Christ's idea." That could be taken as a working definition of what free love signified to Victoria, but Theodore would have fainted away before he accepted it.

Neither Victoria nor Tennie ever saw the inside of Plymouth Church, but thousands did after they'd caught the ferries across the East River—"Beecher Boats" was the term for them—then stood around for hours waiting for the ten-minute bell and a seat in a pew or in one of the galleries or on one of the folding chairs that clogged the aisles. Beecher, nearing sixty, put on as good a show as might be seen in any Broadway theater, swirling his robe, pounding the pulpit that was supposed to be made of wood from Gethsemane, bellowing and weeping. It roused the congregation higher than an all-night camp meeting.

He prophesied hell and damnation as a certainty for everybody who didn't practice "the all-inspiring love power," and he had just finished writing *The Life of Christ,* but he hadn't a word to say in favor of votes for women. "That's halfway understandable," Tennie jeered, "when he'd wooed and screwed enough of them to ruin him if they had ballots to cast." But Tilton did have a vote, as well as a reputation as a public speaker, a voice in the *Independent,* and five thousand dollars a year as editor of the *Brooklyn Union.* Theodore knew too much. Beecher made up his mind to break him.

His candidate for the job was Henry Bowen, not the most likely choice on the face of it, except that Bowen had let Tilton in on the secret reason for Mrs. Bowen's early death—and immediately regretted the confidence. If news got around that Beecher was a practicing free lover, shares in Plymouth Church would be a drug on the market. When Beecher passed the word that he wanted Tilton fired, Bowen was happy to oblige.

One sniff, and Tilton smelled a rat. He hurried off to Beecher to upbraid him for getting him fired as well as for intruding on his

marriage. After shilly-shallying for a while, the reverend admitted
there might be cause for Tilton to complain. Beecher virtually confessed as much in a letter before he did another somersault and said
it was all a parcel of lies.

Theodore took off again, this time to a friend named Francis
Moulton, a rational being and a rarity in this small circle. Moulton
came to the conclusion that there were two kinds of balm for soothing Tilton: a magazine of his own and a promise from Elizabeth that
bygones were to be bygones and only her husband had rights to her
bed.

Moulton raised the capital for a new magazine that Theodore
christened the *Golden Age*. Among the funds was a check from
Beecher, who promised to patch things up between the Tiltons by
having Elizabeth repeat her marriage vows and sign another confession canceling her first. But now she was in a tizzy about it. Pauline
Davis could foresee the whole house of cards come tumbling down
at the first puff of wind, as she hastened to explain:

"I came away from that house, my soul bowed down with grief at
the heartbroken condition of that poor woman, and I felt I ought
not to leave Brooklyn until I had stripped the mask from that
infamous, hypocritical scoundrel, Beecher." It seemed to Tennie
that Pauline, decked out in the usual snood and diamonds, wouldn't
know where to begin.

Victoria heard a similar account from Mrs. Stanton. She told of
running into the Tiltons at *The Revolution*'s office, where Susan and
Laura Bullard were wringing their hands because it was clear their
paper was on its last legs. While Theodore ate supper at the Bul-
lards' along with Mrs. Stanton, he related the whole story of Elizabeth's trysts with Beecher. Meantime, Susan had gone home to eat
with Elizabeth. When Tilton got back to the house, he berated his
wife until Miss Anthony retreated to the guest room. Elizabeth
raced after her, bolting the door in Theodore's face. He was pounding at it to smash his way in when Susan warned, "If you enter this
room, it will be over my dead body."

Altogether, it was a situation Tennie could only describe as
"gaudy." "Up to then, we'd been under the impression it was only
Claflins who carried on like mad dogs when they got their dander

up. It was amazing what you learned when women took to gossiping or when men of *principle* turned downright ugly."

The *Golden Age* published such twaddle that income was as short as readers. Tilton's answer was to take aim at Bowen in an article accusing him of blackening the name of Dr. Beecher by spreading wicked rumors about him and Elizabeth. But this item got no further than the typesetters. Tilton took the printers' proof along when he went to pay Bowen a call. That pillar of Plymouth Church could hardly wait to write out a check for $7,000 to buy Theodore's silence.

"And then," Tennie reported, "another Beecher stuck her snout into the trough. Sister Catherine, a wrinkled old sow who lived in Hartford, Connecticut, was the eldest of a litter of seven. She knocked on our door at East 38th Street with a note from the youngest, Isabella, asking Sis to do the honors during Miss Catherine Beecher's trip to New York. Our house was in the customary state of pickle, so Victoria ordered the carriage to take her for a ride through the park. She had it in for Victoria the moment the wheels got rolling, snorting about the evils of free love and how no decent woman could regard marriage as anything less than God Almighty's design for the human race."

There was no holding Miss Beecher. With white ringlets bobbing under a lace cap, she kept up the attack until Victoria ran out of patience. "You talk as though I am the only free lover in the universe. I will point out for your benefit that love takes a minimum of two for its practice. I assure you there are legions of us, but not all can summon up the moral courage to acknowledge it."

"Have the goodness, pray, to name one other for me."

"Your saintly brother, Dr. Henry Ward Beecher."

Victoria thought the old harridan was going to throw a fit, but she finally composed herself. "I will vouch personally for the taintless way in which my brother observes his sacred marriage vows, unsullied and respected by one and all."

"You may learn better one day. You can't keep a pig in a poke forever, you know."

"I will strike you for this, Victoria Woodhull. I will strike you dead."

"You can but try, Miss Beecher—and your pious brother will help you, I'm sure."

From that day on Sister Catherine never mentioned the Claflin sisters except as "the two prostitutes," which Tennie took to be one more sign of blind ignorance. "We used to turn down many an offer of cash in advance in return for a tumble because it was a point of pride with us to pick and choose when the sap got to rising. There was nothing wrong so far as we could see in a man showing appreciation after the main event, provided there'd been satisfaction on both sides. I'll admit I fell on my ass in judging a man now and then, but nobody can claim to be perfect."

She came a cropper with one Wall Streeter, Luther B. Challis, who hung around her for a time. He promised to take her and Victoria to a masked ball at the Academy of Music on 14th Street, but then called it off at the last minute. They made up their minds to go anyway. When they arrived, they saw Challis and a friend with two girls too young to have finished school.

"My blood began to boil, but I didn't learn until afterward what a bona fide, snot-nosed, lobster-eyed, bloody-handed son of a bitch he really was," said Tennie.

Throughout these weeks, the Beechers—all of them, that is, except Isabella—were hounding the Claflins. The *Christian Union* and the *Independent* alike had them marked down for trouble. Another of the sisters, Harriet Beecher Stowe, wrote about Victoria as if she was Mrs. Simon Legree. In Plymouth Church, Beecher himself tore her to shreds for selling her body while she clamored for the vote. Totting it all up, the Claflins found they had a considerable score to settle.

That's where things stood when Anna left East 38th Street to move in with Polly and Benjamin Sparr at the Washington Hotel. She'd been feeling as sorry for herself as Utica ever did, though Anna had the sense to shy away from hard liquor. Victoria and Tennie put her trouble down to their neglect of her, with Broad Street and the *Weekly* taking up most of their time and Victoria using what was left of it to deliver a lecture to anyone with the price of a ticket. Anna was like the rest of them in craving attention. It was bad luck that the three of them in the hotel were playing tricks, firing off letters in Tennie's name to any number of prominent men, saying the *Weekly* would start throwing mud at them unless they were ready to pay hush money in advance.

But Victoria was still the apple of Mrs. Stanton's eye. She wouldn't listen to a hostile word against Victoria from any quarter, though complaints were raised at every point of the compass when the thirty-first anniversary of the first suffrage meeting at Seneca Falls came up in May and Mrs. Stanton gave Victoria pride of place on the platform in Apollo Hall. She sat Victoria between herself and another of the veterans, Lucretia Mott, who felt disposed to overlook Mrs. Woodhull's reputation for the overall good of the Movement.

The papers labeled it "The Woodhull Convention." Tennie had never seen her sister in better form. "If the very next Congress refuses women all the legitimate results of citizenship, we shall proceed to call another convention expressly to frame a new Constitution and erect a new government." The cheers rattled the windows. "We mean treason. We mean secession, and on a thousand times greater scale than was that of the South. We are plotting revolution. We will overthrow this bogus republic and plant a government of righteousness in its stead." She had them on their feet, shouting approval, waving handbags and jiggling their parasols. She liked that speech so well she ordered a hundred thousand copies from the printer.

Four days later, she received a different kind of notice. Anna went down with a lawyer to Essex Market Police Court to ask for a warrant for Jim Blood's arrest, and the papers couldn't wait to pounce on the whole family.

Tennie thought her mother's brains must have rattled loose. "Judge, my daughters was good daughters and affectionate children until they got in with this man Blood. He has threatened my life several times, and one night last November he came into the house and said he wouldn't go to bed until he had washed his hands in my blood."

That was embroidering the facts a bit. What he *had* said was, "If you weren't my mother-in-law, I'd turn you over my knee and spank you."

"If my daughters would just send this man away as I always told them to, they might be millionairesses riding around in their carriages. I came here because I want to get my daughters out of this man's clutches. He has taken away Vicky's affection and Tennie's affection from their poor old mother. So help me God, Judge, I say here and I call heaven to witness there's the worst gang of free lovers in that house that ever lived. Stephen Pearl Andrews and Dr. Woodhull and lots more of such trash."

Sister Polly swore everything Anna said was true. She also claimed, which was a lie, that there was "something mysterious and unnatural" between Anna and Tennessee. What truly existed between them stirred Polly's envy; this, strangely enough, was affection.

Jim was next on the stand, and the lawyer cat-and-moused him. "When did you marry Mrs. Woodhull?"

"In 1866."

"Was Mrs. Woodhull divorced when you married her?"

"I do not know."

"Were you not afterwards divorced from Mrs. Woodhull?"

"Yes. In Chicago in 1868."

"How long were you separated from her?"

"We were never separated. We continued to live together and were afterwards remarried."

"Have you seen Dr. Woodhull?"

"I see him every day. We are living in the same house."

"Do you and Mrs. Woodhull and Dr. Woodhull occupy the same room?"

Jim avoided answering and his own lawyer stepped in. "Please tell the court that Dr. Woodhull lives in the same house, and who supports him."

"The firm of Woodhull, Claflin and Company has supported the whole of them. Mrs. Woodhull's boy received a fall when he was young. He needs his father's medical care and treatment." Byron was sixteen, but he'd no more mentality than he'd been born with.

Next morning, it was time for Victoria and Tennie to put in an appearance, with Victoria up first before the judge. "Colonel Blood never treated my mother otherwise than kind. . . . I never knew him to put a hand on her. She left my house on the first of April and went to the Washington Hotel to board. All bills for her maintenance were paid by Woodhull, Claflin and Company." She had the receipts to prove that.

Then she laid the blame where it belonged. "Sparr and his wife induced my mother to leave for their own protection and to excite public sympathy. I have always pitied my mother. She always seemed to have a desire to have her own way and seemed to know better what her children wanted than they did themselves. My father is still living with me.

"Sometimes she would come down to the table and sit on Mr. Blood's lap and say he was the best son-in-law she had. Then again she would abuse him like a thief. The whole trouble was Mother wanted to get Tennie back to going around the country telling fortunes, and Sparr and his wife were always telling Mother that as long as Blood was around, she couldn't get the girl back."

After more explaining by Victoria about how Woodhull, Claflin Company footed the bills for a multitude of Claflins, Tennie had her say. The men from the newspapers were given a smile as an appetizer, and then she let rip. "My mother and I always got on together until Sparr came to the house. He's been trying to blackmail people through Mother. I've been accused of being a blackmailer myself. I've a lot of letters here supposed to have been written by her to blackmail different people in this city. But my mother can't read or write. They were written by Sparr.

The judge butted in. "You and your mother have been on most intimate terms?"

"Since I was eleven years old. I used to tell fortunes with her, and she wants me back with her in that business. But my sister and Colonel Blood got me away from that life, and they're the best friends I ever had. Since I was fourteen years old, I've kept thirty or thirty-five deadheads."

She should have quit then and there, but she got carried away. "I am a clairvoyant. I am a spiritualist. I have power, and I know my power. Commodore Vanderbilt knows my power, too. I have humbugged people, I know, but if I did, it was to make money to keep these deadheads. You'd better ask some more questions, Judge." That would be one way to give her a minute to pull herself together. But all the man on the bench did was goggle and tweak his nose.

"Judge, I want my mother. I'm willing to take her home now or pay two hundred dollars a month for her in any safe place. I'm single myself, and I don't need anyone else with me but her." She couldn't hold back any longer. She nipped down to give the old girl a hug that would have squeezed the wind out of a horse. Everything was getting kind of blurry because she was dripping tears like a leaky bucket.

Jim Blood's arm went around her shoulders. "Do retire, my dear. You are only making yourself conspicuous."

The outcome could be termed a draw.

The judge could see no cause for arresting Jim Blood, but the Sparrs kept their hold on Anna for the time being, and that wasn't the worst of it. Tennie knew she had to be off her head to blab about the Com. Tips from him about the stock market came to a sudden end, and the profits from Woodhull, Claflin & Company took a nose dive. "Maybe it was his doing, or more likely his missus's, but I'd put the ax to the golden goose. Things got so tight pretty soon that we had to peddle some of the furniture from East Thirty-eighth Street, and the deadbeats moaned because the cupboard got awful bare."

The papers made hay of the Claflins' day in court. *Unsavory piece of scandal . . . shameless effrontery . . . vile story. . . .* The Cleveland *Leader* hit Victoria square in the eye: "At Cincinnati, a year ago, she was the same, brazen, snaky adventuress that she is now. She is a suffrage advocate because being so made her notorious and her paper profitable."

The National Women and the American Women, who'd been ready to argue over what day of the week came next, found one thing to agree on, and that was to scarify Susan Anthony and her friends for courting Victoria, who was blacklisted by both sides. She'd had four months in the limelight; now they aimed on consigning her to darkness.

What angered her most was the gall of Henry Bowen in attacking Susan, Mrs. Stanton and Isabella in the *Independent* for giving "a prominent place to Mrs. Woodhull, about whose private affairs all gossip is needless," while he sneered that *"Woodhull and Claflin's Weekly* with its coarse treatment of all the sacred things of human life is enough to condemn anyone whose name is associated with it."

If Beecher and his pack were looking for a fight, she'd oblige them with one, and she'd get her blows in first. Most of the letters she sent simultaneously to the *Times* and the *World* were written by Andrews, but the venom in them was hers.

> I advocate free love in the highest and purest sense as the only cure for the immorality by which men corrupt sexual relations. My judges preach against free love openly, practice it secretly. For example, I know of one man, a public teacher of eminence, who lives in concubinage with the wife of another public teacher of almost equal eminence. All three concur in denouncing offenses against morality.
>
> So be it, but I decline to stand up as the "frightful example." I shall make it my business to analyze some of these lives and will take my chance in the matter of libel suits.

Both papers printed her letter. "I can picture Beecher wetting his drawers when he reads it at breakfast," said Tennie. They got in another jab in a column in the *Weekly:*

> Civilization is festering to the bursting point in our great cities, notably in New York and Brooklyn. At this very moment, awful and herculean efforts are being made to suppress the most terrific scandal in a neighboring city which has ever astounded and convulsed any community. Clergy, congregation, and community will be alike hurled into more than all the consternation which the great explosion in Paris carried to that unfortunate city if this effort at suppression fails.
>
> "We have the inventory of discarded husbands and wives and lovers, with dates, circumstances, and establishments. Bankers in Wall Street and great railroad men come early on the schedule. Confidences which are no confidences abound.

Maybe that would make the Commodore sit up and take notice, too.

On the other side of the East River, Beecher locked his door against the reporters. He had a meeting with Tilton and Frank Moulton to determine what could be done to save his hide. What they landed on was to have Theodore soften up Victoria and talk her into holding her fire.

He showed up at the *Weekly* wearing a floppy necktie under his collar and a face that Victoria thought would have been improved by having muscle to it. He was sturdy, though, and something of a ladies' man. First thing she did was hand him a copy of her letter to the newspapers. "I wish you would read it aloud."

He fumbled his way through, and then she was at him. "Do you know, sir, to whom I refer? I refer to the Reverend Henry Ward Beecher and your wife. I read by your expression that my charge is true."

Tennie left at that point. Her sister could handle him better single-handed. Just how well she did in winning him over was plain in the next issue of the *Golden Age*. The title of the piece he wrote was "A Legend of Good Women." The biggest bits of blarney about her said: "If the woman's movement has a Joan of Arc, it is this gentle but fiery genius . . . little understood by the public, she is denounced in the most outrageous manner by people who do not appreciate her moral worth. . . . Anyone who imagines her to stand below the whitest and purest of her sex misplaces a woman who in moral integrity rises to the full height of the highest."

"There was no mystery," Tennie said, "about what happened to turn him ass over teakettle. Sis knew how to work the *Kama Sutra* trick whether she was in bed or stretched out on our office couch."

Nobody could accuse Tilton of being a run-of-the-mill libertine. Instead of keeping quiet about himself and Victoria he wanted everything out in the open, so he took her over to Brooklyn for a bite of supper with Mrs. Tilton.

Victoria described her as being mousy in appearance but good-looking for all that, "with a bust of a size any billy goat like Beecher couldn't wait to get hold of." She was sitting sewing a checked silk dress for one of the Tilton girls when Victoria walked in with Theodore.

"Elizabeth, beloved, this is Mrs. Woodhull, one of the most upright, truthful, religious, and unsullied souls it has been my privilege to meet."

Elizabeth's thumb got in the way of her needle. "I am honored to make your acquaintance, madame."

"She has been wickedly traduced in the press and also, alas, by certain members of her own family. What is more, she knows everything about us—you, myself, and that lecherous scoundrel."

"Theodore! One should not say such things about a man of God. You have told her *everything?*"

"I felt it my bounden duty. Yet you still defend Beecher!"

Victoria sat herself down in a chair beside her. "I have been privileged to receive your husband's confidences. Now I look forward most eagerly to sharing yours."

As Elizabeth put down her sewing and started to weep, Victoria fell on her knees in front of her. "You are not to let guilt burden you, my dear. You have a pure and simple heart—I can see that. Believe me, it is no sin to give yourself to more than one man in the name of free, unbounded love. Do not wince when society in its ignorance casts stones at you, as it so often does at me. What I am striving for is change—change in society, change in the world so it will understand that love beyond the bonds of marriage is not a crime."

Before the three of them put their feet under the supper table, Mrs. Woodhull had Mrs. Tilton pouring out her heart and eating out of her hand. Victoria promised to print not a word about Beecher and the Tiltons in the *Weekly* "lest the innocents be hurt," and Elizabeth gave her a book of poetry with "To my friend Victoria C. Woodhull" scratched on the flyleaf as Victoria took off for the ferry and home.

Tennie reached her own conclusion. "Theodore must have been hungry for another cut of the cake, because quick as winking we had him as another lodger in our house on a more-or-less permanent lease, and Mrs. Tilton's chumminess toward Sis lasted no longer than grease on a fire. Sis offered me a crack at him as I'd had with Jim, but I reckoned I'd save that up till later, since I was still thick with Johnnie Green of the *Sun* and one or two more, besides. I wondered how Jim Blood would take to the new setup, but he was a good sport who never complained."

Victoria was starry-eyed over Tilton all through that summer, and she didn't try to hide the fact: "A woman who could not love Theodore must be dead to all the sweeter impulses of nature." He rented rowboats to take her out on the Harlem River. They billed and cooed their way in a carriage to Coney Island one steamy night when she concluded that a dip in the ocean stripped of their clothes would do them a world of good.

They cooed at each other around the house to the point where Tennie got tired of watching. If it stayed hot after the sun went down they'd drag a mattress up onto the roof and keep going at it up there. "He sleeps every night in my arms," Victoria said, and she wasn't bragging.

What she asked in return from him was a book about her to tell readers and future voters what a miracle she'd turned out to be. Jim Blood had taken a stab at it, but his version clung too close to the facts to satisfy her. Theodore went to work in the back parlor, putting together a story that was to fill a whole issue of the *Golden Age.*

The trouble was that she'd led herself to believe every word she relayed to him. She protested if he'd skipped anything when he came out to read his words aloud to the family. "But you've left out the most important parts."

"Do you really wish me to write that you restored a dead child to life?"

"Of course I do. It was Byron."

Back he went to try again. "During a severe illness of her son, she left him to visit her patients, and on her return was startled with the news that the boy had died two hours before. 'No,' she exclaimed, 'I will not permit his death.' And with frantic energy she stripped her bosom naked, caught up his lifeless form and sitting thus, flesh to flesh, glided insensibly into a trance, in which she remained seven hours; at the end of which time she awoke, a perspiration started from his clammy skin, and the child that had been thought dead was brought back to life—and lives to this day in sad half-death. It is her belief that the spirit of Jesus Christ brooded over the lifeless form, and re-wrought the miracle of Lazarus."

The angels in the attic had to be included, too. "In her tenth year, one day while sitting by the side of a cradle rocking a sick babe to sleep, she says that two angels came and, gently pushing her away, began to fan the child with their white hands until its face grew fresh and rosy. Her mother suddenly entered the chamber and beheld in amazement the little nurse lying in a trance on the floor, her face turned upward toward the ceiling and the pining babe apparently in the bloom of health."

The "pining babe," who'd been Utica, didn't pay much attention at present to anybody or anything except a bottle of absinthe if she could lay hold of one. Failing that, she'd settle for a swallow of perfume filched from a dressing table.

Demosthenes entered the running, and Theodore set down Victoria's account of how that ancient had spelled out his name and steered them to Great Jones Street, though Tilton hedged on this. "She believed him to be her familiar spirit—the author of her public policy, and the inspirer of her published words. Without intruding my own opinion as to the authenticity of this inspiration, I have often thought that if Demosthenes could arise and speak English, he could hardly excel the fierce light and heat of some of the sentences which I have heard from this singular woman in her glowing hours." After hearing this flight of fancy, Tennie reckoned Sis would be burying any bone she had of picking up votes if this masterpiece ever got into print.

Victoria spurred him on to lay the whip to poor Woodhull— "habitually unchaste and given to fits of intoxication"—then snatched the bit between her teeth and went after most of the family. Anna, who was home again after quarreling with Polly, was afflicted "with a fickleness of spirit that renders her one of the most erratic of mortals." She wouldn't take that too hard, Tennie reflected, since all Anna could read with any certainty was her own name. But Buck got a shellacking for interfering in their office affairs, and he was as good at reading as you'd find.

"The father, at times a Mephistopheles, waits until the inspiration of cunning overmasters his parental instinct and, watching for a moment when the ill word to a stranger will blight their business schemes, drops in upon some capitalist whose money is in their hands, lodges an indictment against his own flesh and blood, takes out his handkerchief to feign a few well-feigned tears, clasps his hands with an unfelt agony, hobbles off smiling sardonically at the mischief he has done, and the next day repents his wickedness."

That was bound to get under Pa's hide because it was the truth, no buncombe.

And the same held for Tilton's slam at the rest of them: "For years there has been one common sentiment sweetly pervading the breasts of a majority toward a minority of the offspring—namely, a determination that Victoria and Tennie should earn all the money for the support of the numerous remainder of the Claflin tribe—wives, husbands, children, servants, all. Being daughters of the horse leech, they cry, 'Give!' " When it came to dragging skeletons out of the closet, Victoria was hard to beat.

Somebody must have picked up a copy of the *Golden Age* that carried Tilton's *Life of Victoria C. Woodhull* and recited extracts to Anna. She was so muddled in her head she fancied Jim Blood was the culprit. She gave the newspapers another field day one morning in June when Jim Blood sprinted out of the house with her on his heels while Tennie and Victoria ran neck and neck behind her.

She was screeching, "You bloody ruffian! You imp of Satan! You vile free lover! You've ruined my daughter. I'll have your life." She was making good time for a beldam of sixty-six and might have caught him if she hadn't swung around sharp to yell, "My daughters, come back to your ma!" There was no need for that—all they wanted was to get her back in before the neighbors raised another ruckus.

He nipped back, but she stayed to sun herself on the stoop, waiting for the press to arrive. As soon as she'd got her audience, she let fly. "My girls are virtuous—I've given them the example of a Christian mother. This hell-bound Blood said, 'Let's start a bank, and all the brokers on Wall Street will take off their hats when your carriage drives up!' Blood says to the girls, 'Let's start a paper. You'll get lots of subscribers and when you ride out all them readers will take off their hats to you!' "

They heard all this from behind the front door, but she had the notion that they had fled the house. "I'll wait here until my dear girls come home. Then I'll run and hug Tennie to my bosom and say her Ma's waiting, and she'll kiss me and let me in."

It was time for her to hush. Tennie opened the door, and the Park Row pack came yapping at her. She was fed up with about everything at the moment, and she told them so. "I've been the ruin of my relations by giving them blood until they turned into leeches. Now they scream like sick cats if I try to get shut of 'em: 'We'll show you up; we'll get you in the papers; we'll ruin you.' "

Notebooks were out, and pencils were skittering. "I told such wonderful things as a child, my father made up to a hundred dollars a day at hotels by letting people see me. Now people come up to me or write letters saying what I told 'em as a child has come to pass. When I got older and the deadheads flocked around, I was forced to humbug. I didn't want to, but I had to, to make money. My mother was always fearful I'd marry and the money would stop. I was never really happy until I came to live with my sister. I made fourteen thousand dollars in six months with Colonel Blood, and in all that time all I bought myself was two calico dresses."

Victoria came out to put in the last word. "We don't want any scandal, but if we'd had the nerve to do our duty years ago, it would have been far better. I believe Tennie ought to use the gift God has given her, but not in the mercenary way she was forced into. She has no right to prostitute her powers."

Any time she felt sorry for Tennie she would dream up something different for her to try. Her scheme now was to get her sister elected to Congress at the same time she walked off with the Presidency. She felt there'd be no stopping the two of them once the dust had settled after the Claflins' latest appearance in the papers. It took some string-pulling by Andrews, but it brought an invitation from the German-American Progressives, a society Tennie could truthfully say she hadn't heard of beforehand, to run as a candidate from the 8th Manhattan District. They picked her, according to Andrews, on account of her "practical wisdom and extensive knowledge shown by her different works on the subject of political reform." She took that to mean her articles in the *Weekly* about streetwalking.

Jim wrote a speech for her to learn, and Andrews threw in some German as a sign of good intentions. They put up posters and spread the word around, and Irving Hall was filled to the brim, men outnumbering women, rows of fat cheeks and fearsome moustaches, and an aroma of beer and sauerkraut. It had been a while since she faced an audience, but she was sure she looked fetching in black organdie without frills or jewelry. The main drift of what she had to say was that women were already entitled to the ballot under the terms of the two new amendments, and she intended to make a test case of it by registering to vote.

The speech went down well enough to bring a round of cheers and a basket of flowers when she was through. Later that night, some of the crowd went to the Claflin house to serenade her on the street outside. She might have been tempted to carry the venture a step further if Sister Polly hadn't started acting up again.

Benjamin Sparr fell dead in a room of French's Hotel. They had to break down a door to get in. They found him naked, drunk as a hatter, cold as a mackerel. Polly howled that he'd been murdered. Why? Because he'd had five thousand dollars in cash in his pockets when he set off on his binge, and not a cent was left on the corpse.

Tennie couldn't believe it. "That was a big joke when she kept him on a string so tight he never had more than five bucks in walking money. Who'd done him in? According to our loving sister, we had, Sis and me, to lift his bankroll. What drove Polly to claim such a thing? Our guess was she was jealous. The goodbye note he'd scribbled before he conked out from apoplexy was a roundabout sort of apology for the trouble he'd put us through. It started off, 'Vicky, Colonel, and Tennie included.' Polly didn't earn a mention."

Even the *Times* found space for mentioning the Claflins on a regular schedule though that Park Row neighbor was dredging up more of the mud in which Tweed and his cronies wallowed at Tammany Hall. One of them, Sheriff James O'Brien, informed on them when the Boss declined to pay him $350,000 that O'Brien felt was his due. One night in July he walked into the newspaper's offices with a bundle of copies made from the Ring's account books, and hell broke loose.

No Claflin could have matched Tweed as a hornswoggler in a hundred years of trying. He'd billed the city for more than $12,000,000 for a new County Court House and $175,000 for carpeting it. Office safes were put down as costing $400,000, and $170,000 was the price for forty chairs and tables. It took the *Times* three weeks to lay all the cards on the table, including a four-page extra edition in English and German. The Boss's reign was over.

There was a meeting of citizens at Cooper Union. The upshot was that seventy of them formed a committee to clean up the city and go after Tweed. First they arranged for someone to break into his comptroller's office and lift all the records to make sure the judge who signed the warrant for his arrest would be sure of his ground.

All of this made fascinating reading for Victoria's crowd, especially Andrews and Jim. "What are we going to do about it?" was her question. They concluded the time was ripe for the *Weekly* to cash in among the radicals, who'd been demanding Tweed's indictment for a year and more. What Andrews claimed as some of the most stirring words ever written deserved an airing. They'd been available in German, but they'd never seen daylight in America, in English.

They printed "The Communist Manifesto" by the German who'd once worked on the *Tribune*; at present, he was the inspiration of something known as the International Working Men's Association in London, England, "The International" for short. Karl Marx wasn't likely to ask the *Weekly* for money, which was another advantage.

Tweed was caught in October and set free on bail. Tennie and Victoria were arrested outside the booth at Number 682 Sixth Avenue for creating a fuss because they weren't allowed to register to vote. The judge let them off with a warning, but Mrs. Woodhull ripped off a letter to the *Times* about it: "The inspectors, under law, are guilty of felony for preventing a legal voter from voting."

"A specter is haunting Europe—the specter of Communism" was how Karl Marx began his Manifesto. "If I'd put my powers to work," said Tennie, "I'd have seen a different sort of haunting ahead for us—the specter of doing time in Ludlow Street clink."

Eight

———❧———

The day when the voters would have their chance to put Victoria in charge of the country was waiting not much more than a year ahead, but no strong support had been nailed down for her. She didn't know where she stood with the National Women and Susan Anthony. She plugged away for herself in the *Weekly,* but making ends meet was uphill work now that Woodhull, Claflin wasn't far short of bankruptcy. Every time she made a speech, most papers mocked her, and the Claflin family as a whole was more handicap than help to her.

What she needed was solid backing anywhere she could find it. The first offer came out of the blue from a quarter she had overlooked. Theodore Tilton's words of praise for her in the *Golden Age* woke the National Association of Spiritualists up to the fact she was one of their own and brought an invitation for her to attend their convention meeting in Troy, New York.

Off she went with Jim, who had the patience of Job where she was concerned, though she had a jealous streak that prompted her to throw a pair of shears at him when she saw him with an arm around Utica as she staggered upstairs one evening. Victoria was in top form in Troy, and after hearing her out, the Spiritualists by a show of hands elected her their president—"the chief honor of my life," she called it without adding "so far"; she still counted on at least four years in the White House.

She flattered the Spiritualists in print every week, adding stern warning to the opposition: "The churches and the politicians may sneer at the intentions of the spirit world, but they will do well to remember that it is up in arms and impatiently waits the signal to move upon their stronghold. All will be action, and whoever joins not in the movement will be crushed beneath its weight." She went hunting for more recruits among the real radicals after they applauded her for printing the Karl Marx Manifesto. The International was in an uproar over events in France the past spring. When the people of Paris took over the city, President Adolphe Thiers ordered the army in and twenty thousand Parisians were lined up against the wall and shot. A lot of Communards had belonged to the International, and there was bitterness among the survivors.

By Andrews's reckoning, Victoria could pick up a following from American members if she flew the right colors and sang the right song, which was "The Internationale." That sat well enough with Tennie, and soon she could match anybody with "Then, comrades, come rally, and the last fight let us face." But the Working Men's Association was split more ways than the suffragists. One faction labeled themselves "Section Twelve," and when they wrote their own manifesto, including recommendation for free love, Victoria published it in the *Weekly*. All she got for her trouble was abuse from every other section, which banded together to expel Section Twelve. It seemed to Tennie that old-fashioned marriage was one chain the workers couldn't break. "Free love might have taken their minds off their revolution."

Victoria and Theodore put their heads together and concluded she could use a champion to win her votes from the God-fearing who went to church on Sundays. Nobody carried more weight in that respect than Beecher, so she set her cap for him, willing to swallow her principles for the time being, since, as Tennie promised her, principles and politics mixed no better than axle grease and water. Tennie forecast, "It'll take some persuading to get Theodore to act as go-between, but she won't need telling from me how to go about it." The ammunition for threatening Theodore with was supplied in a note he sent her from his office after a night spent on the Claflin tiles: "My dearest Victoria: I made haste while yet able to sit up, for I am giddy with ———— this morning. Theodore."

Another letter told her he'd done her a different kind of service. "My dear Victoria: I have arranged with Frank [that was Moulton] that you shall see Mr. Beecher at my house on Friday night. He will attend a meeting of the church at ten o'clock and will give you the rest of the evening as you desire. Meanwhile, on this sunshiny day, I salute you with a good morning. Peace with you. Yours, T.T."

Tennie reflected, "I'd have given my eye teeth to see the two of them, Sis and Beecher, circling each other like cats warming up for a fight. They both knew she had the goods on him, but she knew she was only after him vouching for her as a candidate for President, which gave her the leg over him. She dolled herself up like she was off to a wedding, and she left with a promise I'd hear all the details as soon as she got back."

It was after midnight when she laid herself down on Tennie's bed. "He looked at me like a snake does a frog the minute I walked in," Victoria reported, "and said I should address him as 'Henry.' He took both my hands in his, and something of his power started flowing into me, mine into him. It was downright electrifying, I can tell you. I suggested at that point that Theodore—'my dear brother,' as he calls him—might leave us and join his wife. He was quite surly about it."

"What did you gab about with Beecher?"

"The size of our skulls, for one thing. 'For many years I have been in the habit of using phrenology as that which solves the practical phenomena of life' "—Tennie judged Victoria was talking the way he did—" 'I cannot but be conscious of a certain admiration for the configuration of your delicate brow.' "

Buck had had a fancy once that his girls should try charging customers for studying the bumps on their skulls as a side line. He bought a chart for the purpose, but they told him they had their hands full raising spirits. "Did old Henry offer to give you a reading?" Tennie asked her sister.

Victoria still smiling in the darkness—"No, it was the other way around, but that came about just before I said goodnight. He'd talked my ears off by then. I found we had more in common than I expected."

"Such as what, for instance?"

Victoria lay very still. "Visions. He said the most transporting experience in his life was when he was coming down with a fever. He fainted away on the floor, and when it was over he saw 'such a vision of God, of His glory, and of the heavenly land that I lay for an hour in a trance of joy and gladness.' I knew exactly what he meant. The same thing has happened to me."

"Yeah, I recollect you saying so."

"He agrees with me about so many things, but he needs his grit stirred to reveal himself. He said 'marriage is the grave of love,' and he feels he's condemning every couple he marries. But he claims if he confessed to that in public, he'd preach to empty pews."

"What about his bumps?"

"I remembered what Pa wanted us to get into. Mr. Beecher wanted me to explore his head 'to confirm what phrenologists of renown have already confided in me.' He put my fingers to the nape of his neck. I really could feel a kind of a thickness there. He said it's proof of 'a propensity for amativeness.' "

"Which means in plain English?"

Tennie knew Victoria's smile was back. "Inclined to make sexual love."

"How about that! Did you get anywhere with him?"

"Not in that sense. I urged him to pluck up courage and speak out for me, but he said he'd have to think about it. 'I have no doubt that when the time does come, God will give me grace to do it.' He asked me to see him again, but not at the Tiltons'."

"Do you reckon you will?"

"I have to, Tennie. I need his help."

She egged him on with a paragraph in the *Weekly* that must have bewildered all but a few of the faithful readers: "The amative impulse is the physiological basis of character. It is this which emanates zest and magnetic power to his whole audience through the organism of the great preacher. Plymouth Church has lived and flourished, and the healthy vigor of public opinion for the last quarter-century has been augmented and strengthened from the physical amativeness of Henry Ward Beecher."

"We'll have to wait and see, Sis," said Tennie, "how Theodore will stomach you taking on the old lecher who'd already had a share in Mrs. T."

Beecher no longer pointed to the Claflin women as examples of iniquity in his sermons, but he couldn't silence his sister Catherine. When Victoria was booked to lecture in the Hartford Opera House, Catherine raised a ruckus in a letter to her hometown newspaper, the *Courant*. Mrs. Woodhull, she said, was no more than a common prostitute "and seeks to introduce into society a sister who exceeds her in indecencies"; no Christian woman should tolerate their company.

Victoria bit her lips but made no response. She was still looking for an endorsement from Beecher, who for his part was baiting her into a liaison with him with his promises that sooner or later he'd find a kind word to say on her behalf to his congregation. At the opera house she gave her usual speech about women's need to go to court to prove their legal right to vote. Then she provided him with evidence of her trust in him by reading aloud his sister's letter and concluding: "Miss Beecher told me she would strike me. She has done so, but now I will present her with my other cheek with the hope that even her conscience will not smite her for speaking so unkindly of me. She may profess Christ, but I hope I may exceed her in living his precepts."

"I never could have brought myself to be as prissy if I'd been in Sis's shoes," Tennie remarked.

Victoria had drawn sizable crowds everywhere she appeared, but she'd left scarcely a dent on New York City. She remedied that by hiring Steinway Hall for the night of Monday, November 20, and Andrews got down to composing a fresh speech for her. After all the time she'd spent with him, she was tired of waiting for Beecher to vouch for her from his pulpit, so she decided she'd put him to the test by inviting him to introduce her from the platform. Since she didn't intend to tolerate more stalling, her note to him was sharp.

You doubtless know that it is in my power to strike back, and in ways more disastrous than anything that can come to me, but I do not desire to do this. I simply desire justice from those from whom I have a right to expect it, and a reasonable course on your part will assist me to it. I speak guardedly, but I think you will understand me. I must have an interview tomorrow, since I am to speak tomorrow evening at Steinway Hall and what I shall or shall not say will depend largely on the result of the interview.

She received an instant reply: he'd see her at his house any time she pleased on Monday morning. She roped Tennie in as a witness, and they hurried for the Brooklyn Ferry, Tennie's curiosity swelling over what was in store.

He was in such a stew she doubted he remembered her being there at all after they'd exchanged a preliminary nod. With long gray hair sprouting over his ears, he looked to her as if he'd been dragged through a barbed-wire fence as he started whining. "Where is the sympathy that ought to be shown by Christians toward an erring fellow man? When a Christian brother is in trouble, there ought to be a pavilion of Christian hearts into which he can enter."

Victoria wasn't buying his moonshine. "There will be no trouble if you keep your word to me."

"I feel as though I were beating hither and thither like a pendulum. I vibrate between sorrow and gladness that you turn to me. In thinking the matter over before your coming, I reached this consciousness: 'Heartache is good for you.' I let the tears course down my cheeks as freely as they would."

He was weeping again, but Victoria didn't seem to notice. "I am not asking that you endorse what I have to say—only that you appear with me and pave the way."

"Jesus knows that for His sake I smite with the sword and with the spear because I love truth and humanity. God sees me, God loves me, Christ is near me as a refuge, and my soul runs in and is at rest. Hitherto, the Lord hath helped me, but, sweet Sister, you ask too much."

"I have even brought a copy of my speech so that you may see for yourself there is no coarseness in it."

"Nay, nay, tempt me not! I have not spirit enough to speak for you! I cannot bring myself to be a rung in the ladder you wish to climb."

She was growing angry. "Is it courage you are short of, or perhaps it is honesty?"

"Do not inflict such questions on me. I cannot doubt for a moment that I am a child of God, but I confess to you that I am a coward, unfitted to appear beside you while you utter what you believe to be the truth."

"I *know* it is the truth, and so do you."

"For a lardy old tomcat nearing sixty," Tennie thought, "he's pretty spry." He leaped up on the chesterfield beside her sister's knees, sinking in the stuffing, and turned the faucets on full force. "I beseech thee, torture me no longer. Have pity. Let me be."

She shook his hands off her sleeve. "You shall have whatever you deserve."

"What is your intention? What are you going to tell them?"

They had scarcely got home before a messenger boy tugged at the doorbell. Beecher had evidently dragged Frank Moulton in as referee, because it was to his house that Victoria was invited for another round with Henry that afternoon. This time, Theodore added himself to the team.

The mixture as before was doled out in Moulton's parlor. Beecher was still pleading for mercy. "After you left me, Sister Woodhull, down went heart, down went hope, and down came tears until I cried them all away. I reflected that it is our duty in this world to work out an exceeding great reward in the world to come. The path before me is all the way full of Christ, and what is His most precious teaching? 'But the greatest of these is charity.' Dear Sister, show charity in your heart and a place will be yours in heaven."

No dice with Victoria. Everybody knew what was on her mind without her dropping hints about it, but Tilton was in no more hurry to be shown up a cuckold than Beecher was to be branded a lecher. Theodore broke in to remind the preacher that he could announce from the platform that while he didn't condone free love, he was a lifelong believer in free speech as guaranteed by the Constitution.

No dice with Beecher. Victoria's stare was as menacing as a

butcher knife. Tears were soaking his collar. "Oh, if it must come, let me know it twenty-four hours in advance that I may take my life. I cannot, cannot face the horror."

Victoria heard enough. "If you compel me to go upon that platform alone tomorrow, I shall begin by telling the audience why I am alone and why you are not with me."

The town had been plastered with posters: VICTORIA C. WOOD-HULL WILL SPEAK AT STEINWAY HALL AT EIGHT P.M. ON THE PRINCIPLES OF SOCIAL FREEDOM, INVOLVING THE QUESTION OF FREE LOVE, MARRIAGE, DIVORCE, AND PROSTITUTION. Everything on the list was a guaranteed attraction, as she knew from past experience. A mob of people was milling around outside the entrance a full hour ahead of time, most as respectable-looking as could be found at the Psyche Club, with a sprinkling of roughnecks jostling them—three thousand in all by box-office count.

Victoria's team—Jim, Andrews, and the rest—was out in force, together with Utica, who'd been nipping whiskey since breakfast time. Theodore was missing, and there was no sign of Beecher, though Tennie couldn't picture him reaching for a razor until he'd been told what Victoria had to say. Victoria looked imposing in black with a tea rose pinned to her collar. Tennie gave reporters a treat of her own by flashing her gaiters for them, worn because it was raining and windy outside.

Just before eight, Theodore arrived with Frank Moulton. Victoria, getting jumpy, clutched Tilton's arm. "There isn't a man in the circle of two cities brave enough to preside here tonight." Theodore got the message: Five minutes from now the audience might learn he was the cuckoo in the nest with Beecher and Mrs. Tilton. When Victoria headed for the platform, he took after her, muttering something about "No one else has the pluck to do it." Tennie climbed the stairs to a box where some of Andrews's Pantarchy followers were sitting with a view straight across the hall of Utica swaying in her chair in another box.

Theodore opened with some valid comments concerning gentlemen he didn't care to name who'd declined the job he was volunteering for. "It may be that she is a fanatic. It may be that I am a fool. But before high heaven I would rather be both fanatic and fool in one than to be such a coward as would deny a woman the right of free speech."

That set the crowd off cheering, but it was nothing like the welcome Victoria was given as she came to the fore, face white but for a patch of red in each cheek. She sounded as prim as a parson's wife as she denounced the way marriage shackled all parties foolish enough to get trapped in it. "The law cannot compel two to love. . . . Two people are sexually united, married by nature, united by God. . . . All compelling laws of marriage are despotic, being remnants of the barbaric age. . . . It is better to break a bad bargain than to keep it. . . . All that is good and commendable now existing would continue to exist if all marriage laws were repealed tomorrow."

She'd been speaking for ten or fifteen minutes, and still there wasn't a mention of Beecher. Tennie debated whether Victoria had let him off the hook by reason of Theodore's stepping forward, or whether she was saving him for frying later. The applause was steady by now, but hissing was breaking out, too. Victoria put aside Andrews's pages and struck out for the edge of the platform. "If any gentleman or lady who is hissing—"

"It ain't a gentleman nor a lady, neither." Somebody cut in on her.

"If they will come up here with me—"

"May I say something?" Utica was on her feet, with help from the brass rail of the box. "How would you like to come into this world without knowing who your father or mother was?" Tennie thought anybody would admit this sister of hers made a pretty picture, except for the circles alcohol had put under her blue eyes.

She broke up the performance for the time being. A fair number of the crowd raised a cheer because she was making a point they agreed with. Men waved their hats and women their handkerchiefs to show they were with her all the way.

Victoria's tone grew shrill. "There are thousands of noble men and women in the world today who never knew who their fathers were." More hisses from one side, more cheers from the other, but in the middle of the hubbub, Utie let go of the rail and sat down. Victoria picked up where she'd left off, delivering the gospel according to Andrews, which wrapped a lot of claptrap around a few small grains of truth.

When Utica piped up again, nobody could make out a word she said in the din. One of Andrews's friends had his own idea of how far she should be allowed to proceed when she was drunk, so he scampered downstairs to fetch the police. Theodore popped up and started to shout, but no one was listening. Victoria screamed up at Tennie, "Can't you get her out of here?"

She was willing to try, but it was slow going, elbowing through the crush. The officer in blue got there ahead of her. Utica let out a shriek. "Let go of me! I'm her sister." Most of the crowd were on her side, and their yelling showed it. "Throw him out, not her! She's got the right! Free speech! Shame! Shame!"

Theodore was beside himself. "Order, if you please! Chair! Chair! Will you please take your seats?" It worked in the end. Tennie told the patrolman she could handle Utica, then helped her out the door and into a hansom, handing two dollars to the driver.

Tennie got back to her seat just in time for the finale. Somebody from the floor bawled at Victoria, "Are you a free lover?"

She was already in a passion, and she answered clear as a bell. "Yes, I am a free lover." That brought on such an uproar Tennie figured the walls would cave in, but Victoria pushed on. "I have an inalienable, constitutional, and natural right to love whom I may, to love as long or as short a period as I can, to change that love every day if I please. And with that right neither you nor any law you can frame has any right to interfere."

She continued for perhaps ten minutes more, but Tennie could only pick up snatches of it. "I love you all . . . disturb your confidence in the old dead past . . . living so nobly that the best cannot fail to be drawn to me by an irresistible attraction." Beecher was let off scot-free.

The two sisters rode home with Jim and Theodore. Nobody had much to talk about, though Tilton shook his head and whispered to Jim, "She said *violent* things."

Next morning, the elders of Plymouth Church made a move to expel Theodore for his part in the evening's entertainment, but he resigned of his own accord. A different situation developed on East

38th Street. They hadn't counted on the landlord evicting them on the grounds he couldn't accept free lovers as tenants at any price. Moving everybody into a boardinghouse on 23rd Street was no particular challenge when most of the fixtures and furniture had been sold already to keep the *Weekly* afloat. But Victoria's speech finally burst the bubble on Broad Street. "Free love," Tennie said wryly, "is a drug on the stock market."

She couldn't consider Victoria a prime favorite in the White House handicap when she'd turned out to have such talent for antagonizing an audience. The sisters were running out of money as well as luck; they hadn't a home to call their own, and the deadbeats still hung on with no thought of looking for paid employment. Yet it wasn't in Victoria then to complain about trouble. When the invitations began to flow for her to travel the lecture circuits, she was off like a shot, glad of the chance to pay the bills from the printer.

Her disposition was soured by the way the world in general treated her. Both she and Tennie saw red, and that literally. It was a satisfaction to march with five or six hundred members and friends of the International from Cooper Union to 34th Street and Fifth Avenue ahead of four black horses hauling a hearse with a kind of shroud on it saying "To the Martyred of the Universal Republic." That meant the Parisians who had been executed by Thiers's soldiers. Every marcher wore a red ribbon or a red tie. They sang out, "The Internationale unites the human race," and Tennie hoisted a red banner calling for COMPLETE POLITICAL AND SOCIAL EQUALITY FOR BOTH SEXES. "As I recollect, it made an altogether dandy day," she reported.

She admitted to having changed. Victoria had a way of doing that to some people, not excluding her sister. Tennie let off steam. "What gets my goat worse than anything now is the bigots who put it over on women, and we've seen more than our share of them. Society's plain rotten to the core when the better half of the citizens, our sex, can be robbed, abused, and trampled on without legal comeback. The churches are a farce when every religion's a HE religion and the only woman who's won much more than a nod from anybody but Catholics is Mother Mary. Every sort of government, whether there's a king or a president on top of the pile, is built on the idea that men are almighty and women only made to serve them. The lords of creation take it for granted that women are weak and they're the strong ones, which is another horse-laugh when a woman's power over men and over herself, too, is greater than anything a man can even guess at.

"Men write the laws to protect themselves when they go whoring; it's always the girls and not the customers who get dragged off in the Black Maria. The swine risk collecting a dose they pass on to the virgins they marry and their children are going to be born diseased in mind and muscle. If it's a disgrace for a girl to screw around before she has a wedding ring, then the same should hold true for men. If it's wrong to mother a bastard, then it's just as wrong to father one. If hookers are treated like dirt, the same should apply to the whoremongers and pimps who run the panelhouses, and the other noble specimens of manhood who prostitute themselves by toadying to their bosses to hold down a job."

Victoria thought it time for Tennie to have her say in public. Ten thousand people jammed into the Academy of Music to hear her lecture on "The Ethics of Sexual Equality." There were women in furs and women in threadbare shawls. There were bankers and bootblacks, stockbrokers and peddlers. Utica stayed home with a bottle. Jim had a hand in writing down some of Tennie's thoughts, but the windup was all her own work.

"Women must *come up,* or men must *come down.* Our mission is but commenced; the battle is opened. We ask no quarter and take no prisoners. Having set our hand to the plow, we will not look back, nor turn aside until our work is done. The world shall know the wrongs women suffer and the men who inflict them. We propose to tear off the hypocritical mask and expose their moral deformity to the gaze of all eyes." She knew enough about some of the men in the audience to bet she'd put the fear of God into them. She was given a round of cheers from the crowd on the sidewalk as the rented hack took her away.

She would have gone on making speeches but for the fact that somebody had to look after earning the bread and butter at the *Weekly* when Victoria was concentrating on casting around for political backing, and it was already January of election year. Victoria had had a stroke of luck when Susan Anthony invited her to Washington for another annual convention of the National Women, though she had to dip into the till to buy the new smart blue broadcloth suit and chinchilla-collared coat she wore in order to look like a winner.

Susan came out strong for her, sitting her at her side on the platform and praising her to the skies. "I have been asked by many, 'Why did you drag Victoria Woodhull to the front?' Now, bless your souls, she was not dragged to the front. She came to Washington with a powerful argument. She presented her Memorial to Congress, and it was a power. She had an interview with the Judiciary Committee. We could never secure that privilege. She was young, handsome, and rich, and I bet you cash is a big thing with Congress." That set them off chuckling, but Victoria didn't so much as smile.

"If it takes youth, beauty, and money to capture Congress, Victoria is the woman we are after. I was asked by the editor of a New York paper if I knew Mrs. Woodhull's antecedents. I said I didn't and that I did not care any more for them than I do about those of the members of Congress. I have been asked, 'What about Woodhull? You make her your leader?' Now we don't make leaders; they make themselves."

When Victoria got the floor, she tried to light every burner. She lauded the virtues of spiritualism and one of Andrews's pet schemes, "a Constitution of the United States of the World." She called for the ladies to form an Equal Rights Party and make her its candidate for President. A woman from Wisconsin stood up to nominate her, but Miss Anthony ruled that this was rushing things. Victoria may have overstepped the mark with her, or perhaps she was disgruntled because *The Revolution* had just folded, but in any event Susan also dismissed spiritualism and Andrews's Constitution. The one and only goal, she said, must be votes for women. It was Miss Anthony, not Mrs. Woodhull, who got a hearing from the Senate Judiciary Committee, but Susan made no more progress with them than had Victoria the previous year.

Mrs. Woodhull crossed swords with one Senator before she left for New York. The suffragists had given up hope that the Fourteenth and Fifteenth Amendments would ever be stretched to cover women. What they were after now was a Sixteenth Amendment that would go off to each of the thirty-seven states of the Union to be ratified. That, at least, was what they counted on. Meantime, Victoria and the rest of the National Women grabbed any chance that came along to buttonhole a bigwig and coax him into a favorable frame of mind for the day Number Sixteen was put into the works.

But she *did* have a talent for antagonizing people without even trying. When she bumped into Carpenter of Wisconsin in the halls of the Capitol, she called him a traitor to the Movement and threatened to stump his State to blacken his name.

"But the women of Wisconsin are all my friends."

"You don't say! And if rumors are true, you've some lady friends in other states, too, not to mention here in Washington City."

"If you don't watch what you're saying, my good woman, I see you winding up in a prison cell."

"If you people think that's going to help you, go ahead and do it. I've no objections. We'll raise five hundred women to go around the country, letting the voters know exactly what kind of men represent them here in Congress."

If her words carried the scent of blackmail, it was not unintended. She and Tennie had given some thought to blackmail on the part of women and judged it to be a legitimate enterprise. When a man could beat a woman half to death, rape her, rob her, and more likely than not have the judge on his side if she took him to court, then blackmail had to be considered one way to get even.

Both of them felt sorry for Josie Mansfield when her previous keeper, Jim Fisk, hauled her into Yorkville Police Court together with her new lover, Ned Stokes, who'd lived in her house on 23rd Street. Blackmail was the charge Fisk laid against the two of them. All they'd done was warn him they would publish the letters he'd written her when she was the light of his eye and his wife was tucked away in Boston. They were driven to that after he cut Josie off without a cent to spite her for pushing him out of her life.

Tennie went into court that morning to take a look at the man she'd envisioned on his deathbed back in the days when the Erie Railroad undercut Vanderbilt and she was the Commodore's darling. It seemed that years had passed since she'd taken a crack at predictions, and she wasn't anxious to try now when there were warmer irons in the fire.

Jim Fisk came up to her expectations. He was rigged out in a navy-blue uniform with lashings of gold braid and double rows of brass buttons. He looked disturbed by the attention he was attracting, but Ned Stokes, a dude in a white overcoat with a diamond ring on one hand and a gold-nobbled cane in the other, was taking it in his stride. Josie couldn't keep her eyes off him except when she was batting them at the judge.

Josie, dolled up in lavender gloves, a feathered alpine hat, black silk, white satin, and a black velvet mantle, was a daisy, Tennie acknowledged to herself. In the matter of appearance, she gave her points over Susan Anthony. Tennie had to respect the courage in Josie, but she herself didn't choose to be a kept woman.

Blackmail was only part of Josie's game. She was busy on one hand suing Fisk for $50,000, which she said was her right for past favors rendered, and, on the other, for libeling her by publishing an affidavit to the effect that she and Stokes were a pair of extortionists.

The courtroom crowd was so obviously on Josie's side that Fisk walked out halfway through the proceedings, and the judge called a recess. But that afternoon, a grand jury indicted Stokes and Josie as blackmailers. The "Prince of Erie," as Fisk was tagged, stopped by later in the day at the new Grand Central Hotel on Broadway and Fourth Street and started up the stairs to the second floor. Stokes was waiting for him there, still in the white overcoat, but he'd exchanged the cane for a pistol.

He put two bullets into Fisk before he was grabbed. Fisk lived through the night in a hotel bedroom, but in the morning he was dead, just as Tennie had told the Com he was destined to be. She thought that for old times' sake she'd go around to Washington Place, remind the Commodore of her earlier prediction about Fisk, and perhaps at the same time collect the Woodhull, Claflin cash he was still holding onto. But the butler wouldn't let her pass beyond the front hall. "Madame's orders," he said.

"My compliments to Mrs. Vanderbilt. You have my permission to advise her to get herself stuffed."

Victoria held her fire until the uproar over the murder of Fisk had quieted down. Then she rented the Academy of Music again, to pull the trigger in a speech billed as "The Impending Revolution"; she was relying on this speech to get as much space in the newspapers as her earlier outburst in Steinway Hall. Every ticket was sold in advance, and an army of people had to be turned away. She wasn't looking for anyone to introduce her this time. She walked out on the stage alone to lay into the tycoons for enslaving their employees.

"A Vanderbilt may sit in his office and manipulate stocks or declare dividends by which in a few years he amasses fifty million dollars from the industries of the country, and he is one of the remarkable men of the age. But if a poor, half-starved child should take a loaf of bread from a Vanderbilt cupboard to appease her hunger, she would be sent to the Tombs."

That put Mr. and Mrs. Cornelius in their place until another day. John Jacob Astor came up next. "If a tenant of his, discharged by his employer because he did not vote the Republican ticket, fails to pay his month's rent to Mr. Astor, the law sets him and his family into the street."

A.T. Stewart, the department store proprietor? "A poor man who should come along with a bolt of cloth which he had smuggled into the country and could sell at a lower price than Mr. Stewart would be cast into prison. . . . These three individuals represent the principal methods that the privileged classes have invented to monopolize the accumulated wealth of the country."

Not a line of the speech was reported in any newspaper but the *Weekly*. The *Times* dusted her off in an editorial: "She is capable of mischief in inflaming the unthinking hostility of the poor to the rich, and in fostering in the minds of the working men who applauded her during her recent lecture the conviction that capitalists have no rights which workingmen are bound to respect."

Victoria flew off the handle. "I refuse to be ignored, and I won't be put down. We'll meet cunning with cunning, fraud with fraud."

In other words, twist a few arms with a touch of blackmail. She left the details to Tennie while she sorted out her plans for a brand-new political party that would make her its candidate.

Jim and Tennie wrote the invitation and had it set in type: "Have you been deceived, maltreated, abandoned or, to comprise it all in one word, beat? Write out your experience, state the plain truth, give names and incidents with all possible particularity. Send these statements to *Woodhull & Claflin's Weekly* that they may be published and sent broadcast over the land—that like Cain, wherever one of these men go, his infamy may follow him, so that the publicity of his crime may incite him to retrieve his dishonor or deter others from his acts."

One letter they printed was signed "Mary Bowles," but "Tennie Claflin" would have been closer to the truth. "Mary" said that at twenty she had been working in a brothel when she discovered she was equipped at her top end with such a head for business that very soon she had a house of her own, keeping a written record of the names, addresses, and requirements of every customer from the day she opened up.

"If you, in the prosecution of your blessed mission as a social reformer, have any need to see more behind the scenes and understand the real state of New York society better, I will give you access to my two big books. You will find in them doctors of divinity to counter-jumpers and runners for mercantile houses."

Tennie put her own name to the answer. The important part came last. "I curse and denounce a virtue which is forced on women as slaves by men who are themselves steeped in the same vice. I have to associate with male prostitutes in my business, in the family, everywhere, and if I then condemn and avoid women of equally bad character, am I not glaringly false and treacherous to the dignity and equality of my sex? In respect to the books you speak of, I do not know what use can be made of them, for my sister and myself have scrupulously adopted the policy of avoiding personalities when possible. But the time may come when that policy will have to be abandoned, for our enemies do not scruple to resort to them in the most scandalous manner."

She explained to Jim: "I calculate there's no shortage of brothel creepers among our male subscribers. If I can get them fretting that they've been listed in the ledgers of Mary Bowles, they'll be ready to cough up hard cash to keep their names out of future issues."

Before there was time for the trick to work, Utica produced another crisis. Woodhull had been poorly served by his own profession. He'd been living for the most part on a diet that came either in bottles or needles ever since Victoria had taken him in. When he started looking seedier than usual in March, she called in a doctor, who took him off morphine. Woodhull managed without it for a month—no longer. Jim spent most of that month nursing him, and he was there at the end.

Utica took herself off to tell the coroner she suspected that Victoria had ushered Woodhull into his coffin. "I want revenge," said Utica, who missed having a companion to drink with. The only thing was to conduct a post-mortem. The verdict: pneumonia. Victoria was willing to let bygones be bygones, and the notice in the *Weekly* praised him as "one of the most skillful physicians." Jim received a pat on the head, too. "These two people were not rivals. They were brothers, and in spite of all the attempts to make them enemies, they remained friends to the last." If Byron missed his father, he never said so—but Byron had little to say about anything.

"Mary Bowles" was a disappointment. Five or six nervous readers dropped in at the office on the pretense of offering their congratulations for publishing such revelations. Tennie kept two thick ledgers on hand strictly for show because the pages were blank, but callers didn't detect that. She pried a few hundred dollars out of them. Then the sisters changed their tack and went after easier money.

None of the women they had set their sights on could be considered a true friend of Victoria's. Laura Curtis Bullard, for instance, who'd tried to bail out *The Revolution,* offered not a cent to help her, and Mrs. Bullard was an heiress to the Dr. Winslow's Soothing Syrup fortune. They felt she deserved to be at the head of the list, so they set about spinning some fables concerning her, sending them to the printer, and having him pull a set of galley proofs.

It was Tennie's job to go around to see Mrs. Bullard and other ladies scheduled for the same treatment. "You might take a gander

at something we've got in mind for next week's issue." She handed
Mrs. Bullard the galleys. "We like to play fair, you know."

Mrs. Bullard primped her hairpiece, squinted through her lor-
gnette, and started to read the article headed "Tit for Tat." "My
Lord, there's not a word of truth in it! How can you write such
dreadful things? I've never been divorced. I am not 'inflated with
pretension.' Who will believe such dreadful lies?"

"Most anybody who reads 'em in cold print."

"What on earth prompts you and your sister to such wickedness?"

"Stark necessity. If you and your kind aim to do Sis in, we'll take
a few of you down with us. You can put that in your pipe and
smoke it."

"You shall not get away with it. I will consult my attorneys."

"You can't squeeze blood out of stones. There's a cheaper
way. . . ." Tennie walked out with five hundred dollars and left the
proofs as a tribute to Mrs. Bullard's charity. "One way or the other,
apart from cracking safes," said Tennie, "I've got to keep the money
rolling in or else Sis will be done for."

Victoria nearly came unstuck at that point. An announcement in
the *Weekly* said that at the May meeting of the National Woman
Suffrage Association, to be held in Steinway Hall, "the undersigned
citizens" would form the "People's Party" to pick candidates for
President and Vice President of the United States. One of the "undersigned" was Mrs. Stanton, another was Isabella Hooker, and
they'd given Victoria their consent in advance. A third was Susan
Anthony, who knew nothing about it, and she protested that she'd
been hoodwinked.

There only was a small turnout for the meeting. Mrs. Stanton
called Miss Anthony "narrow," and Isabella said she was a "bigot."
But they stopped short of fighting with hatpins, and Susan was
elected number one among the Nationals in place of Mrs. Stanton.
Victoria said the People's Party wouldn't object to sharing the self-
same hall, but Susan declined the suggestion. That left Victoria to
scurry around the street outside looking for a place of her own to
hire, which she found in Apollo Hall.

Mrs. Woodhull went back in to face Miss Anthony and lure the
audience from Steinway to Apollo for tomorrow's session. Susan

worked her gavel overtime to knock down the proposal, but Victoria kept talking. Susan proved who was in charge at the moment by slipping off to find the janitor and order him to turn the gas off at the main to put out all the lights. That was the end of everything between her and Victoria. But Tennie had this to say for Susan: "Not a brick was slung by the old mare when they were raining down on us thick and heavy."

They counted five or six hundred people in Apollo Hall the following morning—Spiritualists, Socialists, men from the International, National Women, free lovers, readers of the *Weekly*, Andrews—but none of the other Claflins. Victoria had to get everything signed, sealed, and delivered that day if possible. Otherwise she'd incur extra rent for a second performance.

The first item of business was to drop "People's" and rename the gathering the Equal Rights Party. Next, Victoria let rip with a speech. "From this convention will go forth a tide of revolution that shall sweep the whole world. . . . A revolution shall sweep with resistless force if not fury over the whole country to purge it of political trickery, despotic assumption, and all industrial injustice." That was calculated to ginger up the sixty thousand men and women on strike to make eight hours the standard workday in New York City. Police nightsticks were being applied to persuade the strikers to return to their jobs.

The result was a foregone conclusion. The moment Victoria sat down that evening, she won the nomination. "All in favor say Aye." The roar they put up might have been heard clear across in Brooklyn City Hall. Hats sailed up to the ceiling. Women wept. Men jumped up on their seats and yelled themselves hoarse. Victoria was on her way, and she deluded herself into believing she might reach her goal.

As an afterthought, somebody remembered they'd overlooked nominating a candidate for Vice President. One man named an Indian because Indians were treated worse than anybody. A woman proposed Jim Blood, so he wouldn't be left a grass widower when Victoria was away in the White House. But they finally settled on Frederick Douglass to balance the ticket, since he'd represent the oppressed race and Victoria the oppressed sex. He would read about that in the morning papers, since he wasn't in the hall nor had he been invited.

Victoria was cock-a-hoop during the next week or so. She told the newspapers she counted a certain million votes safe in her pocket, with more coming in every day. She told one reporter about floating a 7 percent bond issue to pay for her campaigning. "We shall raise two hundred thousand dollars or twice or thrice that sum if needed." She imagined she could win hands down over Grant, when half the Republican Party was hostile to giving him another four years in office, and as for Horace Greeley, the Democrats' choice, why, he was such a dud, nobody in his right mind would vote for him.

Theodore Tilton went out to Cincinnati to help nominate Greeley, and Victoria couldn't forgive his treachery. Tennie had a feeling that Greeley was doomed to lose when a picture in her head showed him laid out in a coffin in City Hall after the ballots had been counted. Victoria took this as another omen of victory in November. There was one handicap that Jim detected, though he decided against telling her about it. A look at the Constitution told him that no one under the age of thirty-five could qualify for President. Victoria was fifteen months shy of the mark.

She had a letter from Frederick Douglass, who had acquired an impressive way with words after freeing himself from chattel slavery in a Baltimore shipyard. "I have never yet been able to find one consideration, one argument or suggestion in favor of man's right to participate in civil government which did not equally apply to the right of women." But he worshipped Lucretia Mott. "I saw before me no more a woman but a glorified presence bearing a message of light and love from the Infinite." Mrs. Mott had declined to extend her hand to Mrs. Woodhull; therefore, Mr. Douglass sent regrets—he couldn't run in harness with Victoria. Yet a black vote and a white vote had equal value. Even without Douglass, she'd round up men of color on her own. Tennie got busy again.

Jim Fisk, enraptured with uniforms as well as women, had been colonel of the 9th Regiment of the National Guard, made up exclusively of Negroes. Tennie applied for the job and was turned down. She thought it was worth another try, and this time she sweetened the bait. The 85th Regiment, also black, was short of uniforms. She offered a deal: Name her colonel, and she'd dress them up like rainbows.

Meantime, another landlord was harassing the Claflins. They were thrown out of 23rd Street because the owner there took offense at the revolutionary tone of Victoria's speeches. When they went house-hunting again, nobody would give them a lease or even pass the time of day. Hotels didn't want them, either, until at last they found a berth in the Gilsey by bribing a room clerk while the manager was out of town.

Four lieutenants of the 85th arrived in a carriage to take Tennie to watch a drill. The manager of the Gilsey watched them pull up. "If you go off with those men, you need not come back." She refused to be bullied. When she was delivered back to the hotel, the Claflins had been locked out of their rooms, with their luggage piled up on the sidewalk.

They walked the streets of New York that night—Victoria, Jim Blood, Byron, and Tennie—for want of anywhere else to go. The sky was pink over the Hudson River when they turned toward Broad Street. The front door of Number 44 was bolted and barred, but Jim climbed over the transom and let them in. They dozed on the office floor until mid-morning, and they went on spending their nights there for weeks. It was a rare way to run in an election. Tennie couldn't scratch up the money to buy the uniforms, so another deal fell through. She never did get to be commissioned a colonel.

Nine

———⟡———

"A fox in a henhouse," Tennie commented, "would have a warmer welcome." The instant the owner heard they were sleeping in his building, he jumped the rent by one thousand dollars a year, cash in advance. They could no more raise that kind of money than fly off to the moon. They trudged the streets again searching for any sort of rental—hotel, house, or office—and got nowhere: Victoria's name was mud. Then Margaret Ann stepped in and put her name on a lease for rooms on East 24th Street and a cheap little cubbyhole at Number 48 Broad.

By then, their cash was gone, and the printer's bills were still piling up. The *Weekly* was all Victoria really had to support her in the race, though the Equal Rights Party had come up with an anthem, sung to the tune of "Comin' Through the Rye":

> *Yes! Victoria we've selected*
> *For our chosen head;*
> *With Fred Douglass on the ticket*
> *We will raise the dead.*

Raising the dead and getting them registered was Victoria's only hope of winning, in Tennie's opinion, but there was no gain in telling her sister so.

By way of the *Weekly*, they set up what they called the Victoria League. Anybody reading about it could only conclude that Mrs. Woodhull was going to run her competition into the ground come November. She had noted in print that "a Victoria rules the great rival nation" and it would be "a new security of peace if a twin sisterhood of Victorias were to preside over the two nations." It took courage to write such stuff when she was no more than a jump away from the poorhouse.

The League had a platform, mostly put together by Andrews. It was devised to appeal to anybody who felt that between Republicans and Democrats the country was speeding to hell in a hack: a brand-new Constitution; a vote for everybody, man and woman alike; schooling instead of prison for criminals; income taxes to hobble the rich; Government jobs for the unemployed; the Government to take over the mines and the gas and water companies; countries settling their differences by debate instead of war, and this as a prelude to their cooperation in running the world for the good of everybody, not only the rich and the powerful.

Then the printer intervened: No more *Weekly* unless he was paid something on account. Victoria took it hard. "They're out to paralyze us, Tennie, in health and strength and purse." The issue of June 28 had to be the last. She wasn't given to weeping, but the tears came the day the sisters announced they were "suspending" operations until further notice.

Victoria deserved better after all she'd gone through, and Tennie did what she could to help. She called on one man with a tale about preparing to expose him as a wife beater. He grabbed her by the collar and hauled her to the top of the stairs, promising he'd pitch her down them if she ever came back. August arrived, and the creditors sued Victoria for debt. They were out of luck. There was nothing left for them to get their hands on, when every stick of furniture in the little office was borrowed and the clothes she wore hadn't been paid for.

She demanded, "Why do they persecute us so? I'll tell you.

Beecher is behind it. Other people demand rights for women. Other people practice free love. But they're not hunted and hounded like coons in the corn. Beecher's the one responsible, but he shan't get away with it. I'll fight fire with fire."

"You might burn your fingers," Tennie said.

"Then I'll glory in it. I'll have stripped off the masks and exposed him to the world for what he is, a damned lecher, a coward, and a sneak."

Her chance came in September when, dejected and intent on quitting as their president, she went to Boston for the National Spiritualists' convention. She ran into rumors that said her only purpose was to squeeze hush money out of some of the members, which was a lie—that sort of work was Tennie's affair. Victoria sailed in to spell out the whole story of Beecher, the Tiltons, and the carrying on at Plymouth Church.

"He preaches every Sunday to his mistresses, members of his church, sitting in their pews, robed in silks and satins and high respectability. I tell you this, my friends, because it is my mission to uncover hypocrisy. If any one of you feels the right to castigate me for it, then let him rise and cast the first stone!"

A down-at-heels little man shuffled to his feet and stood for a second under her stare. The crowd hissed like a nest of snakes. *Put him out! Let her finish!* When she was done, they voted her another term as leader of the association.

She restored herself, but only briefly, as a seven-day wonder. The printer dropped in with a proposition for her to mull over. If she would publish the Beecher story with no holds barred, he'd extend her credit, vowing that a special edition of the *Weekly* would set sales records. She'd be out of debt and back in business.

She debated the proposal with Tennie, Jim Blood and Andrews, who was living under his own roof at last on Sixth Avenue and 54th Street. Tennie liked the smell of easy pickings. "It's a cinch, Sis. Remember what the McFarland murder did for *The Revolution?* Beecher'll do ten times better for us."

Andrews chewed on his fingernails. "I am inclined to agree, although we should not stoop to submitting our decision to mere expediency. The paramount consideration must be how best to continue our advocacy of the principles of the Pantarchy—"

"Shove you and your principles!" Tennie hollered. "Nobody wants principles stuck down their craw every week. Why did the *Weekly* fold? Because it got too damn sluggish. What people like to read most is scandal, hot juicy scandal that'll make their hair curl. If we do it right, I warrant we can sell a hundred thousand copies."

Jim, too, had his say. "It may be Victoria's last opportunity to be heard before election. The more readers we attract, the more likely they are to cast their ballot for her. It's as simple as that. If scandal and sensationalism are required, as Tennie believes, let us serve them in good measure. In my judgment, the ends justify the means in this instance."

Victoria and her conscience fought it out again. "If I withhold the facts, am I not conniving in seething falsehood and hypocrisy and, in a sense, partaking in those same crimes? If Henry Beecher is exposed while there is still time, might he not be shamed into declaring that he stands shoulder to shoulder with me in endeavoring to hasten a social regeneration which he himself believes in. I have the power, I think, to compel him to go forward and do the duty for humanity from which he shrinks."

"So it's settled then?" said Tennie. "Let's get on with the washing. I've got a bit of dirty linen to hang out on the line myself."

Victoria and Andrews filled page after page with an account of Beecher's villainy, including a rundown of what the Tiltons and Mrs. Stanton and everybody else had said, while Tennie set about paying off someone else she'd had dealings with.

When Buck applied an ear to the keyhole and heard Tennie was taking aim at Luther C. Challis, broker on Wall Street, he advised her to drop it. "You and your sister had better watch your step or you'll land in the poop for sure. Whether you know it or not, there's a new law in the land since your paper went under. It says on no account can you send obscene literature through the mails."

"And just what do you reckon they mean by 'obscene' literature?"

He winked his eye. "I'd say half the stuff you write might qualify."

Perhaps she should have listened to Buck for once in her life, but she'd lost all patience with him. "The Philosophy of Modern Hypocrisy—Mr. L.C. Challis the Illustration" was the title she chose for her contribution to the *Weekly*, due to go on the street and into

the surviving list of subscribers' mailboxes on Monday, October 28
—eight days left before the election.

She told about going with Victoria to the masked ball at the
Academy of Music and meeting Challis and his friend. She needed
no prompting to remember everything. "We made ourselves known
to them, and they joined us, accompanied by two young girls not
more than fifteen or sixteen years of age. These girls had come on
fresh from school in Baltimore, in the best society of New York had
fallen in with these middle-aged roués, and had in their innocence
been led by them in the ways that lead to ruin. Wine was called
for, and while the men drank but little, these young girls were plied
with it. . . .

"You may be sure I followed these girls up and got the history of
their connection with these men. They were seduced by them. This
scoundrel Challis, to prove he had seduced a maiden, carried for
days on his finger, exhibiting it in triumph, the red token of her
virginity. We would ask why men should not be held up equally to
the scorn of the world instead of people being called the 'worst
women' and the 'best men.' "

Andrews and Jim had qualms about laying into Challis, but she
stood her ground. Andrews wrote a long-winded introduction to her
report which she felt took much of the sting out of what had poured
out so fast and fresh. Victoria dropped a hint of things to come into
her own masterpiece: "We have five hundred biographies of various
persons in all circles of life, many of which persons are the present
oracles of society, the facts of which biographies are similar to those
presented in this article."

American News, the company that had handled the distribution
of the *Weekly* before, backed away after someone there inspected a
copy straight off the press. American News concluded the stories
about Beecher and Challis made a combination too hot to handle.
Consequently, the whole press run was dumped at Number 48
Broad. But word got out that trouble was about to pop, and the
lineup of dealers and newsboys blocked the street as they waited to
pick up bundles of the special.

They couldn't sell them fast enough. By the end of the day,
150,000 copies had been distributed, and the printer was running

off more. Victoria opened up half a case of champagne, and Jim forecast sales would hit the million mark or even two by the end of the week. Four cents was the newsdealers' share of the dime a reader paid; Woodhull, Claflin & Company got the rest. All being well, they might have a hundred thousand dollars to share between them. From a variety of friends who stopped by, they heard that copies were already going for fifty cents apiece, which left Tennie wishing they had at least doubled the printed price. They also heard that Beecher and his cronies were buying *Weeklys* by the dozen to keep them out of other hands. "That's no skin off our noses when all it does is fatten the bankroll. There hasn't been a peep so far out of Tilton or Challis, has there?"

Since American News still stayed clear, all shoulders had to be applied to the wheel. Help from any friend was welcome as the two sisters, with Jim and Margaret Ann, spent Tuesday through Friday trotting around in cabs and carriages, dropping off more copies at newsstands. Such a mountain of cash was piling up they could afford to laugh when they heard that a single copy was changing hands for ten, twenty, forty dollars, and some early customers were renting theirs for a dollar a day.

There was one reader they had overlooked. Anthony Comstock was chief scout and executioner for the Committee for the Suppression of Vice set up by the Young Men's Christian Association—the Young Mules' Concubine Association, as Victoria termed them. Just what hand he was playing was unknown to them until the weekend. What happened, in fact, was that after he'd lingered over the stories about Beecher and Challis, he consulted with Henry Bowen at the *Independent*—who had sent one of his clerks to the Broad Street office to pick up some copies and put them in the mail to Comstock so he could invoke the obscenity laws.

The first the sisters knew about it came just after the clock on Trinity Church had struck noon on Saturday. Tennie and Victoria were sitting in a livery-stable carriage, as it turned out of Broad Street, with three thousand fresh *Weeklys* at their feet. Two United States marshals flagged them down with a warrant for their arrest that also called for seizing every last copy of the paper, breaking up the type, and commandeering their ledgers. One marshal perched himself up beside the driver, the other sprawled across their laps in case they were tempted to make a run for it.

Next stop was the Federal Building, United States District Court —three days to go before the polls opened. The sisters picked up a few tidbits of information during the course of the afternoon. Challis was after them, too, with a Jefferson Market Court warrant on a charge of libel. Jim Blood was in for it, and so was Andrews, though he was swearing that he'd broken all connections with the *Weekly* as far back as last January and knew nothing of Challis until today.

The idea was that, for a start, the two women would be examined in private, but neither of them would accept that. "We wish the public to be thoroughly acquainted with every fact in the case," said Victoria. "We are not unaware of our rights, women though we are. We demand counsel." It took a while for them to persuade old Judge Reymart to defend them, but then the pace picked up.

The Assistant District Attorney, General Noah Davis, would have had them convicted on the spot if he'd had his way. "Not only have the defendants, by circulating an obscene publication through the mails, committed an offense against the law, but they have been guilty of a most abominable and unjust charge against one of the purest and best citizens of this state or in the United States, and they have as far as possible aggravated the offense by a malicious and gross libel upon the character of the gentleman, whose character is well worth the while of the Government of the United States to vindicate."

He had to mean Beecher, not Challis, yet Beecher wasn't claiming they had wronged him as far as they had been told. Davis was muddying up the water for his own ends. Reymart soon caught onto that. "The idea of the Government vindicating or defending the character of a gentleman is entirely outside of this case."

United States Commissioner Osborn, serving as judge and jury, was another of Davis's kind. "An example is needed, and we propose to make one of these women." He set the price of bail at eight thousand dollars a head. "Hearing next Tuesday morning, ten o'clock," said Osborn. The clerk reminded him about the election, which had him advance the date to Monday afternoon.

Reymart thought they'd be better off without bail. "In all likelihood you would be arrested on the Challis warrant as soon as you put your foot outside these doors. That could mean your being confined in Jefferson Market prison, which is a hell hole, if you'll forgive the expression. This way you'd go to Ludlow Street, which is considerably more comfortable."

They took his word for it, and he wasn't far wrong. Cell Number 11 was a tight fit for two, being no more than eight feet by four, but the sheets were clean and the iron cots comfortable, the food turned out to be palatable, and the deputy warden proved his heart was in the right place by lending them a book of poetry by Alexander Pope, and reading aloud excerpts containing words much bawdier than "token of virginity." By now, poor Jim was fighting off bedbugs and catamites in the Jefferson Market jail, known to the regulars as "the black hole of Calcutta."

Thanks to their jailer, Bill Gardner, they had the Sunday papers served with breakfast. Considering how much space went to Grant and Greeley, they were happy to see they hadn't been forgotten. The *Mercury* asked a deacon of Plymouth Church what Beecher had a mind to do about them. "He ain't going to say anything about it. He's going to cut the whole thing and let it go." The same paper claimed that Tennie smoked cigars, cursed like a mule skinner, and wore men's britches, so she didn't set much store by what the *Mercury* reported.

The *Dispatch* was more to her liking, talking about her "ruby lips" and "splendid teeth," and concluding, "Tennie is a pretty-looking woman, round faced, with well-cut features and a bright, animated expression." She knew what to expect from the *Times,* so she dipped into that last: "The female name has never been more disgraced and degraded than by these women."

It was a scary feeling, spending the day behind bars with the law peering at them as if aiming a shotgun with both its triggers cocked. They could make good use of the smartest lawyer in town, and that, in Bill Gardner's opinion, was William Frederick Howe of Howe & Hummel, 89 Centre Street, directly across from the Tombs. "Mind you, he won't be cheap, but he'll defend anybody for a price—cutthroats, thieves, bigamists, pimps, madams—he usually gets 'em off, too, and makes $300,000 a year at it, or so they say."

Howe was the man for them. They sent a message to his office, hoping he'd get it in time to bring him to Ludlow Street in the morning. He showed up, fat and friendly, with the look of a circus barker, in a purple coat, pantaloons patterned like a horse blanket, and a blue satin scarf with a diamond pin the size of a walnut. He said he didn't need telling about the fix they were in, because he made a point of keeping up with the news, and he'd been anticipating their call.

Davis and Osborn were back in their places in the courtroom, both disappointed that a grand jury had whisked the two prisoners out of their jurisdiction by coming up with a bill of indictment on the libel charge. Howe decided to put on a performance for everybody's benefit just the same. "My clients, these two delicate creatures who are so cruelly castigated, are the victims of a vendetta, of private malice and evil desire for vengeance on the part of persons in high places who durst not confront them before the bar of justice."

His accent provided evidence that he'd been born a London cockney. "If the creation of their devotion, their business acumen, and their passionate faith—if the *Weekly,* I say, is to be excluded from the postal services of the United States, then I foresee an evil day when future generations are denied the ineffable beauty, the boundless consolation, the immortal inspiration that uplifts the 'eart in the works of William Shakespeare, Lord Byron, and 'oly Scripture itself. I raise my voice to call upon the press throughout the land of ours to fly to the defense of these maligned but innocent women in the name of equity and the sacred cause of freedom."

Osborn called them up front to say they were discharged, but that happy state of affairs was over in a flash. Two marshals were standing by to nab them on the grand jury's bill and rush them back to Ludlow Street; there was no mention of bail. Tomorrow was Election Day, but neither Victoria nor the Equal Rights Party had been listed on any ballot; any vote for them would have to be a write-in.

She wouldn't take a bite of breakfast after Bill Gardner brought in the Wednesday-morning papers. Grant had walked all over Greeley, who was on his way to making history by collecting not a single vote in the electoral college. "If Jesus Christ had been running against Grant, He would have been defeated," Victoria cried. "If

He'd voted for you, they wouldn't have counted it, anyway, so far as I can judge," said Tennie.

They waited all week for news of how many had backed her. Susan Anthony and fifteen other women got into the booths without any squabble in Rochester, New York. All but one of them favored Grant, and the holdout wasn't for Mrs. Woodhull but for Greeley. When the final figures were in, Ulysses's score was 3,597,070, Horace's 2,834,079. According to the tally, nobody, not even Andrews, had voted for Victoria. Jim didn't get the opportunity, since he was still a prisoner.

Before the sisters were released, Greeley was dead, as Tennie knew he'd be, and Grant went to the wake in the City Hall, but by then Victoria's interest in politics had faded.

On the Friday after election, the Black Maria carried them to Jefferson Market Court and Judge Fowler to meet Luther Challis face to face. Jim would be up, too, and they intended to get him off the hook if they possibly could. Howe couldn't see why they shouldn't pin Jim with the blame for everything until Victoria explained: With him on the outside, they might manage to keep the *Weekly* going, which was her main ambition now. Howe recognized this as the only way for them to pay his bills and stay afloat, but he said he wanted Zulu Maud in court under orders to look downcast and shed a tear or two any time Fowler looked her way.

As soon as they were seated at a long wooden table, Tennie spotted Challis. "There's lobster-eyed Luther behind us, chinning with that bull-necked joker in the rumpled black suit, bow tie, and copper's boots." Victoria knew the latter right away. "That must be the self-appointed agent of Christ, Anthony Comstock."

Howe threw in a word. "In cases such as yours, the law rewards the stool pigeon by giving 'im 'alf of any fine the court may impose. Anthony Comstock looks out for 'imself as well as for the Almighty."

Tennie craned her neck to catch what Comstock was saying. "Debasing publications are sold on the streets as freely as roasted chestnuts. They are feeders for the brothels. I assure you, sir, I feel like I am stationed in a swamp at the mouth of a sewer."

Challis wagged his head, as pious as a monk. "Have no fear. I am willing to spend $100,000 if need be to see the pair of them convicted."

The clerk got them onto their feet, His Honor banged his gavel down, and they were off. When Howe's turn came, he put on a show as good as anything Beecher staged in church. First, he gave another airing to his argument that nothing worse about Challis had been printed than could be found in Shakespeare or in the Bible, Deuteronomy, Chapter Twenty-two, in particular. He borrowed the clerk's copy to find the page and read in a voice like an organ:

"If any man take a wife, and go in unto 'er, and 'ate her, and give occasion of speech against 'er, and bring up an evil name upon 'er, and say, I took this woman, and when I came to 'er, I found 'er not a maid: then shall the father of the damsel, and 'er mother, take and bring forth the tokens of the damsel's virginity unto the elders of the city in the gate."

Zulu Maud started to sniffle, and Comstock turned red as a beet. It only struck Tennie then where the words she'd written had come from—she'd remembered bits like that in the Bible Anna kept around the house.

"The poisoned Challis," as Howe called him, took the stand. According to his testimony, he had never met Tennie except at the ball, never kissed her, never given her silk underwear, never done more to the two schoolgirls than split a bottle of wine with them and his partner. He had a string of witnesses on his side to vow he was pure in heart. The most unlikely of them was Buck, who, with a grin on his lean jowls, related how he had warned his daughter about printing accusations against Challis after he'd listened in at the keyhole to her plans.

When Tennie was called before the judge, she swore Jim wasn't connected with the *Weekly*, and when Victoria followed her to the stand, she told the same story. Howe made another speech along similar lines, but Jim contradicted all three of them. "I am the agent of Woodhull, Claflin and Company, and I regard myself as subject to punishment as the principals, should the court conclude that a crime has been committed."

Comstock sat through the hearing running his fingers through his whiskers without being invited to testify to anything. The judge decided to reserve his decision, and the three accused went back behind bars, the women to take a dip in the bathtub, which was more comfort than Jim had available.

Victoria was in her clothes again and perched on the edge of her cot when the reporters paid a call. Tennie was only half dressed, but she figured that might be more help than hindrance in the circumstances. Her sister let them have a piece of her mind, feeling out of sorts with the day's proceedings.

"*O Liberty! Liberty! What crimes are committed in thy name!* Gentlemen, I am sick in body, sick in mind, sick at heart. I ask you whether, because I am a woman, I am to have no justice, no fair play, no chance through the press to reach public opinion."

One of them interrupted. "Have you heard from Theodore Tilton?"

"I have not. It is no concern of mine, nor perhaps of yours. Let me ask another question. How can anybody know why I am accused, arrested, imprisoned unless the public are allowed to see the alleged libel? If the *Weekly* is suppressed and I charged with crime, in what way can I substantiate the truth when the judge before whom I only appear as a witness constitutes himself plaintiff, prosecuting attorney, and jury?"

They were too hard-boiled to record any of that. Another butted in. "What about Miss Anthony? Is she going to help you out?"

"She is as silent as the rest. Is it not astonishing that all Christian law and civilization seems to be scared out of their senses at having two poor women locked up in jail?"

A man from the *Mercury* had a question for Tennie. "What have you got to say for yourself?"

"No more than this: You said in print I smoke cigars and use bad language. Tell your readers from me that's a goddamn lie."

Since they weren't restricted in the matter of visitors, the corridor outside the bars often held a crowd: *Weekly* readers, Victoria Leaguers, free lovers, and Spiritualists—including a woman with a black veil who was always cautioning them that their food was being poisoned—but no Tilton and no Andrews, who had dropped them like hot potatoes. The biggest crank among those visitors was George Francis Train, mentioned by Mrs. Stanton after he wanted to buy space for his preaching in *The Revolution*.

"Looking at him," said Tennie, "you'd be slow to judge there's a tile missing." He was a handsome spark, in his forties, with curly brown hair and gray eyes sharp as needles, got up in a flashy blue coat with brass buttons, white vest, black trousers, patent-leather boots, lavender kid gloves, and sealskin coat.

"Every man who throws a vote for a Negro and not for a woman has insulted his mother, his daughter, his sister, and his wife. That is my creed, and I am ready to sacrifice sacred honor, fortune, and life itself in your support. What may I do for you, no expense spared?"

His fortune was his strongest qualification. He had once had a fleet of sailing ships, and he was supposed to be worth $1,000,000, but for all that he said he was a Communist. In point of fact, he walked both sides of the street, helping to organize the Credit Mobilier with his right hand, and the Commune in Marseilles, France, with his left. Had he made his money by being crazy or was it his money that had addled his brains? Tennie couldn't decide.

"I am sure you ladies yearn to be freed from this dungeon. I shall be happy to do everything within my power to help you."

This was early November. Victoria told him about wanting people to read what the *Weekly* had originally printed so they'd appreciate the Claflins' predicament.

"I shall attend to that question by establishing a publication of my own. In it, I shall reprint your words from the *Weekly,* rejoicing in the opportunity to challenge our contemporary Titus Oates, Master Comstock, and the law, which is forever an ass. I shall bombard the newspapers with letters on your behalf, sharpening my quill and unsheathing my rapier the moment I leave you languishing in sorrow here. I am satisfied the cowardly Christian community will destroy you, if possible, to cover up the rotten state of society, but I do not intend to let them. The truths you are telling are eternal."

Victoria cooed, a turtledove. "You have been the first to come to our aid; we shall be the last to forget it."

"Speed is of the essence, and I am familiar with its exigencies. Did you know that two years ago I took it upon myself to circle the globe by land and water within the span of a mere eighty days?" No, she didn't. "Well, that was my accomplishment, and Jules Verne is relating the whole story—disguising my name, of course —in *Le Temps* at this present time."

He was in and out of the cell every day while he prepared the little paper he was going to call *Train's Ligue* for reasons he didn't bother mentioning. He was blown up with his own importance whatever he did. "Perhaps you are aware that I, too, have lived behind prison bars?" No, they weren't. "Dublin, Sixty-six; Habeas Corpus Act suspended. The war here was over, and as one of the Feinian Brotherhood I sailed to Ireland in freedom's service there. I was incarcerated, and I a friend of Louis Napoleon, the Empress Eugénie, and the Queen of Spain."

He reprinted the *Weekly's* articles about Beecher and Challis in the first issue of *Train's Ligue* as promised and felt let down when Comstock raised not a whimper. It crossed Tennie's mind to have a word with Train about Deuteronomy, Twenty-two.

"Capital idea! I pledge my word my next issue shall be an Old Testament special. Lot, Abraham, David, the Song of Solomon—I shall quote chapter and verse and demand the arrest of every Bible publisher for polluting public morality with disgusting obscenity."

One week stretched into another, with a third and fourth to follow. They checked off the hours by the clock on Essex Market until they grew so used to the chimes they scarcely heard them any more. They tried every day to get news of when they'd come up in court again, but all they heard from the warders was that the date hadn't been settled. Victoria fell deep in the dumps and talked about cutting her wrists if she could lay hold of a razor.

Every time Anna dropped in, she had them down on their knees between the cots, praying for a miracle to turn the locks and leave the doors ajar. After one session Victoria burst out, "Did you see how the walls glowed with spirit light, Tennie? I could sense myself soaring toward the throne of grace, then Jesus came to me and said, 'Stay thy hand, my child. All these things are committed to My charge. In the fullness of time, all hidden things shall be revealed, and you shall be justified where you now stand condemned.' "

"I didn't notice anything except how wicked hard this stone floor is. For my part, I'm starving for a man, but I draw the line at shacking up with jailers."

Getting bailed out, if only for an hour or two, was her main ambition. Train was so wrapped up in Bible studies that they hesitated to put out a call to him, so Howe arranged with two of

Victoria's admirers—a Dr. Ruggles and a Mr. Kiernan, both living in Beecher's parish across the river—to stand bail for the sisters at $8,000 a head.

It was the first of December when Howe, in checkerboard tunic and a gold-braided yachting cap, rolled in to take them to the Federal Building. The woman with the black veil over her face and poison on the brain was lurking in the corridor. She had a new alarm to sound today: "Don't you go! They're out to chain you up in Jefferson Market prison and set fire to the place to put an end to you."

Howe got rid of her; they went and shook hands with the bondsmen; and they were free for all of five minutes before an official with a moustache big enough to sweep the floors with approached them. "I am an officer of the Jefferson Market Court, and I have a warrant for your arrest." Challis had them whipped inside again on the old charge of libel, but this time he was calling on the laws of New York State instead of those of the United States Government.

They spent four more days in jail trying to make head or tail of the warrants that were raining down like leaves. It was always Challis and Comstock working in partnership to keep them cooped. "I'll wager my last cent," said Tennie "that Beecher and Henry Bowen have got their grimy paws in it someplace, too."

Howe was bellowing about freedom of the press while he scouted around for more bond money. On December 5 there was another hearing, the extra bail was raised, and they were out at last, just in time to get the *Weekly* out again before Christmas. Jim was free, too, on a writ of habeas corpus.

But it was a case of one man out, another in. George Train's quotations in his Old Testament issue incited Comstock to attack. He had Train indicted on the same charge as he held against the sisters: sending obscenities by mail to subscribers. Train jumped at the chance to be a martyr, wouldn't put up bail, and found himself in the Tombs, which made Jefferson Street prison look a home for waifs and strays.

Victoria poured her heart out in her Christmas issue, reciting the wrongs they'd been done until space ran out and she was forced to promise, "To be continued in next number." She committed herself and Tennie to take to the road to "sow the seed of social revolution, which, springing up, shall sweep the despots like chaff before the fan from their thrones built upon the liberties of the people. Stop the press they may, but our tongues, never!" She had a livelier turn of phrase than Andrews ever had, once she'd learned how to coin them. She laid it on, too, for Train to have his say, and he had much to complain about. Tennie explained why. "They're giving him the full treatment in a cell on Murderers' Row too small to swing a cat in, no tap water, and only a bucket to do his business in, while he calls himself champion of the people. His mates there, twenty-three of them, all due to dance for the hangman, have elected him their president."

He wrote about his experience for the *Weekly* during the five months he was in there under the heading, "Hark! From the Tombs!" In the end a city commission poked through the place and found almost every word was true.

The newspapers had raised a storm about the cat-and-mouse game the law had been playing with the sisters, which brought cash flowing in from new subscribers and sympathizers who felt the two women had been given a raw deal. There was no shortage of invitations to lecture, either. Their first engagement put them on the platform together at Cooper Union on January 9 to tell what was billed as "The Naked Truth."

They hadn't reckoned with Anthony Comstock. The minute he heard about the booking, he was after their scalps. His trick was to have a colleague in Connecticut write in for back numbers of the *Weekly* dated November 2, the one that carried the Beecher and Challis stories. In their innocence, they mailed them off and landed themselves in the mire once more.

On the morning of the lecture, Comstock put his head in around the door at Number 48 Broad with a stocking tied around his neck, looking for the three of them as before. Only Jim was there, along with some volunteers who were helping out. Jim took it calmly. "Oh, so we're arrested again, are we?"

The stocking was wrapped around a sore throat; Comstock couldn't raise more than a whisper. "In my heart, Mr. Blood, I feel God approves and what care I more? If He be pleased, I care for nothing else." He applied a sleeve to his treacly eyes. "Oh, just to do Thy will, Oh, God; just to please Thee!"

He couldn't hoodwink Jim. "Was it Beecher or Challis who put you up to this?"

"I heed no Beecher or Challis but vindicate the laws and protect the young from the leprosy of vile trash. A carriage waits for us downstairs."

Jim had a private word with one of the volunteers which sent her hurrying off in a cab to the house Margaret Ann had rented on Fourth Avenue, where her sisters had just finished breakfast. Victoria had first call on whatever time was left. Tennie scurried around packing a bag for her and getting her off the premises before Comstock and the police got their boots in the door. The cab bearing her off to the 23rd Street ferry for a breathing spell in Jersey City had barely turned the corner when they started banging the knocker.

Tennie was damned if they'd catch her like a sitting duck. "Hey, Ma! Where's the best place to hide?"

"Here in the kitchen, *liebchen*. There, you climb inside this laundry tub. I set this other one on top, so. Mind you lie still, and leave the rest to me."

Tennie heard her mother run water in the sink before she answered the door, boots following behind her as she came back. "See for yourselves, officers. My girls is gone; I do my washing. If you got nothing better to do, you get out, if you please." Boots tramped through the house for a while, then she padded into the hall to let them out, humming to herself, "*Ach, du lieber Augustin, Augustin, Augustin. . . .*"

Tennie laid low for the next three days, so she had to rely on Sis for details of the fracas that developed at Cooper Union after she'd skipped back from across the river. Patrolmen and United States marshals watched the doors to turn the crowds away: "No lecture tonight." But not everybody had faith in a policeman, and most people pushed on inside. Forty or fifty more of New York's finest were stationed within the walls on the chance Victoria would risk it. An old lady in a Quaker-gray cloak and coalscuttle bonnet hobbled down the center aisle to a front-row seat.

A bosom friend of Victoria's, Laura Cuppy Smith, tried to calm the audience after they grew restless and started clapping and stamping their feet, feeling cheated because they'd paid for tickets and received nothing in return. "The enemies of free speech have another order of arrest for Mrs. Woodhull. She cannot appear tonight lest she be thrust again into an American Bastille." Mrs. Smith said she'd fill in by reading the speech Victoria had planned on giving.

That was the cue for the ancient Quaker woman to totter up the stairs onto the platform and duck behind a pillar. Some of them seemed to think this as funny as playing hide-and-seek. Then, quick as a shot, she was in front of them—Victoria rid of cloak and bonnet, back from Jersey City, hair in a tangle, raring to go. The crowd went wild. The watchdogs stood baffled.

She stretched up her arms toward heaven and orated. Comstock was Beecher's stool pigeon, she said, and Challis his vessel of wrath. How long would it be before some mother was charged with adultery "for kissing her own baby boy"? She was intending to reprint the entire November 2 issue, and what did the law propose to do about that?

She held them spellbound for over an hour and finished up talking about "the new gospel. . . . Rising up out of our false notions of propriety and purity . . . coming to know that everything is proper which enhances happiness and injures no one and that everything whatsoever is pure that is healthful and natural . . . we shall prepare for the perfect and pure blessedness of the coming millennium of the absolute liberty of the human heart."

After a bow to the three marshals who'd stationed themselves in the wings, she held out her wrists for them to clamp the handcuffs on. "Jim Blood was already in the Ludlow Street cell Warden Gardner popped her into," Tennie reported ruefully, "which made her luckier than me in some respects, since I had a soft spot for Jim, too."

It was only an overnight stop for Victoria and Jim this time. When they were up in front of Commissioner Davenport the next morning, Howe harped again about Deuteronomy, Twenty-two, and had a bondsman ready to bail them. Two days later, Tennie decided to bite the bullet and give herself up. Everybody in court except Victoria had imagined Tennie was holed up in Jersey City. With the usual sweet smile to the man on the bench, she explained she hadn't left New York, feeling the need to nurse Margaret Ann, which was a fact—Margaret Ann had a weak stomach for the up-and-down life her sisters had involved her in.

Howe had brought in his partner, little Abe Hummel, as well as a brace of other lawyers, one from California, the other an old scallawag with liver spots on the backs of his hands. Tennie wouldn't venture a guess to Victoria about how fast their bills were being padded. The lawyers attempted to convince the judge that what had been published about Challis was no different from words in the Bible or in classics of literature. Tennie was compared favorably to Tobias Smollett, eighteenth-century novelist and ship's doctor who'd been jailed on false charges just like her because of the books he wrote. They brought up a poem, *Hudibras,* by Samuel Butler, which Howe said related "the sordid vices of the sectaries, their 'ypocrisy, their churlish ungraciousness, their greed for money and authority, their fast and loose morality, their inordinate pride, yet it is universally accepted as a masterpiece of learning and subtle casuistry."

Comstock in his undertaker's suit took the stand, and the judge made no move to check the outpour of venom. "When we arrest these people, we habitually find the most disgusting set of free lovers. The women are thin-faced, cross, sour looking, each wearing a look of 'Well, I am the boss,' and 'Oh, for a man!' The men, unworthy of the name of men, are licentious looking, sneakish, mean, contemptible, making a true man blush to be seen near them."

Howe broke in to complain that the witness was prejudicing the court against Miss Claflin and persecuting her out of sanctimonious malice. Comstock squared his shoulders. "Sometimes we serve the Master by bearing patiently, sometimes not. Something each day for Jesus? Yes, so let it be."

That touched Howe off faster than a struck match. "O Liberty, where are thy defenders? O Tyranny, are we to be again subjected to thy sway that such outrages can be perpetuated without even the pretense of legality? And is there no voice outside of these who suffer which dares raise itself to denounce it? Verily the days of Republican institutions are drawing to a close. Must it be as the poet says, 'Truth forever on the scaffold, Wrong forever on the throne'?"

Tennie marked that round as another draw, but an admirer, Dr. Ruggles, pledged five thousand dollars more in bail money, and she was let out until next time. They had one more issue of the *Weekly* on the street and another in the works when the sheriff walked into the office to collect them eleven days later as the clock chimed half past four. Challis had been trying Comstock's boots on for size and found them a fit. To top the charge of libeling him, Lobster Eyes was having them booked for sending what he termed "an obscene article" about him through the mails. Bail wasn't granted anybody when they got to the District Attorney's office through the pouring rain and found him gone for the day.

The Tombs, Centre Street, was their address that night, a long, tall, narrow building that from the outside appeared to be a likely spot for some pharaoh of Egypt to murder his mother. Inside, the whole place reeked of carbolic and stale sweat. There were four banks of cells, one above the other, going around an echoing hall and joined by bridges; guards were yawning and spitting everywhere. The turnkey who took Victoria and Tennie clattering up three flights of iron stairs to the top said they were on the finest floor in the house. Jim didn't fare so well, being locked into male quarters on the ground level which the jailer said was usually reserved for blacks, as there was a problem with rats that gnawed at the prisoners toenails while they slept. "You're just about the jolliest feller I ever did run into," Tennie told him, grinning.

She painted the scene for Anna later. "The little iron door he opened would have served just as well on a coal furnace, but there was a chronic shortage of fire and heat once he'd slammed it shut on us. A skylight, bolted and barred, was all we had to see by but for a glimmer of gaslight coming through a slot in the door that made the mildew on the walls glow green. We had an iron bedstead, a blanket, and a slop pail apiece, one rickety chair, a splintered wood table, and that was it."

Victoria took the chair, and Tennie tried out the lumps in a dirty straw mattress. "Well, leastways we've a taste of what George Train's putting himself through. I wouldn't mind paying him a call if they'd let us."

"They'd sooner torture us with hot irons or dangle us on a gibbet in the prison yard."

Tennie could understand her sister's misery. She felt that way herself, though saying so wouldn't bring much benefit to either one of them. "Where do you reckon they'll store us if Howe can't get us off, Sis? Not in here, I hope."

"Martyrs aren't allowed to choose their own stake or the kind of cordwood. But I know I must see it through to the end, and I pray for the strength to continue."

"You mean *we* must. I was the one who got us into this on account of Challis."

Water was trickling in around the edges of the skylight and dripping between the beds. Victoria got up and came over to stretch out beside Tennie. "Not *we*. The spirits have entrusted me with a mission. What I have done and shall do is a sacred duty. You work for an altogether different reason—because you believe in me. You've suffered enough. As soon as we're out of here, *we* is going to be just Jim and me."

"I like to spit in their faces, too, you know, sons of bitches! You also happen to be my sister. You've done a mountain of things for me. I owe you—always will."

"It's going to wear you down, Tennie. You'll grow weary and thwarted as I do in the middle of every night. You've spent your life supporting people. You deserve better. I'll shoulder responsibility for everything." The kiss she gave Tennie sealed the bargain for the present; Tennie never knew a more determined woman.

One closing item crossed Tennie's mind. "Ever thought of pulling in Ben Butler? He'd be handy with his hooks in a fight like this." Victoria promised she would write a letter to him as soon as she got to pen and paper. Tennie dozed off in her sister's arms, listening to the rain, waiting for the fleas to bite.

In the Court of General Sessions next morning another judge set bail at one thousand dollars for each of them and twice as much for Jim. Howe screamed that sixty thousand dollars, or the sum total of charges, was staked on their combined heads now, whereas Boss Tweed was out for nine thousand less, and he'd looted the city of millions. His Honor didn't want to hear about it. Fair play between the sexes took another beating when a bondsman stepped up for the women, but nobody would do that for Jim, who was hustled back to his ground-floor cell.

They were left with so much to do to bring out the paper according to timetable that Tennie went on working as she had before. Jim's brother George came in to help, but there was more space in the pages to fill after April when George Train was tried after five months of imprisonment. "Hark! From the Tombs!" dried up when the judge ruled George was insane and committed him to the madhouse in Utica, New York. Comstock was in court, mopping his eyes to see him go and leaning on Challis for moral support.

It was close to summer by the time Victoria got to keeping her pledge to the public to reprint the Beecher story. They were used to living on bail, and they'd given up hope of ever coming up for trial. She spent a lot of time and thought pondering how to spell out what she stood for as a matter of *principle* in the May 17 issue. The result didn't ring many bells with Tennie:

> As an ultimate, the Complete Organization
> of the peoples of the World into
> THE GRAND HUMAN FAMILY
> and thereby begin actually to live the
> doctrines and teachings of
> JESUS OF NAZARETH
> who was the first and greatest of all
> COMMUNISTS
> whose disciples "had all things in common"
> in love "professing one another"

Tucked away in a different column was a notice Tennie had sweated over. "My robust constitution is unequal to the terrible pressure that has been made against it, and my health is shattered. I bid our many readers my affectionate adieu." She was supposed to be retiring in order to save what was left of her skin. Woodhull, Claflin & Company was done for, and all Tennie's right, title and interest in the *Weekly* was now in her sister's keeping.

There was one thing Tennie stuck to doing for Victoria, who was delivering her "Naked Truth" speech here, there, and everywhere and pumping most of her earnings into the paper. Asking for contributions from the Spiritualists, the Socialists, and the Pantarchy drew a blank. "They leave me to starve on the streets," she said. "My paper must live to express what I have to say or I shall spend fifteen years in Sing Sing."

Tennie ran her errands around the bankers, the stockbrokers, the sporting men, and the prostitutes, collecting from them in one way or another, wheedling and bullying and doing whatever was necessary to raise the cash. "How it's done is my business, nobody else's," Tennie told her mother. But for a spell the *Weekly* was like Miss Claflin, out on the streets regular as clockwork every week, rain or shine.

Ten

Paying Howe and Hummel was water poured down the drain, but weeping wouldn't bring it back. Howe had been on the wrong track with his windy harangues about Deuteronomy and Shakespeare and freedom of the press, but it took Ben Butler to make the point, with some unintended help from Comstock.

Victoria's first reading of Ben's reply to her letter gave her the impression he was turning a chilly shoulder. "I shall not be able to find time from my public duties to take part in the trial of your case. I cannot believe that in the prosecution of yourself and sister for sending obscene literature through the mails in the Courts of the United States there is the slightest need for my services or my counsel."

Then he went on, "The statute was meant to cover, and does cover, sending that class of lithographs, prints, engravings, licentious books and other matters which are published by bad men for the corruption of youth. . . . If I were your counsel, I should advise you to make no further defense but mere matter of law. I do not believe that a legal wrong can be done you in this behalf before any learned and intelligent judge."

Tennie jeered, "If such a living wonder can be found on any bench in the land we haven't come across him yet." Both of them were slow to catch the meaning of "mere matter of law." All they could scent was more trouble from Comstock. After nosing around Washington City for months, he had wheedled Congress into passing a bill tightening the rules that governed what could or could not be sent through the mail. The same act, dated March 31, 1873, gave him an extra $3,425 a year in salary as the new watchdog of the Postmaster-General. It seemed everything was set to spur him on to hamstring the two women.

Victoria's spirits drooped when notice was served that on June 26 they would be coming up at last before Justice Blatchford on the obscenity charge. They had rid themselves of Howe by then. "All he's done," said Tennie, "is keep us popping in and out of the lockup for six months, and his bills are enough to knock your eye out." They had a new lawyer in Charlie Brooke, an Irish dandy, who'd managed to win bail for Jim—but for all Howe's nonsense they felt lost without him.

On a Friday afternoon they paid a call on Johnnie Green at the *Sun;* Johnnie still stood high on Tennie's list of sweethearts. Victoria asked a favor of him—to talk his editor into printing another complaint from her about the rough justice they were experiencing on what seemed to be a straight road into Sing Sing. He'd do what he could, he said, resentful of her pushing him. On the horsecar going home she said she felt peaked, but Tennie blamed that on the weather, which she, too, found bothersome hot and sultry. After nothing more than a cup of tea for supper, Victoria made steps for bed. Halfway up the stairs she fainted and came tumbling down, eyes wide open but rolled back in her head, showing only white. Her skin was cold under Tennie's fingers. Jim tried Victoria's pulse, but there was none. "Tennie, fetch a looking glass." She held it close to her sister's parted lips, and nothing misted the glass. "There's only Byron in the house, and he's no more use than the fire irons. What do we do?"

Jim carried her up to their room while Tennie ran to get a doctor. She told herself over and over that Victoria couldn't possibly be dying because Tennie would have known in advance somehow if

that was coming and she'd envisioned nothing of the kind. Then a
different thought struck her: Had she lost the power after being so
long out of practice? If anybody had to die, she wished it would be
herself instead of Victoria. That was hard to understand because
Tennie always counted herself as selfish. Supposing death had called
already? What if the stop after next would have to be the undertaker? Her throat was tight, and the tears were streaming down so
fast she was stumbling along half blind and bumping into things
without feeling any twinge of pain.

The first doctor she brought back said Victoria was a lost cause;
her heart had pumped hard enough to rupture itself, he said, and
she might not last the night. Tennie cursed him for a liar and raced
off to find some other man of medicine who'd have a word of hope
to offer. This second doctor was panting after running the three
blocks with Tennie nagging and nudging him.

Anna had entered the scene, and now Victoria was lying on top
of the quilt with hot mustard plasters covering most of her body,
feet wrapped in steaming towels, both hands held firm by Jim in a
bowl of near-scalding water. A basin plumped down in the pillow
was catching a little stream of blood seeping from a corner of her
mouth.

The doctor let this treatment continue without interruption as he
prodded and tapped and applied his stethoscope. Victoria lay like a
rag doll. His face was grim as a tombstone. Tennie remembered
what came next. "I heard somebody scream, and it must have been
me, since Ma was down in the kitchen mixing more mustard. I
wanted everybody in the whole God-awful world to know they'd
killed her. I burst into a Western Union Telegraph office around
the corner to send a wire to Johnnie Green so the *Sun* would have
the news in time for the first edition.

"We watched the dawn come up, Jim and me, as we sat by her
bed, changing the towels and the plasters that the last doctor reckoned were as good as anything might be, since it wasn't her heart
but one of her lungs that had acted up. Pa had shoved Ma out of
their room for kicking up too big a din with her praying, so she was
in with us, keeping it going with Jesus, Joseph and Mary. Sis didn't
stir, though her breath was back, and a pulse was fluttering in her

wrist. We took turns to eat breakfast, and I went out to pick up the papers, which she normally liked to start the day with, always anxious to see her name."

Every one of them carried Victoria Woodhull's death notice. She would have enjoyed the *Graphic:* "Her influence over people of intelligence and refinement, women as well as men, amounting in some instances to fascination and in spite of theories and actions they condemned, is a phenomenon which has yet to be satisfactorily explained." But the *Sun* hadn't done well by her at all: "If Mrs. Woodhull had been born and educated in a different sphere—if her surroundings had been refined and inspiring—she would have developed into a great and glorious character. As it was, she simply leaped from one excitement to another, wasting her life."

Sunday, Monday, Tuesday went by in much the same way. She'd wake up, then drop back to sleep again like a tethered boat on the flow of the tide. When her head was clear, all she could talk about was the trial and Ben Butler and what would happen to the *Weekly* after she was dead. When she'd floated off, she'd sometimes wear a smile like a baby's.

Early on Wednesday morning, Tennie was dozing in her chair by the bed when Victoria roused her with a hand on her sleeve, looking better than she had for a week. "Tennie, He came to me again, our Lord Jesus Christ. He laid His hand on my forehead and willed me better. *For many are called,* He whispered, *but few are chosen.* See, I am well again."

Tennie smiled. "It's a pity to have missed it, but I've been nodding."

They had visitors a day or two before they were due in court. Henry Bowen led a shorthand writer and a deputation from Plymouth Church to question Victoria about her involvement with Tilton and Beecher. Bowen was in a passion because Theodore had told the papers about the three-way deal between himself, Beecher, and Bowen to cover up the tracks left by Mrs. Tilton, the late Mrs. Bowen, and the rest of the ladies Beecher had wooed and won.

Victoria was tucked in under an afghan in the parlor when Tennie let them in. Utica had to be disposed of before they got down to business, since she was roaring drunk. Red spots burned in Victoria's cheeks as soon as she began to speak. "You are all millionaires. You and the press with few exceptions have hounded and black-guarded me as no other woman has ever been hounded. But I have touched bottom. I'm on the incoming tide. Why come to me to vindicate you?"

Bowen insisted that it was her Christian duty to protect the innocent, pretending he wasn't certain she even knew his pet preacher or his darling Theodore.

"Did I know Theodore Tilton? I stayed with him at his house days and nights. And I know Henry Ward Beecher. I have stayed with him at his house days and nights, too, and when I say I stayed with him, I mean no myth."

Bowen was not in the habit of taking any woman at her word, particularly this adventuress. Where was the proof of her uncon-scionable allegation concerning the reverend?

"I have his love letters."

"*Love* letters?"

She disdained his stupidity. "Anyone with a grain of sense would know that, after several months of intimacy, our correspondence was not one of mere platonic affection."

"Are you prepared to show them to me?"

"So that you may suppress them in the interests of your good shepherd?"

"Madam, you wrong me," he protested. "Never in my life have I acted against my conscience even for the sake of a man so beloved by all who harken to him."

"Tennie, fetch me the strongbox." Victoria unlocked it and pro-duced two sheets of notepaper, which she carefully folded so that only the signatures could be read, before she held them out for Bowen's inspection. "That should satisfy your curiosity for the pres-ent." But she dangled more bait in his face. A date had been set at last for Victoria, Tennie, and Jim Blood to be tried on the Federal charge of circulating obscene printed matter. "My case is set for next week," she said. "I shall reserve my evidence until after that, but if you will get that trial out of the way, I shall produce it."

She looked worn and wan, sitting in the crowded United States District Court, with Jim Blood imperturbable on one side of her and Tennie on the other, focusing her attention on their new attorney, handsome young Charlie Brooke, who got swiftly off the mark by citing the learned opinion of Ben Butler that the law, as it stood at the time of their supposed breach of it, did not apply to the *Weekly*. The statutes, he argued, applied to a "book, pamphlet, print, or other publication," and "other publication" was too woolly a definition to support an attack on a newspaper. The jury, following the judge's recommendation, returned a verdict of "Not guilty." If the scales of justice had been in any way tilted by Bowen, Beecher, or anybody else, there was no proof of it—only rumor.

According to his sister Isabella, Beecher had told Bowen that one letter to Victoria was about his refusal to appear with her at Steinway Hall, the other his rejection of a request from her to contribute a few dollars to the National Women's campaign. On both counts he was bluffing. He didn't have Tilton's grasp of language, but as Tennie put it, "the epistles of Brother Beecher to Sister Victoria sounded like the braying of a lovesick jackass."

Though Challis was still out to get the two of them jailed for life, Victoria's concern was how to drum up more subscribers for the *Weekly*. Her method was to supply the same editorial mixture as before and at the same time to shore up her reputation in front of live audiences. Tennie explained afterward, "Back in those days, remember, most everyone else doled out slop about a girl *knowing her disgrace* if a man offered her a slap and a tickle and she *yielded to his solicitations*. After she'd let him in, *fears and hopes agitated her* and *her heart sank within;* she was supposed to feel lower than a rattlesnake's belly. A few samples of Sis's handiwork were all anybody needed to see she held a different view. A spade was a spade to her."

Mrs. Woodhull promised her readers she'd reveal the truth about girls' boarding schools "and cause you to realize that you have permitted your daughters to acquire a vice which when once fostered upon them is impossible of eradication. They will tell you that when very small, perhaps no more than eight, nine, or ten years of age, they were taught by someone already acquainted with the vice the act that led them to destruction. They will tell you of dreams at night and of involuntary action upon slightest excitement by day and altogether such a tale of horror as to make you wonder that you could have been blind to it all this time."

She traveled six hours on trains and ferries to attend a camp meeting of Spiritualists in Vineland, New Jersey, to mortify them with a speech she called "The Scarecrows of Sexual Freedom." Jim, who went with her, was drawn into the act when she introduced him: "This is my lover, but when I cease to love him, I will leave him, though I trust that will never be."

Her words were fiery enough to set fire to the tents the campers had raised among the pines. "What does it matter whether a child or anyone knows who is its father? . . . What is it to you whether I live upon fish or flesh? . . . I would rather be the labor slave of a master with his whip cracking continually about my ears than the forced sexual slave of any man a single hour. . . . They say I have come to break up the family. I say amen to that with all my heart."

The Spiritualists begged for more, and she repeated her performance at their annual convention in Chicago before they voted her in again as their president. She pulled all the stops out then. "I declare I never had sexual intercourse with any man whom I am ashamed to stand side by side with before the world. Nor am I ashamed of any desire that has been gratified, nor of any passion alluded to. . . . If I want sexual intercourse with one hundred men I shall have it. And this sexual intercourse business may as well be discussed until you are so familiar with your sexual organs that a reference to them will no longer make the blush mount to your face any more than will a reference to any other part of your body." She proved she meant what she said in that respect when Utica died.

One day Utica, who had been on the bottle day and night, took offense at something Margaret Ann said, and went after her with a kitchen chair. Margaret Ann ran out of the house and came back with the police, and another brawl was reported in every newspaper. Utica was howling about being overshadowed all her life by Victoria, and Anna was clawing at Jim. Then Victoria took over, saying that as long as Utica packed up and left, with a promise not to return, Margaret Ann should forgive and forget. That seemed to patch things up for the time being, but Utica broke the bargain, and there she was, back again, drinking hair tonic and complaining to reporters that she had been physically abused by Victoria and Jim.

Utica saw one more week out, and then it was all over. The whole tribe of Claflins hung around her bed, with Victoria in the front row. "Do you realize how I have always loved you? Don't you know I would willingly give my life for yours?"

Utica's eyes stayed closed, and they had to strain to catch what she was muttering: "One kiss is worth a thousand kicks." She said not a word after that. Victoria was so tense that she took off for the office and spent the rest of the evening working. She was on a horse bus coming home when the clock struck eleven thirty and Utica was gone. Victoria insisted that she'd heard from her at that very moment: "Vicky, it's all right now."

"Maybe she did, too, but I've got my doubts," said Tennie.

Nobody could accuse Claflins of being close-mouthed. In the middle of the lamentations, Polly speculated that Utie had probably died of a chancre, while Anna figured she'd been poisoned, meanwhile keeping a sharp eye on Tennie and Victoria. The two didn't have to rack their brains to know what all this meant; if they didn't make a move to check the other women, they'd be causing an uproar in the morning just to see their names reappear in the papers. The only answer was to arrange for the medical examiner to step in, which was a job Tennie attended to before bedtime.

The *Weekly* ran the autopsy results on July 26: "The uterus and the vagina were pronounced by Dr. Cushman as natural as those of a virgin." Victoria let herself go in Utica's obituary. "Though dying for love which she could not have in slavery, she cursed those who would have labored to set her and all other women like her free." She told a few home truths about some other relatives, too. Margaret Ann: "Good at heart but angular in disposition and weak in moral courage." Polly Sparr: "The most eccentric and altogether unfortunate of the family, she is as much inclined to suspicion and hate as the sparks are to fly upward."

Jim came out trumps. "A nobler man never lived than Colonel Blood; his light is steady as the stars." And as for Tennie, she had "unbended benevolence, an exuberance of animal spirits and a ready tongue, but seems to lack the interior life and inspiring power of her sister."

There were also a few lines she pretended had come from Utica, a kind of conclusion she'd reached before Bright's disease ruined her kidneys: "Deal gently with those who stray. Draw them back by love and persuasion. One kiss is worth a thousand kicks. Kind words are more valuable to the erring than a mine of gold."

Once she had her teeth into anything, Victoria hung on like a bulldog. She kept up the wake for Utica and the gibes at the Claflins for weeks. A writer on her staff interviewed Victoria "weeping over the remains of her sister" and had her asking him, "Do you wonder, my brother, that I should feel desperately in earnest to reform the evils of our social life when I remember what I have suffered in my own family? Opposed and misunderstood by my parents and sisters, compelled to bear an idiotic child by a drunken husband? Oh, my God, and the world thinks me only ambitious of notoriety!"

Tennie recognized another ambition her sister developed at the time, and that was to stave off her own end as long as possible or even, as she imagined it, forever. An inkling of what was on Victoria's mind showed up sometimes when she'd worked herself up and started letting off steam.

The "Scarecrows" speech before the Spiritualists had brought invitations for her to repeat it elsewhere. A troop of Claflins rode the trains with her for appearances out of town: Anna under orders to sit on the platform in the lecture halls and keep a still tongue in her head, Jim to peddle books and pamphlets published by the *Weekly*, Zulu Maud to open the proceedings by reciting some poetry, Tennie to stand by and take over if Victoria didn't feel up to it. Anna broke out only once, in Philadelphia, where she wigwagged her umbrella and screamed, "My daughters are not responsible for what they do; they're psychologized by that devil Blood."

Victoria never failed to give a crowd its money's worth, such as "If I want sexual intercourse with a hundred men, I shall have it" or "It would be better if a woman bore twelve healthy children by twelve different men than twelve such children by one man" and "I am seeking the truth about sexual intercourse, and I will follow it if it lead me either to heaven or hell."

But she counted on finishing upstairs rather than down. This is how she put it: "In a perfected sexuality shall continuous life be found. So also shall life not come to an end when its springs shall not cease to send forth the vitalized waters of life. Then shall they who have in ages past cast off their mortal coils be able to come again and resume them at will, and thus also shall a spiritualized humanity be able at will to throw off and take on its material clothing, and the two worlds shall be once and forever united."

Tennie mused, "You risked being thrown off at the turns when she went tearing up the track. But if you clung on tight you could catch her message. Free love in large helpings is the ticket to eternity. She'd given up on votes for women, which in her judgment was nothing but threshing old hay, and the revolution had lost its place on the agenda, too, which was a disappointment to me when Spiritualists couldn't hold a candle to Socialists in the rowdy songs they sang, and I missed parading through the streets with a red banner."

After "The Scarecrows of Sexual Freedom" had worn out its welcome, Victoria turned to another lecture called "The Elixir of Life," which went over just as well as the first. She was changing in looks as well as thinking—thinner, more wrapped up in herself, yet still a woman to attract a man.

"The juice flowed strong in her, too," Tennie reminisced, "though she was finding it helped to have a partner young enough to be taught the ins and outs of the game. A prime example was Bennie Tucker, who was nineteen and a virgin when she first hopped into bed with him in the room she was sharing with Jim at the Parker House, Boston. As usual, she kept me up to date on developments."

Bennie was bashful and green as grass, a student whose head swam with dreams of reforming the world. He'd worked alongside Jim in setting up lectures for Victoria in towns close by, and she asked him around to express her appreciation. Two lady Spiritualists were already there together with Jim, but Victoria dismissed them all, locked the door, and hung her wrap over the knob to cover the keyhole. Next, Bennie received a kiss, and she planted herself across his lap, urging him on by telling about the times she'd had with Tilton and Beecher.

She let Jim back in at the end of the afternoon, and he wondered whether she'd like some supper. "Oh, no!" said Victoria. "We've just had refreshment you don't know about." Bennie went off to his lodgings with her promise of a return engagement tomorrow morning, Sunday, at ten o'clock.

Jim was off on some errand when her new conquest turned up for his appointment. "Do you know I should dearly love to sleep with you?" said Victoria. He turned bright red and confessed he'd never had any particular use for girls, which he'd have walked a block to avoid up to now. She took a break for lunch without him but had him back in the afternoon when Jim was writing letters at a table in a corner and she had spread herself out on a lounge, ready for action.

Jim grabbed up his papers. "I must go down to the reading room to finish. There's altogether too much magnetism about here for me."

Young Bennie piped up. "Is it possible that you feel it way over there?"

"I should say I do." Jim let himself out without further fussing.

It took about an hour to work Bennie up to par. He said he'd never felt so proud and happy, though he detected a worm in their apple: "What will Colonel Blood think of this?"

She couldn't make out why he fretted. "That will be all right. Why, only the other day he wrote to me of you in glowing terms, declaring, 'I know very well what *I* would do were he a girl.' " She had two things to ask of Bennie: Would he come back for an evening performance, and would he also oblige her by dropping into the reading room on his way out to let Jim know the coast was clear?

Jim gave them free rein that night by dragging the lounge into the bathroom, leaving the double bed for Victoria and her youthful lover, whose conscience acted up three hours later. He climbed out, put on his clothes, and departed, to give Jim his turn between the sheets.

It was just as well, Tennie reckoned, for her sister to find something to take her mind off her troubles, which were blowing up another storm. The tour was a dud—not enough cash taken in to pay for the halls—and it came at a time when the *Weekly* was feeling the pinch, too, after the collapse of Jay Cooke & Company on September 18, which set off panic on Wall Street.

Everybody had regarded Cooke as a Rock of Gibraltar, but he'd overextended himself on loans to the railroads, exactly as Vanderbilt had forecast. When one of the roads defaulted on a note for $1,000,000, Cooke was done for. Before the day was over, nearly forty more banks and stockbroking houses had gone under with him, and the New York Exchange was shut by order of the board of governors.

Rain was streaming down in buckets when Tennie drove with Victoria to the new office they'd taken on Nassau Street, where Byron spent his time in a back room in George Blood's care. Tennie felt a touch of sympathy for the poor devils who were hammering on bank doors, drenched to the skin, demanding their money or, failing that, a settlement by way of a lamppost and a length of rope. She could smell hard times ahead for one and all, though she didn't expect them to last as long as the five years that dragged by before the sun shone again on Broad and Wall. More than five thousand businesses were bankrupted in the crash of '73. Wages were cut in half, and beggars swarmed in New York streets. Most people who held onto a job were so fearful of being deprived of working fourteen hours a day that the International and everything it stood for was laid away in cold storage, and women didn't stand a chance of winning their rights to the ballot box.

The *Weekly* caught it from all sides. There was a pullout of advertisers who'd been filling the front page before, and a slump in sales as former readers were struggling to keep a roof over their heads, bread on the table, and boots on their feet. To crown it all, spice itself went out of style. It seemed people felt that bringing sex out into the open as Victoria had been doing was somehow responsible for the fix they were in, and Comstock's breed of killjoys came into their glory.

The Commodore was still sitting on the sisters' nest egg. Tennie contemplated sending out an SOS for at least a nibble at it when she read about his being called in by Ulysses Grant, who'd come up from Washington to stay at the Fifth Avenue Hotel while he brooded over what might be done to get the country back on its feet.

Vanderbilt was willing to throw in ten million dollars of his railroad bonds if Grant would unfreeze thirty million from the Treasury, but Grant declined the offer. Then Tennie heard via the grapevine that the Commodore was welshing on $1,750,000 he owed the Union Trust Company because otherwise he'd run short of cash to meet his payroll. "Trying to squeeze as much as a nickel out of him would be a fool's game. We'll have to sit back, bite the bullet, and bide our time."

The only love letter Bennie Tucker had written in his life arrived for Victoria a day or so after their encounters in the Parker House. The reply went off from Jim instead of her, which spelled the end of the correspondence. The two of them were winding up a lecture tour out West, and Tennie had just sloshed in through the wet snow that was piling up on Nassau Street, when Bennie opened the office door to provide her with her first look at him. "You're a handsome young rip right enough, and I judge you know the ropes when Sis has been your teacher. She thinks the world of you. She'll be awful glad to see you when she gets in tomorrow. But isn't this weather terrible? Just look at this."

Tennie hoisted her skirts, and his eyes bulged at the flash of white thigh between the top of her soaking stockings and the lace of her underwear. George Blood had to interfere at this point by walking Byron in, which firmed up her fancy to try Bennie out some other time. It would be worth adding him to the list of deadbeats on that account, if nothing more.

Bennie made himself useful around the office as well as the house for the next five or six months, running errands, fetching the suppertime beer in a washstand pitcher, sleeping with Victoria but never with her eager sister, though Victoria didn't hesitate to put in a good word toward that end, telling him, "Nobody can love me who doesn't love Tennie."

"I wasn't shy about coaxing him myself, either," Tennie related. "I'd ask him to help me off with my shoes and into slippers, but he didn't know left from right nor his ass from his elbow. I came straight out with it more than once and said we shouldn't hold back from enjoying a tumble together."

"Are you in earnest about that?" Bennie asked.

"Of course, I am. Do you think I wouldn't do a little thing like that for you?" It was still no deal, and a considerable aggravation to her.

Along with Anthony Comstock and Luther Challis, Bennie was in court every day of the ten the sisters were on trial for libel, starting on March 4 of the following year. Victoria, Jim and Tennie were locked up every night in the Tombs because Judge Sutherland refused bail. He let Challis's lawyer, William Fullerton, who was one of Beecher's cronies, introduce whatever he wished in the way of evidence, including the events of the cancer clinic and Tennie's woman patient who had died after treatment there.

Fullerton cross-examined Victoria on the subject of free love. "In your opinion, should a woman desert her husband and live with another man if prompted by such a desire?"

"If her will takes her away from a man, she surely ought to go. I hold that any man or woman married or unmarried who consorts for anything but love is a prostitute."

"And has a right to break it off at will?"

"There is nothing to break but hate. When they hate each other, it is already broken."

Zulu Maud was also a fixture installed by request of Charlie Brooke. She stared at the stand the moment Victoria stepped up, and she shook with sobs while Fullerton was browbeating her mother. Howe and Hummel couldn't have asked for a better performance, but every tear was genuine. Tennie put an arm around the girl's shoulders, and Victoria was on the verge of weeping, too. All three of them had cause to wail when the judge seemed to be railroading the Claflins, even though in sixteen months of searching, Fullerton had found nobody to prove that what had been written about Challis was anything but total truth.

They felt they were doomed after Sutherland finished tying the knots on Friday the thirteenth and the jury retired at noontime with a warning from him that the only verdict could be guilty.

"Comstock," Tennie whispered, "has the look of a cat dipping a paw in a bowl of goldfish. I can just about hear the gates of Sing Sing Prison slamming shut behind us."

The jurors were still debating at suppertime, and the prisoners were tucked away for another serving of hardtack and another night in their cells.

At eleven o'clock next morning, the jury shuffled back into place, red-eyed from a dearth of sleep. The foreman's hands trembled as he spoke. "We wish to express our unanimous and most hearty concurrence in the sentiments expressed so eloquently by Your Honor, but decide to yield to the defendants that charitable presumption of innocence where there is a reasonable doubt." They'd gone through a hundred ballots to reach their conclusion: Not guilty.

It was hard to say which of them—Challis, Comstock, or the judge—was suffering the most. "They couldn't be more crushed if they'd been flattened under a steamroller," Tennie exulted. She was ready to plant a kiss on every juror. "It is the most outrageous verdict ever recorded," Sutherland snorted. "I am ashamed of the jury who rendered such a verdict."

Jim and Bennie credited the "magnificent style" of Charlie Brooke, while Victoria put the victory down to the hand of the Lord. Tennie was more inclined to give praise where it was due, which was to the tears of Zulu Maud.

The old *Weekly* staggered along under a burden of debt that would have broken the back of a camel. The printing stock was as cheap as could be found, and the pages were down in number from the previous sixteen to eight. The photographs of Victoria, Jim and Tennie that previously sold for a dollar a head were offered at a dollar the set. "And there aren't enough takers," said Tennie "to keep us in flypaper." Victoria launched an appeal for $1,000 but it pulled in a minimum of contributions. She saw no choice but to take to the road lecturing to garner whatever she could. This time, traveling alone, she pushed on to California, which she hadn't seen in fifteen years, with a new attack on marriage, "Tried as by Fire." She wore herself out, delivering it every night to a hundred different audiences, catching her rest in rackety railroad cars and cheap hotels.

Bennie's family had booked passage for him on a trip to Europe, which he was willing to take, since he'd learned to manage again without Victoria in his bed whenever she felt the need. She was so exhausted by the time she came back that she conceived the idea that she and Tennie might both be improved in health by taking a vacation along with Bennie. It wouldn't be the first time readers survived without the *Weekly* for an issue or two. Where to scrape up the necessary cash was the stumbling block, but not for long.

The tar Victoria had spread over Beecher still stuck fast, driving him to handpick a committee of six church elders to investigate in private and, if they lived up to his expectations, lay on the white-wash. "Anybody with half an eye," Tennie said, "can see Tilton's scheduled to come out the villain of the piece, especially since his wife's left home at Beecher's urging, and she's primed to testify Theodore's lying in his teeth when the only place the good shep-herd's ever had his hands on was her forehead, giving a blessing."

One woman was prepared to tell a different story, and that was Victoria. If she disclosed the facts, the game would be up for the pharisees of Plymouth Church, as they well knew. So Tennie found there was missionary work to be done over in Brooklyn. Then on another day she paid a return visit together with her sister and Jim McDermott, a new addition among Tennie's Brooklyn circle, who edited the *Sunday Press.* In all seriousness, Victoria asked the com-mitteemen whether they might care to hear from her. They deeply appreciated the gesture, they said, but no thank you, Sister.

One more errand came Tennie's way. She scuttled around the steamship offices, bargaining for cut rates, since she and Victoria were journalists. The French Line sold her four cabins on the *Lafay-ette,* a double apiece for Victoria and Jim; Anna and Tennie; singles for Zulu Maud and Bennie, who cashed in his original ticket. Beecher was standing treat for them all.

With Victoria bought off and his letters to her probably long since tossed into the fire, he could afford to set his opinions down on paper and hand them over to his cohorts on the committee, who in turn passed them on to the reporters. Theodore got the worst of it. "I can see now that Tilton is and has been from the beginning of this difficulty a reckless schemer, pursuing a plan of mingled greed and hatred, and weaving about me a network of suspicions, misun-derstandings, plots, and lies, to which my own innocent words and acts—nay, even my thoughts of kindness toward him—have been made to contribute."

Beecher knew better than to give Victoria a flick of the whip, but "the circle of which Mrs. Woodhull formed a part was the center of loathsome scandals, organized, classified, and perpetuated with a greedy and unclean appetite for everything that was foul and vile."

All this came about while she and her company were out of the

way, bound for Le Havre and then two weeks in Paris. Tennie
scribbled a note to Johnnie Green: "The skies are clear, the waves
just enough to roll you to and fro in your berth and stir a taste for
company. I hadn't tried it in a ship at sea before, and I figured a
few drinks in Bennie might help light his torch. The steward
obliged me with a bottle of whiskey. Bennie was already under the
covers when I sashayed into his cabin, but I'd no more than perched
beside him before Sis poked her face in, looking daggers at the sight
of the hooch. She begged and threatened and wrung her hands in
her belief it was a sin to take a man under false pretenses when he
was potted. I got an earful about me being her nearest and dearest
and how wicked it would be to follow in the path of Utie, which
struck me as totally ridiculous. I didn't look for an argument,
however, but merely took one small shot to prove to her I could
handle it, then put myself to bed in the bunk upstairs to Ma's,
regretting one more lost opportunity."

Paris was supposed to be the city of love; her main complaint was
that she didn't get any. Jim and Victoria shared a room in the
Grand Hotel, Zulu Maud was put in next door with her aunt and
her grandmother, Bennie had a single down the hallway. Tennie
gave it a last try one afternoon when she strolled in on Bennie.
"Why, your bed's plenty big enough for two, isn't it?" The ox
declined to take the hint, and she wrote him off for good.

Aside from that, plus never understanding the language, she was
fascinated by Paris. It was a relief to be free from lawsuits and
scheming and wondering when she might be picked up again for
another turn through the mangle. She kicked up her heels, inspected buildings on the guidebook's list, watched the fishermen
dangle their lines in the Seine, admired the flowers that filled the
parks, and only wished she had the money to go shopping on the
Rue de la Paix.

Victoria didn't see things in quite the same light. She approved
of the general appearance of a city that came straight out of the
pages of the history books with spires and towers and archways and
monuments stretching as far as her legs would carry her. But the
wreckage of the Tuileries, battered and burned at the time of the
Commune, disgusted her. Communards and Communists were one

and the same breed of evildoer, she said, and she'd never forgive them for the damage they'd caused. To Tennie, this sounded out of place, coming from a woman who once had marched in sympathy for the Parisians who had been executed, but Tennie let it pass. "She'd gone through a lot lately, and if she was showing signs of fitfulness in her thinking, I could understand it when middle age was creeping up on her."

Bennie was left behind when they sailed for New York, and that was almost the end of him where they were concerned. After everything Victoria had done, and Tennie had hoped to do, for him, he was an ingrate, a churl, a niggard. According to what they heard at second hand later, he'd taken to saying things like "However worthy the ends the Claflin sisters claimed to be pursuing, the means to which they resorted were unjustifiable and even disgraceful." They weren't sorry to be rid of him when they were on the receiving line for abuse from all sides.

They had a rough crossing home, but the weather was nothing compared to the storm that was thundering over Beecher's head. The investigation committee had done its duty and reported him pure as snow, but Tilton had beaten them to the punch by swearing out a complaint in City Court, accusing him of stealing his wife and demanding $100,000 in compensation.

Victoria was beside herself with worry. She'd seen enough of the law at work to last her lifetime, yet one side or the other seemed bound to drag her in. If they could subpoena her, she'd be under oath to tell the truth or force jail for lying. What she must do was leave town and stay away until the dust had settled. Back on the road, lecturing to pay her way, she'd be a moving target, hard to hit. She was in no condition to manage it by herself, which meant Jim and Zulu Maud traveling with her while Tennie pushed on ahead, booking halls and lodgings, sticking up the placards, coaxing editors to publish a favorable mention. George Blood would have to be in charge of bringing out the *Weekly* as best he could. Whatever help he might scratch up would have to be willing to whistle a while for their wages.

Fall came, and the team kept going. Tennie always said she felt bright as paint, but Victoria was ready to drop. In Philadelphia she was all in. The doctor's order was for her to drop all engagements until her lungs cleared up and some of her strength returned. Filling the bill for her there, Tennie won good notices for "inimitable freshness and audacity," having a voice "astounding to hear when at full capacity." She would go on holding the ends together for her sister so she would have time to recover her health.

When the Beecher trial opened in Brooklyn City Courthouse in January, Victoria's name was bandied back and forth every day. The mobs that jammed the morning ferries crossing from Manhattan and the evening boats bringing them back were paying as much as five dollars apiece for a seat in the courtroom. The marshals turned droves of them away at the door, leaving them to circle around outside among the hawkers of souvenirs, popcorn, and pretzels who'd set up their stalls as if at a fair.

Tilton had engaged three lawyers, Beecher five. Tilton's trio brought in a dozen witnesses, Beecher had half a hundred faithful followers vouching for him. Both sides were traveling the same route, making Victoria out to be the scarlet woman who'd brought on Theodore's downfall, which had resulted in his wife's walking out on him. But nobody could track down Mrs. Woodhull when she and her entourage were slogging on through Illinois and Kansas, Missouri and Nevada, Iowa and Michigan in the name of free love, booed in some places, applauded in others, yet somehow keeping their heads above water.

Then Victoria's health gave out again, her constitution hit hard by the winter freeze that struck the Midwest. The cruel wind that near blew them off their feet as they got off the train one night left her struggling to breathe before they reached shelter in a run-down hotel. Her throat was so clogged the rest of them could barely make out what she was gasping. "It's like somebody's tightening an iron band around my chest." Tennie could see only one choice. "We'll call it quits and head home; a prison cell will have it all over an appointment with the undertaker.

The wolf was back howling at the door, and the sheriff was likely to be standing next in line. The only place Victoria could think of to turn to was Number 10 Washington Place. A messenger bore the letter off to "Dear Commodore."

It was you, Commodore, who first extended your hand to aid two struggling women to battle with the world. It was you who encouraged them to break away from the fetters that held them captive to public opinion and to go out into the world to claim a recognition as individuals upon the talent they possessed. To you they owe their all. . . .

But there needs to be some great Patron Saint to endow the work to give it vitality and material strength. Commodore, we appeal to you to become this great Patron Saint. To do all this would require a paltry sum only when compared to your many millions. . . .

Let us again beseech you to become the Patron Saint of this great cause and, by so doing, build for yourself a monument of fame before which all future ages will bow with blessings on their lips and with gratitude and reverence in their hearts.

They both signed it "Affectionately yours," then sat back and waited and went on waiting. No answer. "There's not a peep nor a crumb out of him or his bitch of a wife or son Billy or any other of his ten whelps," Tennie snapped. "All we've got for our trouble is a feeling we've made ourselves cheaper than dirt."

The trial dragged on, with more space given to it on Park Row than anything that had creased the country since the war. On the days Beecher took the stand, his followers dressed up the courtroom with lilies to point up his purity of heart, while he clutched a bunch of violets to provide the jury with a hint of his character. He blew a shower of kisses, but the hissing and the cheering balanced each other, which was a sign that the dirt was still sticking. His "Don't remembers" and "Can't recalls" added up to nearly a thousand by the reporters' count.

If Victoria had laid low, she might have escaped. But she couldn't restrain herself when Tilton testified that he'd only rendered her favors to keep her quiet for the sake of his wife and Beecher. "My relationship with Mrs. Woodhull was a foolish one and a wrong one, and I do not ask any man to defend me for it, but I say here before God that Mr. Beecher is as much responsible for my connection with Mrs. Woodhull as I am myself."

To set the record straight, she hit back at him in the columns of the *Herald.* This was the nub of it:

No matter how inconsiderately he has treated himself—not me —in regard to his relations with me, I forgive him heartily all his intended harm now that the defense are making use of those relations to crush him in this case, and I do what I can to relieve him from the effect of this testimony upon the public, not having the pleasure of denying it in a better way upon the stand. . . .

That he now regards his action as having been "foolish and wrong" I have no reason to disbelieve. But the attempt to make Mr. Beecher equally responsible with himself for that which made it foolish and wrong is preposterous and absurd. It is little schoolboy's sniveling, "He made me do it; if it hadn't been for him, I shouldn't have done it." I have said before that I believed Mr. Tilton would make quite a man if he should live to grow up. I confess to considerable skepticism upon that point since reading his evidence upon his trial.

The subpoena she was served with came from Beecher's team. What they were after were Tilton's love letters to throw in his face. Spring was here already, and to celebrate it there was a tea rose pinned to the collar of Victoria's blue silk suit as she set off for the ferry with Tennie—who was not at all sure she wouldn't be alone on the return trip and her sister in prison again either for telling fables or refusing to talk at all. There was no sign of the evangel or the savior in Victoria's manner today; she was simply flummoxed over how to handle the correspondence she was carrying in her morocco-leather pocketbook.

Beecher was missing from the courtroom, but the sisters had their first peek at his wife, glittering as to eyes, hostile as to manner. Tilton stared hard at Victoria and she flushed bright red. A lawyer for Beecher asked for the letters. Not without an order direct from the judge, said Victoria. Tilton's legal team started an argument, objecting to anything Tilton had written her being entered as evidence unless she was sworn in as a witness, which was precisely what she intended to avoid.

The wheels were spinning in her head. She walked across to whisper to the same William Fullerton who had denounced her at the Challis trial and was now in Tilton's hire. Heads craned every way for a better view, but nobody in the crowd ventured a word for fear the marshals would evict him. At a nod from Fullerton, she took another step forward and bowed to the judge.

"I have only a few, unimportant letters which are entirely credit-able to myself as well as the gentlemen that wrote them. Others, I believe, are in the hands of the defense as well as of the prosecution." Then for a second she gave them the rough side of her tongue. "I have been imprisoned several times for publishing news of this scandal, and my office has been ransacked and much of my personal correspondence carried off."

The judge ordered her to hand over whatever she had. There were no more than six, and every letter a careful choice from her collec-tion. The farthest any of them went was: "My dear Victoria: Put this under your pillow, dream of the writer, and peace be with you. Affectionately, Theodore Tilton."

A Beecher lawyer flipped through the bundle. "These won't do, Mrs. Woodhull."

"Very well, sir, I am not to be the judge of that. They may not do for Mr. Beecher, but you were anxious to have them." Not anxious enough, Tennie said to herself, to make a cash offer to see the livelier specimens from Theodore's hand that are stored away.

They let her go without more pressing. Why she wasn't put on oath to have her say was a mystery only until one calculated the damage she might have chosen to do both parties if her bluff had been called.

June was almost over before the judge delivered his closing ad-dress to the jurors, and July before they concluded, after fifty-two ballots, in a deadlock, nine to three in favor of Beecher. He shouted victory and led his flock in special evening service, singing "Christ leads me through no darker rooms/Than He went though before." Both men dived into the lecture business, Tilton to work off his debts, Beecher to charge a guaranteed one thousand dollars a perfor-mance which was ten times more than Victoria ever made.

Tennie noticed peculiar things in her sister that a fancy doctor might have cured if they had the money to pay him. "She'd grown so pale these past few months you could have sworn her blood was draining away, which in point of fact it was, by virtue of her losing pints of it where most women get off luckier. It preyed on her mind and cramped her style with Jim, as you might well guess. Being what she was, gabby and willing to cause a stir, she didn't hesitate to sling the whole subject at her audience in the *Weekly,* then at anybody eager to see her in the flesh as she pulled this fresh skeleton out of the closet and preached about menstruating."

As far as anyone could gather from listening to her, and it wasn't always easy, female troubles had begun as far back as the Garden of Eden, a corner of the world where Victoria had felt herself at home. Everything there would have continued rosy if Adam and Eve hadn't fallen into what she termed "improper physical habits," namely cohabiting for pleasure instead of limiting the exercise to the pro-creation of babies. She pointed the finger at Adam, not Eve, for that, which, she claimed, was the root of menstrual problems, brought about by "an undue excitation of the ovaries." The "river of life" went to waste in only two kinds of creatures, humans and monkeys, leading her to believe this resulted from walking about on two legs instead of four like the rest of God's menagerie that never knew what menses meant.

"As if this wasn't enough to knock you off your rocker," Tennie reflected, "she got religion, too, worse than ever, and only Ma should be stuck with the blame for that." The old beldame, an Evangelical all her life, turned Catholic. The only possible reason Tennie could come up with was that it gave her something to fill in her time. She was off to Mass every morning before the birds were up, and she thumbed her beads all day. The Infant of Prague lit by two candles presided over her bedroom, hers alone now that Buck was living in separate lodgings on Third Avenue. Instead of having to wait for a camp meeting to send her into raptures, she had everything she needed at hand, and Victoria followed in her mother's footsteps.

In her sister's case, it didn't take Tennie long to figure why. "The Pope and his church showed respect for a woman, Mary, and they're forever gassing about the precious blood of Jesus. Those two things together must have struck a chord in her." Victoria took to dressing like a gospel preacher, wearing flowing black silk, long hair, and a lace veil over her shoulders, no rings on her fingers, but a Bible in her hands.

The new fads got mixed in with the old and she hashed them up together in her speeches or in the *Weekly.*

Search the Scriptures. They point out the way to eternal life. I have given you the key. The holy temple is the human body, is the male and female perfectly united and joined together in Christ. He showed the way and the keys to unlock the temple, so that its now hidden glories may be realized, are the tree and the river of life, blending their fruits and waters to become the healing of the nations —that is, all the ills to which the flesh has made us heirs.

The Book of Genesis had a firm hold on her thinking—if that was the right word for it when her brains seemed to have sunk somewhere below her navel. She'd recite the Bible story about "a garden eastward in Eden" and the four streams that flowed out of it as an introduction to speculating that "the long-lost Garden of Eden is the human body." She explained: "Its four rivers, which have their source in the extension of the mouth, are the Pison, the blood; the Gihon, the bowels; the Hiddekel, the urinary organs; and the Euphrates, the reproductive functions."

Then she'd get down to details concerning intimate human functions before the temple, and Jesus Christ showed up again for the finale. "When we catch glimpses of thy perfection, do we indeed see them through the door by which He entered once into the holiest place and is set forever at the right hand of God to invite us all to seats beside Him? Shall we enter through the gates into the holy city by the straight and narrow way and find eternal life in the sunshine of thy everlasting glories, O enchanting garden?"

Tennie remained a skeptic. "Sis might sound less cracked if she had a man entering *her* on a steady schedule, but as it is, her readers and listeners can't help concluding she's going daffy." Subscriptions to the *Weekly* were canceled right and left, and the lecture halls were only half full on the best of nights.

There was a hint of things to come when she took Anna along in place of Jim on a lecture tour that lasted all winter through New York into Vermont, down into Pennsylvania, then across the Midwest as far as Wisconsin. The leather-bound Bible and a plaster statue of the Virgin Mary were part of her luggage. Only God spelled love to her now; the free variety was committed to the past, and she claimed she'd never had time for it, anyway.

The first thing she did when she was home again was to renounce spiritualism. She sat down with Tennie and wrote a series of articles exposing every trick they once learned: how to slip out of knots, conceal what they needed in chairs, turn cheesecloth into ghosts— the whole works. She followed this up by handing in her resignation as president of the spirit raisers. That was the last straw. She'd shucked off one by one the free lovers, Andrews and the Pantarchy, the Socialists and Communists, like Salomé stripping off her veils. With nobody left to buy it, the *Weekly* died with the issue of June 10, 1876.

Next to go was Jim. The original Mrs. Blood had moved away from St. Louis into Brooklyn, short of money, low in health. When Victoria discovered he was helping the unhappy woman as much as he could, it was over. Anna worried at her daughter until she sued for divorce on a charge of adultery, which he didn't fight—though the witness Victoria paid to swear he'd gone whoring with him was a man Jim had never met. Tennie regretted that ending. "She thought no more of ridding herself of Jim than of losing a loose tooth, but I was sorry to see him go. He'd always been an open-hearted, honest, real gentleman to me, which made him one of a damn small handful."

Eleven

"Another one," Tennie continued, who'd never been less than fair and square with me all the time we were chummy was on his way out by a different door. Nobody had seen the Com outside his own walls since April. The only place he was likely to be on view again was in his coffin when he'd just passed his eighty-second birthday, but he was in no hurry to be lowered away."

In a room across the street from the Vanderbilt house, Johnnie Green had a *Sun* reporter on death-watch duty, living on sandwiches and beer with a deck of cards for amusement while he counted the comings and goings of the clergy, the doctors, and the family, all after their share of the old man's fortune. Beecher jeered that the newspapers "noted the rises and falls of Mr. Vanderbilt's temperature as though they were part of the daily weather report."

The daughters were in and out of the house every day as he lay in bed, howling in his misery, then pausing to join in a hymn. It wasn't pity that took them there but the desire to get a new will drawn to increase their share of the inheritance. The youngest son, Cornelius Jeremiah, had the same thought, though he wasn't on the calling list, not being on speaking terms with his father.

Johnnie Green heard that Vanderbilt was begging for more magnetism, and Tennie debated whether she should offer her services as
a means of getting a foot in the door. She left it until it was too
late; young Mrs. Vanderbilt swallowed her pride and hired a prac-
titioner named Frederick Weed.

Since they wouldn't let her try to ease the Com's suffering, the
big question for her was how much longer would he hang on. She
had lost hope of collecting from him personally what was owing the
Claflin sisters. Once he was gone, she would take a crack at Billy
and waste no time about it, for the sand was running out and the
cash had fallen to a trickle, since Victoria was so persnickety these
days.

Tennie would have accused anyone except Victoria of being
downright selfish in giving up on everything except life eternal.
One turn around the track was all Tennie looked for. "I didn't find
playing a harp in heaven any more appealing than being fried in the
fat down below. Once I got planted, I reckoned I'd stay planted.
The only use for a set of wings would be here on earth, where I
could spread them and see something more of the world than I had
so far. She might have her head in the clouds, and her *principles*
might be half-baked, but I'd stuck by her in the past, and it was no
time to change now that the going was so rough."

On January 4, the Vanderbilt butler hung black crepe on the
front door, and flags all over New York were lowered to half-mast.
One of the last things the Commodore mumbled was, "I shall never
cease to trust in Jesus. How could I ever let him go?" Tennie would
have welcomed a final look at him packed in ice in his satin-lined
coffin. Since there was no chance of that, she stood shivering in the
snow, gawking like the rest of the crowd at half a dozen mutes
shouldering him out on a bier. She was turned away at the Church
of the Strangers—no ticket—but she tagged along in the procession
behind the hearse as far as the Staten Island ferry.

He left $105,000,000 free and clear, almost 90 percent of it
outright to Billy, roughly $250,000 apiece to his eight daughters,
and no more than the income from $200,000 at 5 percent to Cor-
nelius Jeremiah. For Tennie there was nothing but the return of the
"Aurora" who looked like the unclad Miss Claflin. But if anybody

imagined the two sisters were willing to be overlooked and to keep quiet about it, they were due for a surprise.

Trouble was underway before they even got into the fight. Two of the daughters, Mary Alicia and Ethelinda, teamed up with Cornelius Jeremiah to claim in Surrogate Court that the will was invalid, since the Commodore's brains had been addled by spiritualism for the last ten years. They chose an attorney named Scott Lord. Tennie and Victoria placed their business with him, too. Somebody had to pay them at least $700,000 with compound interest, and their candidate for the handover was Billy.

Tennie's note to him was brief and polite, but it opened the door to his private office. He sat there behind a mahogany desk, a lawyer on either side of him, an undertaker's black suit on his back, gray side-whiskers fluffed out beyond his ears.

She gave them a glimpse of ankle as she took a seat, uninvited. "How's everything going at the house? It's been a while since I stayed on the premises."

Billy huffed and puffed like a yard engine. "What is it you're after exactly, Miss Claflin?"

"My right as a woman and the same for my sister. I calculate that to be seven hundred thousand dollars. Leastways, that's what the court will hear when we file the papers tomorrow morning. It's an obligation of your father's to us."

For a moment, she fancied the balloon was about to burst, but he controlled himself. "Just how was this debt you claim incurred?"

"Starting when you installed me in the house to steer him away from the maids. Then you got him married off to Miss Frank Crawford. That could have been me, not her, you know."

The three men put their heads together and she caught words like "preposterous" and "outrageous" and "blackmail." One of the lawyers took the helm. "May I ask whether you hold any receipts or other documents to substantiate this solicitation?"

"Nary a one. That wasn't the way he did business, as Billy knows. He trusted me and I trusted him. As a matter of plain fact, he promised to leave me and my sister half a million dollars, which we've yet to get a smell of. I do have one thing, though, come to think of it."

Billy again: "And what might that be?"

"A lock of his own hair. He handed it over as a mark of confidence, believing anybody who had it held power over him."

"Set your little mind at rest—it gives you no power over me. If that's the extent of your proof, you'd best be on your way."

"Oh, I've more than that—that's no more than a keepsake, sort of sentimental. How many witnesses do you want—my sister, the servants, and your stepmother for openers? They might relish a day in court. And we can always apply for an order to give us a dig through his personal files, can't we?"

"Are you by any chance daring to threaten me?"

"Threatening? I wouldn't stoop to any such thing. What I know is that you've come into about ninety million dollars, and like as not want to hold on to it. That might turn out tricky if your brother and sisters prove that when he wrote his will your father was off his nut because of spiritualism. My sister and I would be happy to testify before a judge and jury about him pestering us to call up your grandmother and the rest of 'em on his behalf. It'd make gaudier reading than Tilton and Beecher."

The second lawyer took over. "You might get more than you bargained for, young woman, if you ventured to place yourself upon the stand. Have you considered that? In all fairness, you should be warned that a witness can never tell what may be forthcoming under counsel's cross-examination."

"If you're hinting more mud might be slung, forget it. I've experience with that kind of trouble. By the by, do you happen to know offhand what the law says about suing a dead man for breach of promise?"

They held another conference, but they were humming a different tune. Now the words to be heard were "scandal" and "prudence" and "settlement." Billy spoke up again. "Tell me, how do you arrive at the sum you have mentioned?"

"Easy. There's the half million that was promised and the seventy thousand he kept for us to build up interest, which must be worth one hundred thousand by now. I understand Frank Crawford's walked off with half a million, as well as the house and furniture, but it's not in my nature to be greedy. I'd say a hundred thousand would be getting off cheap for breach of promise. And finally there's my sister's career to be considered. She's been drumming her fingers for months, waiting to get this business cleared up when she could have been making one hundred thousand, at least, lecturing over in Europe."

Then the haggling set in, as she had expected it would. Their first offer was fifty thousand, which was the best joke of the day to her. They agreed to double that, so she dropped the point about the losses her sister had taken. They said they'd fight tooth and nail to bar any meddling with the Commodore's private papers and the sisters would be old and gray before the courts handed down a decision. Tennie said a silent farewell to the half million, but stood firm on breach of promise.

It was settled for two hundred thousand dollars plus a signed pledge that she take herself and Victoria off to the other side of the ocean. They must stay there until Billy had extricated himself from the suit to break the will. They were never to breathe a word about the deal to anybody.

"Considering the hand we had to play," Tennie declared, "I was satisfied even after it cost Billy a cool million to quiet his brother down and half that much for every sister."

They had four first-class cabins, a brace of servants and Victoria's son and daughter with them when they sailed for England in August aboard the *Lafayette.* When reporters came buzzing around the pier before their departure, Mrs. Woodhull did the talking. "Mr. William H. Vanderbilt has no more to do with our departure than a child unborn." One of her first appointments in London was to be with the best doctor in town, and she spoke of being "sick at heart, sick in body, sick in mind" at leaving the United States. But Tennie made a habit of looking on the sunny side. "Regret was as much a stranger to me as the love she used to preach about before inclination disappeared. I couldn't wait to bury the past and see what a brand-new country had to offer in the way of men and maybe money and a vote for women."

Twelve

London, capital of England, where a woman's place in society was preordained and the only female with an admitted voice in politics was the plump and peevish little queen, who declined to show herself in public. August 1877. Summer dust flying up under the wheels of carriages as they trundled through the parks. Blue sky blurred by smoke drifting from factory chimneys and kitchen stoves that were never allowed to cool. The fire of women's suffrage reduced to embers after four thousand of the faithful, treading Susan Anthony's path, had met with the same refusal as she when they tried to register to vote. A city where Victoria and Tennie, reputations unknown, could sink into anonymity if that was what they wanted.

They didn't. Victoria had expected the British press to dance attendance on them when the ship docked at Liverpool, but she was disappointed. With Tennie she rented a flat on Gilston Road in the London suburb of West Brompton, an address that only their closest neighbors regarded as fashionable. Respectable, yes, but nowhere in the same class as Mayfair, Belgravia, or Eton Square.

The first months there Victoria spent in the care of the medical specialist. When treatment was over, he pronounced her as sound as a bell, a condition that surprised him in a woman past forty. By December she was eager to go again. She hired St. James's Hall on Piccadilly and dusted off one of the standards: "The Human Body: The Temple of God." She also made sure that the advertisements for her lecture bore a flattering likeness of her plus a Bible text.

Tennie found that evening as dull as dishwater (which she seldom deigned to dabble her hands in). Victoria relayed some home truths about a mother's duty to enlighten her children about the facts of life below the waist, but that was all. She succeeded in engaging the interest of one member of her audience, however. Tall, bearded John Biddulph Martin was a partner in Martin's Bank, Lombard Street, which had been in business longer than the Bank of England. "You'd never think he'd turn out to be a stagedoor Johnny," Tennie said, "but, by God, he did."

Whenever Victoria delivered a lecture, which was often, he was there, a bachelor three years younger than she and still tethered to his gray-haired mother's apron strings. On his first call, rose-red and shy, at the West Brompton flat, he drew Tennie aside to declare his intentions. "I am charmed by your sister's intellect and fascinated by her manner. Mrs. Woodhull has such verve, such sparkle. If she will accept me, I shall make her my consort. In having your services toward that goal, may I rely upon your help Miss Claflin?"

Miss Claflin's ears were only slowly adjusting to accents that sounded to her as if they owed a lot to a mouthful of mush. "How's that?"

"Your sister. It is my ambition to marry her."

"Why didn't you say so at the kickoff?"

"But that is precisely what I attempted to do."

"Then I didn't catch your drift. You reckon you've got something in common?"

"Need I say more than that I have long held similar views to those of John Stuart Mill?"

"Yes, you need. Who's he when he's home?"

"He died, alas, four years ago. He was philosopher, economist, prophet. When reading his treatise, *The Subjection of Women,* I concurred with every word. I regard his writings as the classical theoretical statement of the case for women's suffrage."

"Did he wear a dog collar like one of them we've got back home, name of Beecher?"

"No. Mill was a founder of the first women's suffrage society, besides being an undoubted genius who studied Latin, Euclid, and algebra at the age of eight."

"Sis keeps a level head on her shoulders, too, you know. She and me, we're both strong for votes for women."

He was doing all he could to understand her. Good head? Strong for? "Your sister, if I may so, is a most remarkable individual."

"You can say that again in spades, though she's slipped and fell on her fanny once or twice, like the rest of us."

"I'm extremely sorry, but I don't quite gather your meaning."

"Skip it. Let's get down to cases. From the cut of you, I guess you can afford her, so there's no concern on that account. But it takes more than money and brains to make a good marriage. Most women look for some steady exercise between the sheets. I know I do, and she's not past it yet, not by a long shot. How are you provided for in that department? Can you get up the ante?"

He spluttered for a moment, dumbfounded. "My dear Miss Claflin, if I interpret you correctly, and I'm afraid that I do, then I must protest the introduction of a subject far too delicate for discussion between us. Ladies and gentlemen, even husbands and wives, simply do not permit themselves—"

"You're all of a doodah, as you limeys put it, aren't you? But there's no cause to get upset. You enjoy yourself listening to Sis spouting in public along the same general lines, so why not plank cards on the table with me?"

He paced the carpet before he answered. "Very well. If it is assurance you seek on what I insist is strictly a personal matter, please allow me to state that I am fully aware of a husband's responsibilities in each and every respect. Does that satisfy your curiosity?"

"Couldn't ask for more. I warrant not to put a spoke in your wheel when you turn up here courting Sis. In fact, when you get right down to it, I'll even hold the lantern for you."

"Miss Claflin, all I can say is that you're a veritable diamond in the rough. I am deeply obliged to you."

"Any time, old cock. Any time at all."

But rocks cluttered Martin's road when Buck reasserted himself,

as the aging Mrs. Martin learned along with every other reader of
the British newspapers. Buck, staying behind with Anna in New
York, envied his two daughters their windfall from the Vanderbilt
orchard. When Cornelius Jeremiah, the youngest son, brought a
fresh lawsuit to wrest an extra two hundred thousand dollars from
his brother Billy, Buck volunteered his testimony to rehash what
Tennie and Victoria had imagined had been laid to rest, and to
inform the judge that Reuben Claflin wasn't the only witness to the
fact that the Commodore had once had his heart set on making
Tennie his bride. So her name cropped up in headline type in the
same size as Victoria's.

The judge cut off further disclosures by adjourning court for the
day. Buck straightaway made a beeline to Billy, and on the following morning announced that since no one in his family wished to
press their legitimate claims against any Vanderbilt, he was taking
off for foreign parts. What bigger treat could he give his dear wife
than to call with her on their two girls in London?

The news that the old couple were en route threw Victoria into
what she was learning to describe as a tizzy. The Claflins and the
Martins had less in common than the Bulgars and the Turks, whose
partiality for slitting each other's throats somewhere in the Balkans
comprised the principal news at the time. John Martin was the
product of generations of wealth, influence, and culture. An Oxford
scholar. Life governor of St. George's Hospital. Member of any
number of top-drawer professional societies. In short, as London
cockneys said, a nob. And the Claflins? Victoria decided that somehow the mongrels had to be supplied with a spurious pedigree.

She let it be known that Dr. R. Buckman Claflin, recently retired
after a distinguished career in the service of Aesculapius, was about
to honor London with his presence, rather than heed the appeals of
his admiring countrymen to enter the field of politics as a United
States Senator.

She had to admit that he lived up to the role she'd created for
him when he presented himself on her doorstep, an aged dude
decked out in a brand-new wardrobe, flourishing a gold-mounted
cane, with Billy's hush money scorching his wallet. Anna, on the
other hand, in a cotton dress that had seen better days, bore a strong

resemblance to a withered walnut. She was hugged, none too suffocatingly, by her daughters. All things considered, Victoria concluded it would be advisable to keep the pair of them clear of John Martin's path.

The smoke that had circled around Victoria's head in recent newspaper stories from New York aroused the suspicions of John's mother, Mrs. Robert Martin, that somewhere out of sight a fire was smoldering. Until her doubts could be allayed she would restrain him from putting to Victoria the question she was praying for: "Will you consent to join me in holy wedlock?" She bared her soul to an American journalist whose acquaintance she had made expressly for the purpose.

"All that stands between him and me is what those papers have said of me. Help me. I love him better than life. He is my all, my everything. Stop those slanders in the American papers. Place me right with the world, and my loved one will come back to my arms."

The task she set herself was to erase the past or, failing that, at least to rewrite it. But the Moving Finger was as cruel to her as to Omar Khayyám: "Nor all your Piety nor Wit/Shall lure it back to cancel half a Line/Nor all your Tears wash out a Word of it."

"I shall leave no stone unturned or unthrown in my efforts," she told Tennie.

"I've always heard that people who live in glass houses ought to be careful in that respect."

Victoria's goal was respectability. Achieving it, she would wrap herself up in it like a cloak, in the hope that Mrs. Martin might then warm to her as a suitable bride. Her trick was to seek out the editors of some estimable magazines and coax them into offering readers her version of her career to date. Then she would put together a new scrapbook to present to Mrs. Martin as positive proof that Victoria was nothing less than a living marvel, a woman of quality.

From the *Christian Union:*

That a woman who had devoted her whole life to doing angel's work should have been so maligned and persecuted, even up to the gates of justice, where alone she received a verdict of blameless, is one of those marvels which the pages of history only can explain and which show that all those who have fought for a good cause, from Saints and Martyrs downwards, have had to pass through their Gethsemane of mental suffering too exquisite for human utterance.

Rereading the clipping, Tennie detected an odor akin to Beecher's from the pulpit.

From the *London Traveller:*

The malice of enemies together with her opinions on the social questions have combined to give her a reputation of sin, but no slanders have been heaped on any human soul with greater injustice. A more unsoiled woman does not walk the earth.

As though these effusions were not enough—or perhaps too much to be believed—Victoria inserted an advertisement in the *Times.*

Mrs. Victoria C. Woodhull, being again compelled to commence libel suits against Americans who are constantly circulating malicious slanders, offers a reward of fifty pounds for every letter that contains enough libel to enable her to proceed criminally and civilly, and five pounds will be given to any and every person who will give information that can be proceeded with legally against persons who are circulating foul stories by word of mouth.

John's solicitors were at her service by then, but bricks could not be built when her offer produced not a wisp of straw.

Next followed a letter to the *London Court Journal:*

My name has been most unrighteously associated with what is known by the name of Free Love. No viler aspersion was ever uttered. No greater outrage could be inflicted on a woman. No deeper harm could be done to an innocent.

Tennie wondered, when this met her eye, how her sister proposed to account for the acres of space previously donated to the subject in the *Weekly.* She read on. These stories had been done, Victoria claimed, behind her back while she was caught up in lecturing.

Articles favoring free love appeared without my knowledge, which startled the readers of my hitherto spotless print. But the evil done did not rest there. I became inculpated as though I was morally responsible for utterances and doctrines which I loathe and abhor from the depths of my innermost being. I now openly avow, with all the earnestness of righteous indignation, that during no part of my life did I favor free love even tacitly. With the feelings that should acctuate every sanctified wife and mother of a family, I regarded it with loathing when once I got a slight idea of its character and the deep infamy to which it led.

Her guile was boundless. When she learned that Mrs. Stanton was in town visiting her daughter, Victoria veiled herself in black to pay an unheralded call on her. As her former worshipper entered the drawing room, Victoria undraped herself with the flair of Sarah Bernhardt. Would Sister Stanton accompany her to Mr. Martin's legal representatives and swear out an affidavit that never in her life had she heard a harsh word said about Mrs. Woodhull's character? Mrs. Stanton replied that she would be happy to attest to her admiration, but truth could carry her no further. Since this fell short of Victoria's requirements, she left after delivering a two-edged blessing: "May the good angels watch and guard you. I will not condemn."

So far, she had relied on peppering the newspapers in England and the United States with her outbursts, sometimes in her own name, sometimes under false ones. Dissatisfied with the results, she determined to plunge back into publishing on her own account. Volume One, Number One of *Woodhull & Claflin Journal,* handed out free of charge, called upon "the whole press of the world to aid us in unearthing those vile traducers who are wanton with our good name which, though nothing to them is to us at all, is dearer than life itself." A second issue never saw the light of day.

However, another older, established publication opened its columns to her in exchange for a donation of twenty-five thousand dollars to its treasury. *The Cuckoo* included among its staff a young Irish poet recently down from Magdalen College, Oxford, where his scorn for manly sports had brought him a ducking in the Cherwell. Tennie found Oscar Wilde's pasty complexion, greasy locks, and air of languor singularly unappealing.

"Had I been asked, I should have said *The Cuckoo* made a curious nest for a hawk of your sister's species," he remarked.

"What's it to you so long as she feathers it? You look like you're in molt yourself."

"What droll expressions you Americans employ! I shall make a point of exploring the fauna in your native habitat at the first opportunity."

"The way you carry on, you'll have to keep a sharp lookout for feathers over there, and a coating from the tar bucket to hold them fast."

Two men Victoria had once idolized—one for valid reasons, the other not—were targets now for her fury. She claimed that Stephen Pearl Andrews, "high priest of debauchery," had put her signature on the "filthy effusions" that had landed her and Tennie behind bars, and that it was Andrews who reigned at the Free Love Club, where "moral leprosy" ran riot until "the civil authorities were induced to interrupt their nightly orgies."

"Stephen Pearl Andrews" she wrote, "I impeach thee before the judgment bar. Pure hearts which might have communed with their Maker in the spiritual Sinai, hast thou by infernal wiles tempted to bow down before the idol of the flesh. With daring hand thou art filling up the measure of human wickedness. Arch blasphemer! All ye who love humanity aid me in rescuing sons and daughters of men from him who would trample all that is ethereal, beautiful, incorruptible and immoral into a pestilential mire of sensual grossness!"

Her attack on luckless Jim was signed "A Correspondent" in case Mrs. Martin might consider it churlish treatment of a man by his former helpmate. "It is well known that from the moment Mrs. Woodhull knew Colonel Blood he adopted toward her a course of deception and treachery. After she had returned from a long Southern lecture tour, his conduct was so flagrant that she felt forced to apply for a divorce. Whilst this was pending in 1876, and she was still his legal wife, he under terrible pressure essayed to defend her for the first time. But Blood's vindication was of little advantage to his wife. It came too late. Had it followed when she was first attacked, she would not now be under the necessity of clearing her character from foul aspersions!"

She had a brickbat of her own to cast at Jim. "It will be known to many of her friends that some years ago Mrs. Woodhull was in precarious health, failing day by day, many persons expecting her death. She has since discovered that she was near being the victim of slow poison. Mrs. Woodhull was treated by an eminent American physician as a pronounced slow-poisoning case." Mrs. Martin's shoulder continued cold. If her John dared to marry this unseemly Mrs. Woodhull, his mother would disown and probably disinherit him.

"Surely," Victoria brooded, "the frost would melt once she realized that I again envisage myself as Presidential timber?" She had been too preoccupied to contest the '76 election, but since both the sisters retained American citizenship, she tossed her bonnet once more into the ring in 1880, blaming corruption in high places and chicanery in the count of ballots for her earlier defeat by Ulysses Grant.

It was the only campaign recorded in the history books in which a candidate refrained from making any personal appearances before the voters. Instead, she bombarded them by mail from London with pamphlets extolling womanly virtue, which was the solitary plank in her platform. Tennie didn't believe there was a hope in hell of besting James Garfield or Winfield Hancock, yet the outcome puzzled her. In a dream the man she saw in the White House was not Garfield, the victor, but his Vice President, Chester Arthur. In any event, it certainly wasn't Victoria, who repeated her earlier performance by garnering not a solitary vote, but she vowed to try once more in '84. Meantime, she pursued a life of new-found celibacy, though Mrs. Martin still declined to receive her.

Tennie's future looked easier when Francis Cook tottered over the horizon. Mr. Cook, as he was then, was endowed with several of the qualifications she was looking for in a more or less permanent beau. He was a widower commanding a fortune at least the equal of the Martins', and his faith in clairvoyance was on a par with the Commodore's. "This old codger's as eager for a touch-up from a warm hand as he is for a chat with the departed," she assured Victoria. "I reckon I'll have it easy."

Like his predecessor, the lean-cheeked, lonely man relied on the spirits for guidance. The more he disclosed about himself, the better Tennie could please him. Cook & Son, with offices in St. Paul's

Churchyard, were importers, their original profit quadrupled by the monopoly they enjoyed in the sale of silk shawls from India. Every woman wanted one after the queen was proclaimed empress of that inestimable addition to royal real estate in 1876.

Cook's home in London, Doughty House on the Thames at Richmond, was the next best thing to an art museum that Tennie had ever seen, hung with canvases she later came to recognize as the works of Rembrandt, Raphael, Van Dyck, Titian, and Velasquez. Taking her on her first tour he stopped in front of a portrait of a golden-skinned woman naked from the waist up.

"Who's the mermaid?" Tennie asked.

"Diane de Poitiers, my dear, the paramour of King Henry II of Navarre, painted by François Clouet, and one of my favorites, I might say."

"You did say. So you've still got an eye hung out for the ladies, have you? I guarantee that one had herself serviced any time she snapped her fingers."

"You know, I detect a certain resemblance in you, about the mouth particularly. Perhaps there's some French blood in your ancestry. I shouldn't be at all surprised if there were."

"I'd be downright flabbergasted. British to the core, that's us. Cavaliers. Bluebloods. One of them shinned down the family tree to take a crack at Oliver Cromwell."

He patted her cheek with a wrinkled hand. "I might have guessed. The fairness of skin. Always a sure sign of breeding."

"And the same holds true all over, head to heels."

"I should dearly love to see you in an evening gown. Jewels at your lovely throat. Shoulders exposed."

"I had a feller paint my picture once. He called it "Aurora." It was a bit drafty sitting there in a half a yard of veiling."

"May I have the privilege of viewing it one day? I should welcome that opportunity."

"Sorry, but I left it behind in our cottage at Newport. I might have another one done over here as a replacement before I get too old and gray for the job."

"In similar costume?"

"Why not? So long as there's a fire going, I'm not fussy."

He was rising like a trout at a mayfly. "It will be my pleasure to introduce you to one or two men of reputation who I am certain would be happy to undertake the commission."

"And you with a seat in the audience? Well, we'll see about that —but one thing you can do is come and help choose something you fancy me in of an evening."

Then, and on her later visits, he showed her his accumulations of Italian majolica, bronzes, ivories, tapestries, and ecclesiastical gold plate. None of it intrigued her a fraction as much as a collection of antique rings crusted with precious stones. Any one of them would satisfy her as a pledge of things to come.

If she could induce him to stand before an altar, just two words, "I do," would give her the instant rank of countess—in Portugal, anyway. Twenty-five years earlier, King Luiz had dubbed him viscount, a courtesy title, after Francis had bought the mountaintop estate of Montserratte, to lay out half a million pounds to restore the palace that stood there and extend the grounds until they rivaled in splendor the royal Palacio da Pena itself on its remote perch on a nearby massif of the Serra da Cintra, and Montserratte was judged the finest example of landscaping on the whole Iberian peninsula.

She wheedled him into telling her about his late wife, his bride before Tennie was born, as a curtain raiser to the production she was planning for him. The stage was set in the library of Doughty House one evening after dinner, Tennie decolletée in one of the new dresses he had insisted on paying for, firelight twinkling on the chandelier and on the crystal decanter and the glasses set out by the butler together with silver salvers of fresh fruit and walnuts.

She had gone through similar performances before, so her opening line was routine. "Would you like a word or two from the departed?"

"My treasure, you well know how much I value your company in that respect."

"Then let's see if we can cast a line to the first of your better halves."

He turned the lights low while she snuggled down in the armchair. She had practiced the accent while learning to trade in pounds and pence and adjusting to traffic on the wrong side of the street. "Francis," the flutey voice called, "can you hear me? Are you there?"

"Present and accounted for, my dove. Are you keeping fit?"

"I'm in absolutely splendid form. I gather you've something on your mind involving that charming girl you've been seeing rather frequently of late."

"Quite right, my dear. I confess I have. I hope you won't think I'm neglecting you."

"On the contrary. I trust the friendship will develop. I feel for you, Francis, being there, woebegone, without me. That is my only source of sorrow. I enjoy total happiness here above. I can scarcely bear to contemplate your being left alone."

Tennie, through her lowered eyelashes, noted as she sobbed in the shadowed room that he had covered his face with his hands. "Oh, my dearest, if there were only some way in which to relieve your anguish."

The voice was firmer. "Francis, there is. Let her occupy the place that was mine there below. Marry her, Francis, for my sake as much as yours. It is no more than we both deserve."

"You wouldn't object?"

"Go ahead, Francis. Nothing to be dreamed of in heaven would please me more."

Ring on her finger and head in the clouds, Tennie dashed off a note to Johnnie Green as soon as she returned to Gilston Road. "I am now engaged to be married to a gentleman who is richer than Vanderbilt and titled and who worships his precious treasure, and Victoria will be married in a few weeks to one of the richest and into one of the noblest families."

Her news was premature as far as Victoria was concerned, but Tennie was rapidly installed in luxury at Number 47 Emperor's Gate, a more elegant address than West Brompton, with both her fiancé and the spirit of Mrs. Cook and colleagues in regular attendance.

Francis had a family of grown-up children who couldn't be expected to hide their doubts when an American adventuress only a hair's breadth from forty was engaged to be married to their father, whom they thought in his dotage at the age of sixty-eight. She wondered whether they realized that he had retained a wicked eye for other women besides his bride, but she herself came to a tolerant understanding with him on that point.

She began to lose track of the number of times Victoria hauled her across to New York with or without Anna, Francis, and John Martin, but always in pursuit of dual dreams: laundering her reputation and election to the Presidency of the United States.

On one such occasion, the sisters had two fleeting encounters with their yesterdays. On a Manhattan street, the pale, drawn face of Jim Blood came into view, breaking into a forgiving smile at the sight of Victoria. She passed him by in silence. In Boston, Tennie ran an errand for her to the *Globe,* which had reprinted one of Victoria's London tirades under the headline "As Big a Lie as Was Ever Told." On the previous day, Victoria had stormed in on the editor, threatening a libel action, then simmered down, leaving behind for his edification other articles of hers—which Tennie was now there to collect. On Victoria's path through the city room, she had walked past an editorial assistant toiling at a desk, face hidden behind a black bush of a beard. She knew him immediately by his eyes, into which she had once peered with unrequited longing. The editor confirmed his identity. "Yep, that's Bennie Tucker. He's the chap who wrote the headline." Victoria went no farther in seeking a printed apology.

She was embroiled in her third attempt to capture the White House before the way would be cleared for her marriage. "This call goes out from England issued by Victoria C. Woodhull, supported by British capitalists," declared the manifesto she addressed to "the people of all the world," urging them to "rally round her standard and support her in her right to represent and work for the people of America." St. James's Hall was the promised site for the convention to nominate her and select a delegation whose steamship fares and transatlantic expenses she undertook to pay.

She dropped the whole affair when John's mother obligingly breathed her last. Victoria became the new Mrs. Martin in a quiet, private ceremony a few days later and set up housekeeping at Number 17 Hyde Park Gate, an ugly house on the outside but its interior something of a showpiece with a forest of marble busts and white bearskin rugs. Though she engaged one of the best cooks in London, she found very few in John's circle willing to partake of her hospitality.

Tennie was content to await her turn until Francis had at least partially overcome the qualms of his offspring at the prospect of having her as their stepmother. How justified she was in her patience was evident one October day when guests swarmed to a Kensington church for the wedding and she moved into Doughty House, taking Anna with her, while Buck, slowed down by a series of strokes, stayed on with Victoria.

Newspapers on the other side of the Atlantic could not desist from exhuming the Claflin history in the course of reporting Tennie's new status. Victoria felt impelled, on her father's death soon after, to dispatch a note to the New York *Sun*. "Sir: My father, Reuben B. Claflin, died of grief caused by the malicious libel published in the *World* of October 24. Has not our family suffered enough? Please insert this notice for our heartbroken family."

Tennie was hypocritical enough to wear mourning for months. Someone else close to her was not entirely overwhelmed by grief, either—at any rate not so overwhelmed that she wouldn't try to make capital out of his death. The poison-pen letter signed by "Justice" was posted simultaneously to the Lord Mayor at the Mansion House and the Fleet Street press. "A mysterious death occurred on the nineteenth of November of a much respected and honored citizen by the name of Reuben B. Claflin. His papers were spirited away as well as the will that is known to have been made by him, including money and bonds. His death was sudden. His sickness and burial were very mysterious."

When a Scotland Yard investigation confirmed that a terminal stroke was the cause of Buck's end, John Martin hired detectives and offered a reward in an effort to pinpoint the source of this latest scandal. Tennie quickly nipped that in the bud. Though it was beyond her to discover which of the servants Anna had evidently bribed to record her words, Tennie had no doubt that Mother was the culprit. Poor Francis! Poor John! They were learning at a gallop what marriage to a Claflin entailed.

If her own social standing had been impaired, the damage was corrected when she prompted Francis to endow with eighty thousand pounds of his fortune a boarding school for young women where the curriculum would be devoted exclusively to music and the arts. This Kensington haven was named Alexandra House in honor of her Royal Highness Alexandra, Princess of Wales, who with her husband, Prince Edward, graciously attended the grand opening. Tennie thought she caught him winking at her, but common sense told her he must have suffered a speck of plaster blown into his eye. Shortly thereafter, her Majesty the Queen awarded Francis a baronetcy. He was now Sir Francis, and his wife, Lady Cook. "As the Poet Laureate attests, kind hearts are more than coronets, Tennie," he puffed, "but both are equally gratifying."

After these triumphs, "my little woman," as he often called her, couldn't place a foot wrong. The world and his wife angled for invitations to her garden parties to be welcomed by her and to stroll by the fountains and the lily pool, to listen to the string orchestra, and enjoy the best that the stillroom and kitchen could provide, served under a large marquee. During one invasion of guests, she summoned the outdoor staff to demolish a fence to allow access to the meadow. She was the habitual toast of those gatherings. "An absolute winner," the men would burble. "Amazingly knowledgeable for a woman, and a Yankee at that. Jolly amusing lingo, too, once you get the hang of it."

Where the English rated her "a brick," "a pippin," "a Dresden doll," she was Lady Bountiful to the Portuguese. Her first day at Montserratte was bittersweet. Four chestnut horses dark with sweat drew the carriage up the stone-strewn road that zigzagged up the mountain through the scented forests of cork and eucalyptus trees. Barefoot black-shawled women pelted her with basketfuls of blossoms to the cheers of their escorts. Apple-cheeked girls and boys, eyes dark as chocolate and clothes bright as flowers, danced as they sang in chorus. Flags of all nations flew from the turrets of the palace, and bats shrilled, dipping in and out of the torchlight. Rockets swooshed up into the starlight at the climax, at which point Baronet and his Lady sipped a last cool goblet of porto branco before they sank gratefully into their two goosedown beds. Tennie lay thinking about children, wishing she had a daughter of her own to care for, before she recovered her senses and dismissed the idea because she had passed the age when it was considered even a remote possibility.

She consoled herself by establishing seven little schools for the neighboring peasants, then over the years sent a dozen promising pupils to further their education in English convents. The poor, hardy perennials of the landscape, were provided with food for their tables and clothes for their backs, the sick with medicine and doctors' care. "In my philosophy," she said in the recently acquired tones of a gentlewoman, "those of us who happen to be blessed with the financial means are under an obligation to share them, not cache the stuff away in a vault like a squirrel smelling a hard winter ahead."

She was selective about her charity. Sister Polly, for example, was widowed now and crippled with arthritis. "But that's her misfortune, not a qualification for a handout, when she's done me not a single good turn all her life."

In Richmond she saw an opportunity for philanthropy of a different order—a home for wayward girls. The announcement of her plan brought a succession of church committees to wait on her, stirring memories of childhood when the Claflins never knew who would come pounding on their door as a prelude to running them out of town. "We beg you to reconsider, Lady Cook. If girls of that class are led to believe that not only they but their babies, too, will be looked after, it will only encourage them in their folly." She repaid them for thwarting her. Not a penny did any church in Richmond receive from her after that.

At Montserratte, she laid in a store of quite different memories to console her in her old age.

The *palácio,* bone-white walls and scarlet rooftops competing in shimmering brilliance under the blistering noonday sunlight, had rooms to spare for siestas with a sturdy companion in cool darkness behind locked shutters. Most of their names were soon forgotten. But not Augusto the forester, strong as a bull, who would come scented with sweat and the cork he cut for a living in the forests along the Collares road, the heels of his sandals ticking like a clock on the tiled floors; they were invariably the last thing he removed before he was on top of her. Then there was Leon, tanned brown as leather, reeking of garlic and fresh-netted sardines, who trudged up the mountain from his cottage by the sea for an hour of panting pleasure, and all of this on tap for a handful of escudos.

The mud of the past might have sunk to the bottom if Victoria had not constantly roiled the water. But she was more intractable than Tennie, impossible to deter from diving into the deep end whenever she heard of anyone daring to question the identity she had chosen for herself as Mrs. John Biddulph Martin, model of propriety, advocate of motherly love, and future President of the United States. On one of those reckless plunges she pulled Tennie in with her, and Tennie barely escaped being borne away by the current.

Thomas Byrnes, Inspector of New York City Police, was the purported author of a front-page article in the Brooklyn *Eagle,* which Victoria received regularly in the mail. Detailing the history of "two adventuresses," it was widely reprinted by other molders of American opinion. At Victoria's urging, John Martin rented a house in Manhattan to enable his wife and sister-in-law to be on hand for instituting suit for criminal libel. "I will incur any inconvenience to obtain justice and redress," Victoria said. "It is not a question of damages. No damages, however exemplary, would be any satisfaction for injuries that cannot be measured by dollars."

Francis, whose feelings on the subject ran somewhat cooler, hied off to Montserratte when Tennie and the Martins sailed on the S.S. *Trave,* taking along Zulu Maud, whom her mother persisted in treating as a child, though her next birthday would see her an unprepossessing thirty-nine.

They drove to police headquarters with a portmanteau full of documents supporting Victoria's claims to respectability and were ushered into Byrnes's office. Bottle-nosed, black Irish, and devoid of charm, he called in a sergeant as witness before permitting Victoria to describe the vendetta her enemies were conducting against her.

She was interrupted after fifteen minutes. "If you have any business with me, madam, please state it." She extracted a fistful of pamphlets, written by herself, but he brushed them aside.

John took up the cudgels. "Don't you refute this newspaper article in some way, Inspector?"

"No."

"I think it does my wife a grave injustice." Byrnes folded his arms. John heaved a sigh. "I'm very sorry you will do nothing."

"I'm sorry, too. But I am a public official, and any statement I make I may be held responsible for. There are the courts to which you can have recourse immediately."

Victoria was trembling with agitation as an officer escorted them to the waiting carriage. Now that John had seen Byrnes call her bluff, libel suits were dropped for the time being. She had one card left to play to convince her bewildered spouse of her innate, lifelong purity. Tennie sensed exactly what she had in mind. She would assure him that no matter what lies were spread about her, she had acted only to shield Tennie. It was Tennie who should be adjudged guilty of sin, not Victoria.

Two days later, the trump card was played with no effort on Victoria's part. The newspapers reported that after twenty-six years the authorities in Ottawa, Illinois, had revived the indictment against Tennessee Celeste Claflin for manslaughter and fraud. The ocean had never seemed so safe and sparkling to her as on the voyage back to England. Francis, spared an explanation of her hasty return, was delighted to have her home.

Tennie should have known better, of course, than to take any further trips across the water with the Martins, but Victoria embarked on yet another bid to put herself in the White House. This time, she would rally support on the spot for her campaign against Grover Cleveland, and she wanted Tennie at her side. Tennie did have the sense, however, to decline a visit to Chicago, which lay too close to Ottawa for comfort. Scarcely had Mr. and Mrs. Martin settled in their hotel there before the Chicago *Mail* began unraveling the story of the Claflins' younger days.

John and an attorney were waiting outside the courthouse before the doors were opened the next morning, seeking the editor's arrest for libel and damages of one hundred thousand dollars. John underestimated his adversaries. Far from being silenced, the *Mail* proceeded to delve much deeper into the record than had ever been done before, citing names and dates as far back as Buck's burning down the mill in Homer. The woman's death in Ottawa, the house of assignation Tennie was alleged to have conducted in Cincinnati —in column upon column, it was all there.

Case Number 103173 in the Cook County Circuit Court, the

Martins versus the *Mail,* never went to trial. The Martins collected Tennie in New York and fled homeward with her. Grover Cleveland 5,554,414, Victoria Woodhull 0—it had been in vain once more.

Tennie avoided her native land for some time after that, preferring to occupy herself with such matters as opening the Doughty House gallery to the public and serving as guide, and then touring with the collection when it was exhibited free of charge throughout the United Kingdom, France, Germany, Italy, the Netherlands, and, of course, Portugal. When she estimated that danger was over, she resumed visits to the States on her own and was always well received, even to the extent of a meeting with the most vigorous of all Presidents, Theodore Roosevelt, whom she found as evasive as his predecessors had been about votes for women.

Victoria, meanwhile, remained preoccupied with her own affairs. From time to time she ventured onto the lecture platform, although without any fresh thoughts to utter. She founded a magazine, the *Humanitarian,* to trumpet her praises under Zulu Maud's lackluster editorship. She precipitated new lawsuits, including a monumental action against the British Museum that removed two hostile publications concerning her from its shelves and brought her twenty shillings in recompense for libel—the only case of its kind she ever won.

Tennie made a practice of taking newfound friends to cheer Victoria up at the Martins' country home in Bredon's Norton, Worcestershire, a retreat she increasingly preferred to London's hustle and bustle. Ivy covered the gray stone walls of the sixteenth-century manor house in Norton Park, and roses flourished in gardens overshadowed at sunset by Bredon Hill and watered by the tiny stream that flows into the gentle Avon. Since John held title to most of the place, she reigned as mistress of the village as well as of a platoon of servants.

One by one, the familiar faces vanished. Byron went soon after the sisters' initial appearance in London, and gave no cause for mourning. Jim Blood's death while seeking gold in Africa they heard of only belatedly, by which time grief was pointless, in Tennie's estimation. Anna died in Doughty House, firm in the belief that heaven was her just reward. She was eighty-five years old; Tennie hoped not to linger that long.

Pneumonia carried off John Martin at Las Palmas in the Canary Islands. He had gone there alone, his wife complaining that "ill health and shattered nerves" kept her from accompanying him. He left her 171,797 pounds after taxes, $835,000 by her sister's calculation—together with everything else he had owned.

His departure set Tennie to thinking. Before marrying her, Francis had been remiss, as it developed, with a certain Mrs. Holland, who upset both the Cooks by suing him for breach of promise. He confessed in court to paying her to cohabit with him in Richmond, but denied any talk of making her his bride. The jury accepted his word and awarded him costs. But were there other Mrs. Hollands lurking in the closets in hope of laying later claims against the old man's estate? And what of Tennie's own legal status? "After all, I didn't bother with a divorce when I got shut of Bartels," she mused. "If my present marriage has got holes in it, I might be left high and dry when Francis's number comes up."

It was all arranged in no time. For a consideration which, prudently invested, was destined to make her a millionairess, she waived further right to the fortune and then led him by the hand for a second marriage in a civil ceremony under a newly drawn contract. He lasted six months more, and then in 1901 his will made her richer by some $120,000, added on top of the $750,000 he had already deeded to her, but she was no longer mistress of Montserratte. He bequeathed that property to his eldest son, Frederick, together with the bulk of the eight million and most of the art collection the family had gathered during the course of four generations.

None of Francis's children caused her any trouble, since they had the lion's share of the inheritance, but more distant relatives, ignored and embittered, made such demands of her that she refused to listen. As any Claflin would have done, she applied to the Home Office for an exhumation order when they spread rumors concerning the speed of his departure, but changed her mind. "If you hadn't convinced me Francis ought to rest in peace," she told her stepsons and stepdaughters, "I'd have gone through with it, mark my words, for if there's anybody I won't give the time of day to, it's a scandal-monger."

Frederick allowed her unrestricted use of Montserratte. She found Portugal increasingly attractive when fog and winter cold descended on London, but her days of jousting in the bedroom were over. Lust and Francis had passed away almost simultaneously.

The years sped by so fast it was impossible to keep track of them. Victoria emulated Tennie and built a new school for Bredon's Norton; Tennie donated funds to the war chest of Mrs. Pankhurst's suffragettes. Victoria offered five thousand dollars to the first man or woman to fly an aeroplane across the Atlantic; Tennie, when war exploded in Europe, gave her imagination wing and envisaged an army of uniformed Amazons, one hundred and fifty thousand strong, entering the field of battle against the Hun. Neither of the projects achieved more than a favorable nod from the newspapers, yet that in itself made a pleasant change from former days.

Tennie found it strange that whereas the struggles of the militants had failed to win the vote for women, the loss in battle of millions of men fulfilled the purpose for which she and Victoria had fought. First in England and then in the United States, women could now march to the polls—although Tennie had a premonition that the new President, Warren Harding, whom the ladies adored and had helped elect, was not too long for this world. It was also ironic to her that the Sixteenth Amendment, which the Movement had hoped would secure women's suffrage, turned out to be authorization for income taxes, and women's right to vote had had to wait until the Nineteenth.

The break with Victoria was a great cause of pain. It developed out of the blue from a remark of Tennie's about Victoria's memoirs. Tennie, who had gone to visit her sister, had misgivings the moment she saw Victoria from the railroad-station platform, wearing a dowdy black hat of cartwheel dimensions, and overflowing the sidecar of a motorcycle driven by a white-clad retainer, behind whom Tennie was to ride on the pillion seat. Tennie extended a hand, forgetting that Victoria avoided physical contact with anyone these days for fear of contamination. Once inside the manor house, they entered the library, where sunlight streamed through mullioned windows onto the items of antique furniture which she had developed an interest in. "You must," said Victoria, "read the opening chapter of the autobiography I commenced during a recent trip up to town."

Tennie read the opening: "Sitting here today in this north room of 17 Hyde Park Gate, London—dreary, smoky, foggy, insulated as you are in the customs and prejudices of centuries—I am thinking with all the bitterness of my woman's nature how my life has been warped and twisted out of shape. . . ."

This was as far as she could go. "Bitterness, Sis? Why should you be bitter?"

"Because I have every reason to be."

"Come on now. You're rolling in clover and have been for God knows how long. What if you never got elected? You'll turn up as a speck on the walls of history. You've had a good run for the money. What more can anyone ask who'll be eighty-three next September? We've both been favored by lady luck, if you ask me."

"You call me lucky when I have been robbed of my destiny? I have been abused, rejected, humiliated, when I might have changed the world as ruler of my people. That was the prophecy."

"You changed things for your own benefit, right enough. I remember when you didn't have shoes to put your feet into back in Ohio."

"You turn on me after all I have done for you—join the multitude that has always decried me?"

"Let's look at it the other way around. Who was it made most all the money when we were children? Who told fortunes, as you never could? Who sucked up to Vanderbilt? Who angled our way out of New York when we were close to starving to death?"

"I have always doted on you, Tennie. Why do you deny me your love now?"

"Know what I think? I think the only person you've ever doted on is yourself." She had been itching to say that for years. "You used to go around spouting how everybody must love and care for everybody else. Then you changed your tune and proved you didn't believe a goddam word you said. The same holds for votes for women. All you gave a hoot in hell for was votes for Victoria

Woodhull. Get your name in the papers; pull in a crowd, fool lunkheads like me into going along with you. Attention was what you craved, and screw the rest of us. I don't pretend to know too much about love—who does? But one thing I'm certain of—you're a selfish bitch and jealous as the devil of me."

Victoria, her face mottled with scarlet, struggled to pull herself up from the wing-backed leather chair. I'm glad she can't make it, was Tennie's thought. "Wouldn't two creaky old hens scrapping on the Persian carpet make a real treat for the servants?" Her sister stared long and hard at her before she burst out, "Upstart! Ignorant, evil, snot-nosed whore! I *made* you, Tennessee Claflin, brought you up, got you started, and this is the thanks I get for my trouble. I'll see you dead, and I'll spit on your grave."

"Doubtless you will, old sow, but you won't have much by way of company."

A tug on the bell cord which almost dismantled it brought Zulu Maud in to summon a taxi for her aunt.

Tennie made herself comfortable on the white wrought-iron chaise that Antonio, the head gardener, had moved out onto the lawn for her from the shade of a towering tree whose name she would have to ask when he came back from his siesta. She wanted to feel the warmth from the brilliant Portugal sky clear through to her brittle bones. She weighed so little now, she left scarcely a dimple on the flowered cushions. She put down the comic book she had been skimming through and picked up a pad of paper. The joints of her fingers ached as she picked up the pencil, but she set her tongue between her ivory teeth and began to write:

It's a pity I have to stir my brains so hard to remember anything these days, but maybe I've been too hasty, anyway, in spilling the beans to the young Englishman who takes down every word I say in shorthand. He's a bit too crawly for my taste with his "Lady Cook this" and "Lady Cook that," but it isn't in me to refuse him when he's bent on telling my story, on the strict understanding, of course, that it will never see daylight until I'm tucked away underground.

He's asked for a few lines from my own hand, so here goes. I must be careful to hide this away out of sight someplace, though. It wouldn't do to let anybody dip their nose in too early when it might upset them.

I'll get down to brass tacks and admit I'm not pretty any more. The powers I had as a girl are almost *kaput,* but sometimes they still bring Sis into view. I see her then as the light fades, sitting bolt upright in her leather chair, waiting for the sun to rise again to save her from the dark for another day. "If more people knew about it," she's saying, "I could get out of this," and she's not referring to that chair.

I've tried many a time to cipher when and where my own number will come up, but I can't catch a glimmer. Perhaps that's the way it's meant to be for everybody, because otherwise we might roll over and give up the ghost. But no matter what happens, I'll find the strength to face it. A woman's nature is stronger than a man's. It's her job to bring life and joy where men take it on themselves to rule and kill, which is what they've been doing ever since Adam humped Eve.

They have the gall to crack down on us when we stand up for equality. And why? Because they're afraid. They know in their minds we're better than they are and intended one day to inherit the earth and the fullness thereof. Meantime, they expect us to *love* them when love ought to be recognized for what it really is: a nonsense that man imposed on woman as a sop to dull the suffering he inflicts.

The nice young Englishman puts the spur to me to sum up what he calls "lessons from life." I can't figure it better than this: Do what you can with whatever you're born with any time the opportunity crops up. You'll lose some, win some— it works out about even. And weeping and wailing about the outcome won't count for more than a single straw in a bale of hay. Poor old Sis. Why didn't she ever cotton onto that?